Under the Wings of the Almighty

Walter Rohloff

Editor: Connie May

Printed in the United States of America

0 1 2 3 4 5 6 7 8 9

Cover design and formatting
Brock Maraee Rohloff

To my
"Herzele"
My eternal wife, friend and companion
In love and appreciation.

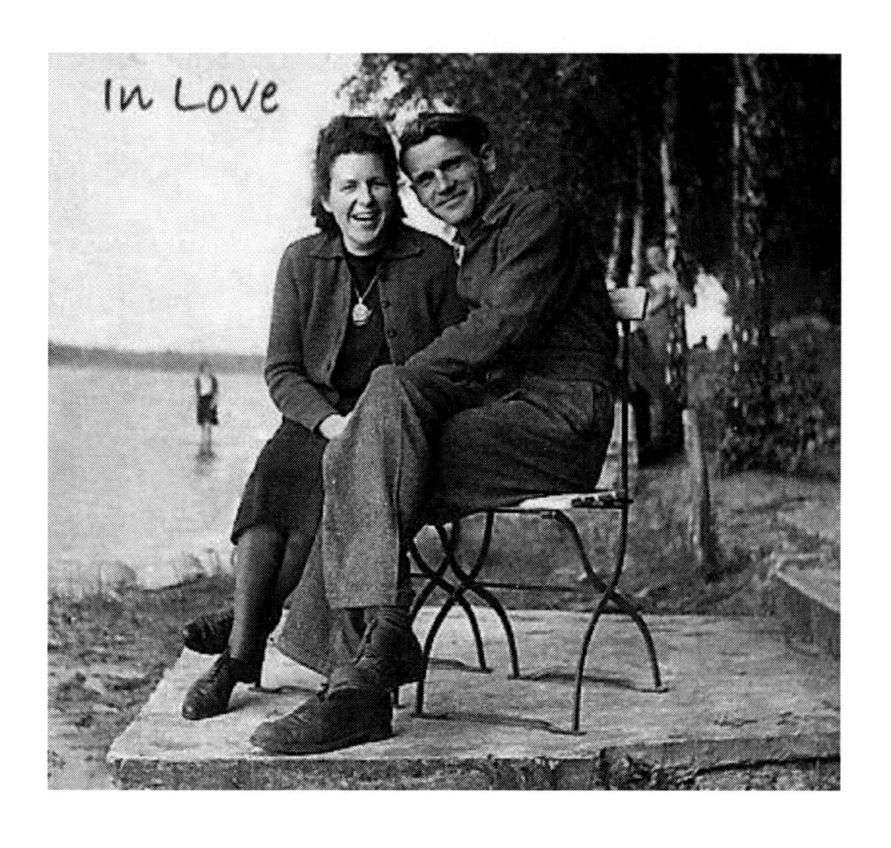

Contents

Acknowledgements

We are indebted and very grateful to friends and neighbors: Albert Brown, Ron Brown, Linda Olsen, Robert Foster, Jeff White, David Monson, Curtis and Ginger Lamb, Gay Burkholz, Mario Rohloff for their friendship, advice, help and encouragements in bringing this book about. We are especially grateful for the Lord's assistance and figuratively speaking "keeping his wings" (Matt. 23:37) over us. How overwhelmed we are when we hear Ludwig van Beethoven's Ode to Joy: "Brethren, above the stars' canopy a loving Father must dwell." We learn of the Prophet Joseph Smith communicating with the Father and the Son and restoring the gospel of Jesus Christ. We sing: "I am a child of God, and He has sent me here." Yes. He has sent us here to prove ourselves. One day we will be judged how good we did on earth. (Rev. 20:12) We are grateful for this God given opportunity. We love our Heavenly Father and his Son Jesus Christ. The intent of this story is to show, first, there is a loving father in heaven who wants to help us, his children; Second in gratitude we will donate all proceeds from the sales of this book to the poor and needy.

Please forgive any grammatical mistakes made in the presentation of this true story.

Thank you,
Walter and Edith Rohloff

Introduction

The story here told shows how true the statement of Paul in Romans 8:28 is: “And we know that all that happens to us is working for our good if we love God and are fitting into his plan.” It tells the story of Walter and his family before and after they joined The Church of Jesus Christ of Latter-day Saints when their own family became their strongest persecutors; the difficulties they had with the Nazi and Communist governments; their activities during World War II and after the war, and experiencing deadly concentration and prisoner of war camps, military attacks, illness, hunger and mistreatment, and because of their beliefs, personal set backs. It also shows how marvelously the Lord guided Walter and his family through those difficult times.

They had to endure great hardships. What looked hard to stand up for the truth and to overcome barriers and contradictions in their lives-proved a blessing for them in the end. They truly did live under the wings of the Almighty.

It is a very special, unique, and true story.

“There is a guiding hand above all things. Often when things happen, it’s not by accident. One day, when we look back at the seeming coincidences of our lives, we will realize that perhaps they weren’t so coincidental after all.”

Thomas S. Monson,
President, The Church of Jesus Christ of Latter Day Saints

1

YEARS OF CRISIS

It was a beautiful Sunday morning. The Christian world was celebrating the day of Pentecost. At the marketplace in the city of Neubrandenburg in Mecklenburg, Germany, a military band would give a concert. Bruno and Irene had made plans to attend and Irene would be wearing her finest attire and her high-heeled shoes. Wearing the shoes would be hard for her, as she was extremely pregnant, but Irene was beautiful and always liked to look her very best.

On the previous afternoon Irene wasn't feeling well. Bruno asked his mother-in-law to find a doctor and his mother-in-law, Auguste Boers, told him to get a midwife instead. “Oh no,” Bruno said, “It is not time for the delivery yet.” He was sure he knew better than his mother-in-law who had brought six children into the world. Besides, he and Irene were still planning to attend the concert.

Bruno and Irene did attend a concert, but it didn't come from a band at the marketplace. Instead, they were an exclusive audience to Walter’s strong voice as Walter was born at 4 am on the 4th of June, 1922. With Walter’s brown eyes he looked at his parents, who lovingly stroked his full head of blond hair. Irene kept a small, curly lock of his hair her whole life. When Walter got older and his hair turned a darker shade, Irene used the lock to prove to him that he once had straw blonde hair. Bruno rapidly made plans for Walter’s future. It was his wish that he become an engineer, but first he needed a name. Irene preferred the name “Egon” but Bruno had a different idea. He wanted him to be named after his brothers “Walter Kurt and Arnold.”

On one weekend in June 1922, Bruno arrived at the "Standesamt" (bureau of vital statistics) to report the birth of his son. A clerk entered Bruno's preferred names and Walter became Walter Kurt Arnold Rohloff. Walter always liked the names his father gave him.

The living conditions didn't change after the birth of Walter. Irene was living with her parents in Neubrandenburg, Germany; Bruno was living with his parents in Pasewalk, Germany about 40km away. They had been married for almost one year, but were not able to find an apartment in Pasewalk. Bruno worked for the city and liked what he was doing. So every weekend he would travel by train to see his wife and child.

Germany had lost the First World War and large territories had been taken and incorporated into other nations. Many people had declined citizenship in the new nations, and had to leave or were driven from their old homeland. People tried to find a place to live in the remaining, much smaller Germany, but housing was scarce. The economy was in shambles. To make the large payments to the victorious nations, Germany printed money that it actually did not have, inflating the prices. In 1923, Germany couldn't make the reparation payments required by the Versailles Treaty. In response French and Belgian troops occupied the Ruhr region, Germany's most productive industrial region at that time, taking control of most mining and manufacturing companies.

Political unrest within Germany took place. Friedrich Ebert a social democrat, tried to establish a peaceful republic, but communists and anarchists revolted against him. The nation faced too many problems.

Bruno's family, who came from Hohensalza, Posen, Prussia, was one of the refugee families. Their home was now, in 1918, part of the restored Poland. Apparently when this land was part of Prussia, the Rohloffs left their family and home in Pomerania, Prussia and moved into this land. That was probably more than 200 years earlier. Now they had to make a decision to either stay and become Polish citizens or they had to leave. They didn't sign a document surrendering their German citizenship for a new Polish one; they wanted to be Germans. In fact, while Bruno was a prisoner of war in France in 1918 to 1920, he was asked many times to surrender his German citizenship for a Polish one. He always declined. It would have brought him home much earlier than two years after the war ended in the spring of 1920.

Grandfather Eduard Michael Rohloff and Grandmother Anna Amalie Zabel Rohloff had to leave their home at Hohensalza Kastellanstr.37 and were imprisoned for a short time in Warsaw, Poland. After that, they settled in Pasewalk, Germany. It was not an easy time for anyone involved in this expulsion, but especially hard for Walter's blind grandfather. However, he had a marvelous wife who carried the burden without complaining. Their trust in the Lord was endless.

In Pasewalk, Bruno (29) found his family and it was there later that he met his wife, Walter's mother. Irene (28) was from Neubrandenburg and at this time was visiting Pasewalk with friends. Both towns were easy to reach by railroad and were only about 40 km apart. Irene's family had been living in the small communities around Neubrandenburg for a long time. The city was founded by Germans' in 1248 in this then-Slavic nation. Walter didn't know from where the Boers family came and in what year they settled near and in Neubrandenburg. The first church records were created in 1703 and the family was living in the area at that time.

After dating a while, Bruno introduced Irene to his parents. The first visit made a deep impression upon Irene. She had a good relationship right away with her future mother-in-law. She was, as she told Walter, "the love in person." It was different with her future father-in-law. Maybe because he was blind his face looked different or maybe he handled things differently. Grandfather had an imposing figure and was very much in charge. In the morning at breakfast he would tell his sons what he wanted them to do. Even Walter's father, who was then 29 years old, didn't object to his wishes.

Irene spent Christmas Eve with Bruno's family. A small program was presented. The birth of our Savior was remembered. Bruno and his father played a hymn together—Bruno on the concert zither and his Father with the violin. The Christmas story was read and Bruno's father gave a talk about the importance of our Savior's birth. Being blind, he remembered the scriptures well and often quoted from the Bible. They all would sing and pray together. It made a deep impression upon Irene, who had never experienced a Christmas Eve like this.

Bruno and Irene were married in the Lutheran church across the street from Irene's parents' place on the 30th of August, 1921. Not much changed in their lives. Bruno was living with his family in Pasewalk and Irene with her family in Neubrandenburg. The condition didn't change when Walter was born. Irene got along well with her mother before Walter's birth, but after he was born, difficulties arose. Irene's mother had a stroke. One day Bruno took his wife and son to live with his family. Walter used the term "family", because there were still adult children in both of their parents' homes.

For a time the young family was living in Bruno's parents' home, Walter was the star of the show. Irene and her mother–in-law spoiled Walter. Irene told Walter (when he was in his teens) that Bruno would come home from work at noon to have his meal and the basket with baby Walter had to be next to him. One day Bruno's mother came in and saw that Irene had put Walter on the chair next to Bruno's chair. She asked Irene to take Walter away and put him in the next room. Irene objected, saying, "Bruno wants to see his boy when he comes." Irene's mother-in-law insisted and when Irene crossed the threshold to the next room with the baby, the ceiling broke right over the place where Walter's basket had been. It probably would have killed him. Irene's mother-in-law must have been inspired.

"Uncle Kurt Rohloff" was Walter's favorite uncle. When Walter was about three years old he wanted to show Walter his play boat which was about two feet long. He took Walter to the Ueker River. It was a deep, wide river with a strong current. They were standing on a platform and Walter watched Uncle Kurt unravel the rope to which the boat was tied. While doing this, Uncle Kurt moved a little back and unknowingly pushed Walter into the river. Walter struggled and when he almost went under water he called,"Uncle Kurt."Uncle Kurt looked at Walter, calmly tied the boat down, and pulled Walter out of the river. That could have been the end of Walter's story but the Lord didn't want it to end at that time. (Walter remembered this incident as if it had happened yesterday.)

There was a great need for apartments in Germany. The economy was in shambles. When Germany printed too much money to pay the Allies, the resulting inflation robbed the people of all their savings. On payday Bruno wouldn't come home with the money, but went right away to buy groceries and items needed. Bruno paid his bills immediately too, because on the next day the money would not be worth as much.

Walter (Age 4) and his sister Elfriede (Age 3)

A comparison of prices over the years:

1914	1 egg = .08
	1 lb potatoes = .04
	1 lb butter = 1.40
1918	1 egg = .25
	1 lb potatoes = 10.00
	1 lb butter = 3.00
1922	1 egg = 180.00
	1 lb potatoes = 80.00
	1 lb butter = 2400.00
Jun. 1923	1 egg = 5000.00
	1 lb potatoes = 2,000.00
	1 lb butter = 150,000.00
Nov. 1923	1 egg = 80,000,000.00
	1 lb potatoes = 50,000,000.00
	1 lb butter = 6,000,000,000.00
1925	1 egg = .11
	1 lb potatoes = .07
	1 lb butter = 2.30

November of 1923 the price for 1 egg
50,000,000.00 Marks

This 50 million mark banknote, worth approximately US $1 when printed in 1923, this sum would have been worth approximately US $12 million, nine years earlier. The note was practically worthless a few weeks later because of continued inflation.

The young family survived fairly well through those years until 1926, when Bruno lost his job. He couldn't pay the rent for the apartment anymore. Hope for improvement went away when Bruno couldn't find a job. Walter's parents were relieved when Irene's father, Wilhelm Boers, invited the family to move into his house in Neubrandenburg, the house in which Walter was born. Walter's family occupied the largest room, the only one that faced the street. It was upstairs and had an entrance from the hallway. Another entrance in the same hallway went to Irene's parents and Aunt Elisabeth's apartment. Bruno and Irene placed their bed, Walter's sister Elfriede's bed (Elfriede was born in Pasewalk in 1923), and a closet for clothes in the room. They found space for a dining table and a small table for Bruno's zither. But there was not enough room for Walter's bed. Walter, about 5 years old, slept with Grandfather in the next room, a dark chamber with only a small window. The wall of the next house was about a foot or two away from this house so only a little light came through that window.

Walter attended Sunday School in the beautiful Lutheran church across the street. It was the same church in which Walter was christened as a baby. The minister would give a sermon and afterwards the congregation would divide into small groups by age. A teacher explained what the minister was talking about. Walter liked to go, but the church was large and the ceiling high and so it was cold. Walter doesn't remember if his parents went to church, but he remembers the family always had a blessing before their meals. Walter still remembers the words of the prayer they used:

"Lieber Herr Jesu sei unser Gast
Und segne was Du uns bescheret hast."

In April, 1928, Walter started school in the "Postschule," but the school was soon closed after only two years. The school was used because the main school had no room for the two younger grades. Then a new school was built and the girls moved into that school, while the two young grades of boys from the "Postschule" moved into the boy's school. Then the town finally had a boys' and a girls' school. While Walter had been walking about 15 minutes to the "Postschule," he now had to walk more than 30 minutes to the "Knaben Volksschule" (boys' school). To reach the school, Walter had to cross a major railroad crossing of about eight tracks (Walter's family had moved to the outskirts of the town). At times the kids had to wait and let trains pass and they were late for school. (Sometimes the children were late leaving their home and, while they didn't have to wait, used waiting at the crossing as an excuse.)

In those years Walter was a quiet boy and liked to play but showed not much interest in learning. In school he learned the old German handwriting, but in 1930 the old handwriting was not officially used anymore. Everyone in Germany was encouraged to use the same script used in every other European nation. Walter can no longer write it, but can still read it. This now helps Walter to read the old church records when doing genealogy research. When Walter left home the letters his mother wrote to him were in the old German script. Walter doesn't think she ever changed her handwriting.

Germany Walter's place of birth: Neubrandenburg

A world wide depression started in the late 1920's and it hit Germany hard. In October 1927 there were 1.37 million people out of work. It rose to 6.1 million in February 1932. With 44% of the work force out of work, Germany had the largest percentage in the world.

Other nations like the USA hat 25%, France 20% and England 18%. It affected almost every third household in Germany. Bruno was very depressed, but it made him look for a purpose in life. He attended many churches, but no one could give him the answers he sought. Bruno had long discussions with ministers, but never got a satisfying answer.

The house in the center was Grandfather Boers home, Walter's place of birth. This is the place the Rohloff family was kindly invited to stay when Bruno lost his job and - kicked out when Bruno joined The Church of Jesus Christ of Latter Saints, called Mormons

2

LOOKING FOR LIFE'S PURPOSE

One early morning in 1929, Walter walked into his parents' room. He stopped. An unusual sight appeared before him, one he had never seen before. Beside the tile-lined oven and where Bruno had his little table with his zither, his father was kneeling in prayer. Walter didn't know then, but now he knows that his father was asking the Lord for help. Being out of work for some years and looking for work and finding no employment was very discouraging to Bruno. His father-in-law was a butcher and bought and sold domestic animals. He wanted to help Bruno and took him along when he bought and sold animals. But Bruno couldn't understand that a cow cost 300.00 DM when he bought and just a short distant later 400.00 DM when he sold the cow. He was not a business and crafts man. Office work was his trade and he could not find work. It had made him depressed and humble and he was looking for a purpose in life. For a while, Walter's mother was afraid the depressed Bruno might take his life. She knew he had a pistol in the drawer of his night table.

The picture of seeing his father kneeling in prayer is still vivid in Walter's memory, as if it were happened today. Little did his father know the changes this prayer would bring into their lives. What must have been going on in his father's mind? How did he plead for an answer? Bruno surely didn't realize that the answer would place their lives upside down. All would be affected by the turmoil and hardships, but in the end it would give him the answer he was looking for and the knowledge that there was a God, a loving Father, and that we all are his children. It would give him and his family the courage to stand up for their Redeemer, Jesus Christ, in the difficult years ahead. It would give peace and happiness to him and all who accepted this message until the end of their days on earth.

Bruno was raised in a good Prussian home where Jesus Christ and the Bible were the foundation of their belief. Bruno had studied the Holy Script intensively and was looking for an answer to many questions he had. He had discussed these questions with friends and the Lutheran clergy in town. He had visited all kinds of meetings and had not yet found an answer to his questions. For him being out of work for some time added to his problems and made him reflect on his life's purpose.

In 1928 Elder Carl Ernst Toebe, who had been living for a time on the lower floor right below Bruno's apartment of Walter's Grandfather Boers house, wanted to visit Grandmother Boers. Mistakenly he knocked on Bruno's door and Bruno opened. (When Elder Toebe and his family did live in this house, this door was the main door to Opa's living quarters. Opa generously had given the room to Irene and Bruno. Bruno lost his job in Pasewalk and Grandpa invited the family to live with him.) Elder Toebe told him he wanted to visit Grandma Auguste Speerbrecher Boers. Bruno invited him in and told him his mother-in-law had a stroke and had lost the ability to speak, but he would call her daughter Elisabeth, which cared for her. When she came Elder Toebe gave her a tract and talked about the restoration of the Gospel of Jesus Christ. Elisabeth told him she didn't know anything about religion, but her brother-in-law Bruno did. She invited Elder Toebe to speak with Bruno. Elder Toebe started a conversation with Bruno, and in the course Bruno explained, "I like to talk about religion but in your meetings you will never see me. All sects and congregations are only splitting up the whole." The tract he left Bruno to read mentioned the Book of Mormon as the history of the Indians and that interested Bruno.

Time went by and Elder Toebe visited Bruno again and wanted to leave a tract. Bruno told him he was not interested in a tract, but when he would bring him the Book of Mormon, which was mentioned in the first tract, he would read it. He also told him he is out of work and couldn't purchase the book.

Sometime later Elder Toebe returned and brought a book but not the Book of Mormon. It was the book A Voice of Warning by Parley P. Pratt. Bruno was very disappointed and told him he was not interested because he had plenty of those books from the Jehovah's Witnesses. He only wanted to read the Book of Mormon and no other book. A few days later he got what he asked for.

Bruno read in the Book of Mormon all through the night and when he had finished reading, he knew it was the word of God. It gave him the answer to what he had been looking for. Of course, now he was interested in visiting a meeting of The Church of Jesus Christ of Latter-day Saint. He told Irene of his intention. She had reservations because she had not heard any good about the Mormon Church.

Not far from the house in which Bruno's family was living was the meeting room of the LDS Church. Bruno went visiting one Sunday and took a seat in the rear. Everything was strange to him. In the front of the room sat two men. One Elder Gustav Ebert conducted the meeting. Later he learned their names. He also saw Elder Carl Ernst Toebe sitting at the organ. Close to the end of the meeting Bruno heard the conducting elder saying to his counselor: "Brother read the Word of Wisdom". His counselor replied, "Brother today is Sunday? We never did that before." The conducting elder said:"Do it anyhow."

Brother Adolf Kuhfeld was reading from the book called the Doctrine and Covenants about a revelation from God "The Word of Wisdom." Bruno learned it was "Given for a principle with a promise, adapted to the capacity of the weak and the weakest of all saints" and "That in as much as any man drinketh wine or strong drinks among you, behold it is not good." And again, "Tobacco is not for the body, neither for the belly, and is not good for man, but is an herb for bruises." Bruno also heard the promise of the Lord, "man shall find wisdom and great treasures of knowledge even hidden treasures; and shall run and not be weary and shall walk and not faint."

No one in the room knew Bruno with the exception of

Brother Toebe. No one knew why the divine message of the Word of Wisdom needed to be given. But on the last bench someone was sitting, who went thoughtful home.

From Bruno's time of being a prisoner of war in France, he having been released on the 3rd of March 1920, he brought home hemorrhoids. With the years it got worse. Only in the evening could he use the restroom because of the hour long pain he always had after his bowel movements.

So was it on this particular evening, as he went to the restroom, that Bruno changed. He had eight cigarettes in his pocket and wanted, as he usually did, to smoke one. He had already pulled one from the box when the thought hit him: "You ask the Lord every day for work and expect the Lord to listen to you. You believe that the Book of Mormon is a book like the Bible. You don't know yet the connection between the book and what the young man read in the meeting. But you know the Lord does not want you to smoke. The Lord said you are strong enough to overcome. He promised you great blessings. In the past you have asked the Lord many times for help and for the truth. Now He is showing you the way."

Bruno put the cigarettes away and never smoked again.

It was inventory time and the city needed extra help. They hired Bruno for a couple of months to help. In the previous week Bruno had loaned a fellow co-worker a few cigarettes. "Here are your cigarettes," said his co-worker on Monday and handed him the cigarettes. "You can keep them. I don't smoke anymore," Bruno responded.

First the man teased him and tried to get him to take the cigarettes, but Bruno stood firm. Then he went into the next room and told the other workers, "Rohloff does not smoke anymore." They all came over and blew the smoke under his nose. Bruno smiled. It didn't bother him anymore. Something had died in him. What he couldn't do by himself - he didn't have the power - the Lord had helped him to overcome. The addiction died in him, as he used to tell Walter. For years before he had tried to overcome, but always in vain. He was often ashamed of himself. From the little welfare money he received, he took money away from his family to indulge in his habit. Now he had overcome the addiction; his prayer had been answered. He thanked and praised the Lord. It was a present from his Heavenly Father and a testimony of the truthfulness of what the young man had read.

This was not the end of the temptations. On Sunday, his brother Kurt came over from Pasewalk. Knowing what Bruno liked and wanting to make him happy he brought a cigar box full of cigarettes. "You will love this," he told Bruno and gave him the box. Bruno returned the box to him and told him, "I don't smoke anymore." Kurt didn't want to take the box and said, "You will change your mind. Keep the box." But when Uncle Kurt went home, the box with the cigarettes went with him.

That was not all. For years Irene had tried to get Bruno away from this filthy habit. "It stinks and it makes the draperies yellow and we can't afford it," she would say. But it didn't help and Bruno kept smoking. Now, in her thinking, this "Elder" Gustav Ebert, a simple mechanic, who was Bruno's conversation partner but didn't have the education her husband had, got him to quit. In addition to Irene's increased anxiety, Bruno had told her he would now become a member of The Church of Jesus Christ of Latter-day Saints through baptism.

Irene was upset to say the least. It caused her sleepless nights and worries about her husband's, what she felt was, a mindless decision. To make the meals for the family she had to use the kitchen she shared with her sisters Olga and Elisabeth, who took care of their families.

Of course, the top subject in their conversations was about Bruno joining the Mormons, the devil's church. Neither she nor any of her family and friends understood Bruno's decision. Irene loved her husband, but did not comprehend what he was doing. She also was influenced by her family and maybe misled by the clergy. She wrote a letter to her mother-in-law. She explained what was going on with her husband and what she had heard about the Mormons. Bruno parents were honest, God-fearing people. Irene's letter had a depressing effect on them because they loved their son.

Their answer came soon. First, Irene's mother-in-law wrote (3rd of July 1929) to Irene and expressed her concern that her son wanted to give himself into the hands of the devil. She wanted to know where and when the LDS church meetings were to be held. She stated that Bruno's father wanted to surprise Bruno and attend a meeting. Bruno's father also dictated a letter and told his son, he couldn't understand why he, being well educated, would join a satanic sect. He called it "Mormon club." Both parents reminded him of his obligation to care for his family and to recall the teachings he had received in his youth.

You couldn't find a good word about the Mormons in Germany at that time. As a teenager, Walter remembers finding a book in his father's library about the Mormons written by a Lutheran minister. It was full of distortions. The book had probably a great influence on the Lutheran clergy; not being willing to inform themselves about the teachings of the LDS church, they took the writings of this minister for truth.

Bruno, after reading the letters from his parents, gathered his last pennies together and went by train to visit them. He took his scriptures along and tried to explain to his parents his new found faith and why he wanted to join the LDS church. Grandfather knew the Bible well and quoted frequently what the Bible said in his letter and Walter is sure, in their discussion. Bruno did not accomplish what he set out to do. He couldn't change his father's attitude about the Mormons. His father showed Bruno the door. Perhaps Bruno in his enthusiasm about his new faith was a little forceful in his approach. He was baptized 29th of July 1929 into the LDS church.

Bruno's mother passed away about five months later (16th of January 1930). She always had a special love for Bruno. Her husband thought she passed away of a broken heart, because of Bruno changing to the Latter-day Saint faith, but the doctor explained to him otherwise and Bruno attended the funeral and smoothed things over with his father. His father was heartbroken over the loss of his wife and never recovered. He had always depended on her. For a blind man, she was his eyes and his connection with the outside world. He didn't want to live any more. He passed away just six months later (28th of July 1930).

These were trying times for Irene. She was in the middle of all that was going on and didn't understand what it meant. On one side was her husband with no income (they were living on welfare) and with new ideas—a new religion and a religion her family didn't approve of.

Irene's sewing skills – a big help in the depression

On the other side was her family who had been helping them and had given her family a roof over their head. The family thought

Bruno had joined the devil's work. They never looked into the scriptures. "What was good enough for their forefathers was good enough for their family too." In their judgment they depended completely on what others said, and there was nothing good said about the LDS faith at that time.

(Continued on page 22)

Below are transcriptions of the letters that were written by Grandmother Rohloff and Bruno's father in answer of Irene's letter:

Dear Irene,

Just now we received your letter. It is awful, what you write us. We are completely speechless. Is Bruno insane or what? He has now already so much misery, and now he wants to make it still worse. How can he commit with his clever head such a foolish thing, instead he should humble himself before God and ask for his forgiveness of his sins. Then God will help him, for God wants to be ask, if he is to give something. He demands our pleading, if we want to live. Instead he runs in the hands of the devil. If he joins this sect, he is lost forever. Father says he can't imagine how it is possible, that Bruno will give us such grief. He knows however completely well, what we have endured already. Does he not consider how his misery lies heavy in our heart we worry enough about you, but we just can't do, as we want. Our business falls asleep completely. Everybody runs into the large businesses. If we wouldn't have the repairs and here and there a small order, then we would not know what to do. But what can we do, one must carry in patience his cross. But we do not want to run away from the school of our Lord because of it, for we can't do very much. God wants to help us, but we must ask him for it, and trust him alone. Dear Irene! Your need lies heavy in my heart. What we can, we will do, but how, we do not yet know. But with God everything is possible. You write Elfi must have a quilt. They have had both (Elfi and Walter) a quilt, or do you mean an inlet? It would be good if we could express ourselves orally. Father will write Bruno. Write everything exactly, which day in the week the meetings occur and at which time and which street and number. Father thinks to surprise him, but he should not know it. Write immediately. I can't comprehend what become of Bruno. Everything else I could have imagined, only not this. Why does he engage which such devilish people? And then he even wants to throw his little children into his ruin. Does he not fear God at all? How should God be with him, if he leads such a life? He should search his soul. On knees he should ask his Savior for pardon, that he gives him power and assistance that he may resist the devil. He should turn back, before it is too late, for then there is no going back. He should however not sell his soul. Now may God be with you. Be you all greeted from all of us.

From Grandfather Rohloff to Bruno his son:

Dear Bruno!
Just now we learn that you belong to a Mormon club. Even more you want to be baptized. Even more you want your children to be baptized also. What shall we think of you? Have you lost your mind? We can't explain your conduct in any other way. What devil has bewildered your senses that you have joint an evil society? Does the Lutheran truth not suffice? Or have you no knowledge?

The dear God has given you a sound mind so that you can recognize the truth. I must conclude from your current conduct, that your whole service here in Pasewalk has been only hypocrisy. You expect from God help and serve the devil. Do not err, God can't be mocked, for what the person sows, that will he harvest also. Truly you should have more necessary things to do than to run to this evil society, for it stands written: He who does not care of his family is worse than a Jew. Do you not feel sorry for your children? Do you not think about a conclusion of the holy commandments, that the sins of the fathers shall haunt the children down to the third and fourth generation? You still want to rob the children of the gift of grace which God has given them through the holy baptism? Still more, do you want to load a curse on you, your family and your grandchildren? Read what Paul wrote to the Galatians: Whosoever preaches the gospel differently that I have preached it shall be condemned. This curse would strike you and your children, if you leave the Lutheran confession. The same apostle writes to the Hebrews: Who once are illuminated and has tasted the powers of the future world and has received the Holy Spirit and apostatized, can never again be enlightened. Dear Bruno, listen to our pleas, avoid the society. Think of it, what kind of heartache you will cause us. What would pastor Wohlgemuth say if he still lived, who has instructed you so truly in the word of the truth? Will he not stand on judgment day before God as a witness against you? Once more dear Bruno, we ask you, leave this sect alone and ask God, to forgive you your sins. Our God says: he who will keep my word will recognize the truth and the truth shall make him free. If you now submit yourself to sinister forces, you attest by doing so, that you do not keep the word of God, and that is so painful to our hearts. Now we want to close. Be you, your dear wife and children cordially greeted from your parents and Arnold. ------

End of the letters

The Eduard & Anna Zabel Rohloff family

Irene's sister Olga, family had just moved into the room were Walter was born, and she made life more difficult for Irene, Walter's mother. It was Bruno's misfortune one day to come into the kitchen where the three sisters prepared the meals for their families. (Irene didn't understand what Bruno had done either, but she loved her husband and couldn't change anything in the situation.) That day Bruno, visiting the kitchen, got into a terrible argument with Irene's youngest sister, Elisabeth. From that day forward she disliked Bruno. This was an almost unbearable situation for Irene. She had to listen to the constant criticism of her husband when she prepared the meals. It is really remarkable that she still stood with Bruno. Walter doesn't know if his father ever fully realized what his wife went through.

Then there was another thing. Bruno brought home the money from the welfare and gave it to Irene. Irene looked at it and saw the amount was less then she had received before. She asked,

> Don't we get DM 10, 50 a week?"

> Yes" Bruno said, "The missing money I gave as a tithing to my church."

That was the straw that broke the camel's back and she aired all her frustration. No one talked to Bruno about his joining this devilish Mormon sect, but everyone talked to her. All the people she knew showed their disapproval of Bruno's choice to her. She carried the pressure. She understood very little about religion or why it was important to leave the Lutheran faith and become a member of The Church of Jesus Christ of Latter-day Saints. What she knew was she had less money to feed and dress her family. She had already taken a house cleaning job at the family doctor's home. It was hard on her and she hated to do it. Bruno listened to her and when she was through he took the money he designated for tithing and placed it with the other. While doing that, he looked her straight in the eyes and said,

"You make a decision today. You go with me or our ways part."

Irene was stunned and after a moment of silence she pushed the money Bruno had designated as tithing back to him.

After that the family all attended the LDS Church. Walter loved his Sunday school teacher. Sister Martha Wehse rapidly captured his heart. She had a nice way of teaching the children to love Jesus Christ. In August 1930, Elder Gustav Ebert, a stake missionary who in his lifetime baptized nearly 100 converts and Bruno's lifelong conversation partner came over. All sitting around the table, he asked Irene and Walter questions about the teachings of the church. He asked if they wanted to become members of The Church of Jesus Christ of Latter-day Saints by being baptized similar to Christ's baptism. Yes, they wanted to be baptized and become members of the Lord's church.

It was a beautiful summer day when they walked to the Tollensesee, a large and beautiful lake surrounded by forest. They stopped away from the public beach at a quiet place. A bench was close to the shoreline, providing a nice view of the lake. Many members of the church went along.

Irene and Walter's place of baptism

Elder Ebert performed the sacred ordinance of baptism, and they "as were baptized into Jesus Christ were baptized into his [dead.]

Therefore we are buried with him by baptism into death: that like as Christ was raised up from the dead by the glory of the Father, even so we also should walk in newness of life" (Rom.6:3, 4). While they later sat on the bench, he confirmed all of the converts as members of the church and blessed them with the Gift of the Holy Ghost. There were eight converts who made a commitment on that day to walk in the Lord's way. Before they returned home, Sister Marie Kruse went to Irene and gave her a bouquet of beautiful flowers. "Oh," said Irene, "they are as beautiful as the flowers on my wedding day." Arriving at home she looked at the calendar and saw it was the 30th of August 1930, her wedding anniversary.

. One day Walter was home from school, sick in bed. During the daytime he was privileged to lie in his parent's bed, but at night he had to return to the ugly chamber, to his bed. He had to gargle saltwater to fight diphtheria. The family couldn't afford a doctor and Bruno did his best to keep the family healthy. Walter didn't like to gargle saltwater, but when Irene his mother offered him a candy, he would do it. In this world wide depression candy was rare in the house. His parents were glad when they could place a meal on the table. Walter remembered well his father cutting an apple into four parts and giving each one of the family a piece. The meals were simple but the children didn't go hungry. If the parents did, Walter didn't know. The Great Depression ruled not only in Germany, but covered the world. Millions of men were out of work. Every third man in Germany was looking for a job. The political parties fought each other and the government changed frequently. No helpful changes came, but then Hitler's party appeared on the scene, and his party gained momentum and grew.

Meanwhile, Irene's family thought they could still change Bruno's mind about religion with force. One evening while Walter was still lying sick in his parent's bed, the door to the chamber opened. In came Irene's father, her brothers Wilhelm and Erich and her brother-in-law, Willy Tank. They came maybe to help her sister Irene and to persuade her husband to leave the LDS Church. Bruno was sitting at his little table next to the large wardrobe and playing the zither. His heavy cane hung from the top of the wardrobe. Walter could hear the men getting louder and getting nearer to Bruno. Then Walter saw his father looking up to his cane and the four men disappeared rapidly. They knew Bruno had defended his bride with that cane, as bad behaving men tried to harm her in a bar before they got married.

The Neubrandenburg LDS Branch. (1931)

Why were these men against Bruno joining the LDS church? They knew very little about their own Lutheran faith and absolutely nothing about The Church of Jsus Christ of Latter-day Saints. They never attended church. The only one in Irene's family who attended was Aunt Elisabeth, who at times attended the Lutheran Church. She gave Irene a hard time when they met in the kitchen, and later became a stout communist and was buried as such.

A few days later Bruno was notified by the housing authority that he had to vacate his room by the 31st of December 1930 or his family would be evicted. Eviction meant his furniture would be placed on the sidewalk of the street. If the furniture remained there at nightfall, the furniture would then be moved by the housing authority to an old, retired railroad car. These railroad cars were placed in the slums of the town. Irene said to her husband

“I will never go there. I would rather die.”

“Don’t be afraid,” Bruno said, “It is for the Lord’s sake. He will care for us.”

3

THE GREAT DEPRESSION

Bruno tried hard to find a small apartment. Whenever he heard about an apartment he went there, only to find it was already rented. It was enough to drive one to despair. Toward the end of the year 1930 he found a short-time job with the city to help with the inventory. Shortly before Christmas a man named Paul Standke walked into his office and asked for Bruno. He told Bruno the housing authority had sent him. He asked Bruno if he would be interested in renting a small apartment, a room and kitchen. Bruno told him he would be at his home right after work. When Bruno and Irene arrived at Pasewalkerstr.11 they saw the landlord had divided a three room apartment into two apartments containing one room and a kitchen or makeshift kitchen. Only a few had the money to pay for a large apartment. The apartment with the kitchen was already rented. Bruno rented the apartment with the makeshift kitchen.

On the 30thof December, 1930, Bruno's family moved into their new apartment. The living room was too small for the two beds Elfriede and Walter used. Bruno moved the kitchen cabinet forward as needed and placed the children's beds behind. It worked out great, just as if it was made for it. Bruno had told Irene not to worry, the Lord would help. He was right, the Lord helped. They praised the Lord. They later rented the whole apartment when the other renters moved out. They lived in this apartment for the rest of their lives.

It was the ideal place for the children. The area was called "Kleckersdorf" because the homes were "kleckert" (meaning here a home and there another one). It had a lot of open space. Not far away was the Datze River and behind the river the hills. Bruno leased a meadow on the river side and made part of it into a garden spot.

Elfriede and Walter thought working in the garden was a great idea and Bruno gave the children a spot to take care of. First they thought it was fun, but then it seemed like work and they didn't like it anymore. Bruno raised all kinds of vegetables. Walter liked Bruno's cauliflower best. Bruno tied the leaves together. That made nice, dense heads of cauliflower. But it also hid what Walter did to them. Walter would open up the leaves and eat the heads then close the leaves again. Bruno never punished him for that. Because he knew Walter loved to eat raw vegetables.

Rest stop on Walter's bike ride to the Ruegen Island
(Walter at right)

In front of the grocery store and the bakery was space for the children to play. In between the display windows hung a nicely decorated mailbox. On the front at each corner it had downward-pointed pins. The children played run and catch. With other kids behind him, Walter bent down and ran underneath the mailbox. He brought up his head too early and one of the downward pointing pins penetrated his head. He doesn't remember anything after that. When he woke up, he was sitting on a chair in his house and the landlord's wife was washing the blood from his head. Walter was unconscious and didn't know how he came to the house or what had happened.

For the kids, the piece of land Bruno leased on the Datze River was the ideal spot in the summer. Bruno had not cultivated all of the meadow. A large part, especially along the river, was left the way it was found. It made a great playground for the kids. They could play in the river except in a few places where the river was too deep. Walter and the kids knew the places well but not one of them could swim well and one day misfortune almost hit them. The landlord's daughter, Erika Standke, got into a deep place in the river and surely would have drowned, but after a short hesitation Walter jumped into the water after her. Both struggled with all their strength and effort and they made it to a safe place.

Walter's 1st year in elementary school (1928, Walter row 3 from the front, marked with an 'O')

Our small branch of the church had a Boy Scout troop and Georg Dauss was the scoutmaster. Walter was too young, only 11 years old, to be part of it. In 1933 the troop planned an outdoor activity and invited Walter to come along. They would go on a bike ride into the hills but Walter didn't have a bike and didn't know how to ride a bike even though his younger sister, Elfriede, already knew how to ride a bike and how to swim. One of the adult members took him along on his bike. They went into the hills, made a campfire in the dark, and warmed up some hot dogs. There was one for each one of the troop. While the scouts were working on some activities, Walter had to watch the hot dogs.

Most of the adult men in the branch were out of work and having a hot dog was a luxury. Walter couldn't remember when he had last eaten one. All that he knew was that he liked to eat hot dogs. Being alone and watching these delicious sausages was too big of a temptation for Walter. Knowing that one was for him, Walter took and ate one. He enjoyed the taste so much and was so hungry he stole someone else's hot dog and ate it too. Of course the scouts were not pleased with his unkind behavior when they returned. On the way back on the trail through the dark forest, the scouts wanted to teach him a lesson. They ran away and left him alone in the dark. Walter had to find his way back to the bikes alone. The scouts waited until Walter arrived by the parked bikes. This was Walter's only scouting adventure. Scouting was later forbidden by Hitler (1 Dec 1936), so he never became a scout in Germany.

In 1932, Germany had 32 political parties. Walter was 10 years old and understood very little of what was happening. On the many election days Germany had, he saw the Nazis sitting at the polling places singing and squabbling. Somehow his friends were divided in parties, too. Of course they were divided into the parties their parents favored: Communists, Socialists and Nazis. Walter's parents never spoke to him about politics and parties and he didn't know which one they favored. However he went with the one his friends favored, the Social Democrats.

Walter and his friends left their favorite playground and marched to their homes because it was raining. They had just one tarpaulin and they held it over their heads and sang. In the summer they would come together and would sing folk songs. But this time they didn't sing just folk songs, they sang songs they had heard the Nazis sing. As Walter came into his house his father was waiting for him. "What were you singing?" Walter knew there was something wrong and he knew it was about the Jewish people. Bruno had talked about the unjust treatment of the Jews to Walter many times. He disagreed with the Nazi philosophy. Walter told him, "We were singing folk songs." "Oh, no," his father said, "You were not only singing folk songs, you were singing songs against the Jewish people." Walter lied and denied it, but it didn't help. "You did and so that you do not forget to treat the Jewish people fairly, I will give you a lecture. They are God's children just as we are." He gave Walter a long lecture and then moved a chair in front of them. Walter had to lie over the seat while his father gave him a good spanking.

Some years later, Walter learned that his father had meant what he said. While reading Gerd Skibbe's books Walter discovered that his father had saved the life of a Jew. In later years Gerd informed Walter that his father had heard in a manager's meeting (Bruno was personal manager) the names of Jews who would be sent into a concentration camp. His father knew one such Jew. In the darkness of the night he did the dangerous walk over to that man's home and informed him about what was going on. Because of this, the family was able to safely leave Germany.

Bruno had previously patronized and been treated well in Mr. Rosenstein's shoe store. Now (late 1933) Nazi S.A. (Storm Troopers) men were standing at the door and wanted to prevent Bruno and Walter from entering the store. They told Bruno, that good Germans wouldn't buy at a Jewish store. Without hesitation Bruno told the men, "The store was good enough and helped us in the depression when we had little money, it is good enough now to be patronized." They went and bought their shoes there.

Once Hitler came to power, people found work. After looking for work for many years, Bruno found work as a carpenter in the nearby town of Trollenhagen. Hitler was building an airport for the new air force. The work was not what Bruno was trained for and not to his liking, but it put food on our table. It was hard on Bruno. He was not used to physical work, but now he could pay the debts he had accumulated over the years.

In 1934, Walter was old enough to join the Boy Scout troop in the church; all youth organizations were not yet forbidden, but rumor's had it soon would be. The effort of the Nazi Party was to get every youth into the Nazi "Hitler Youth." Saturday's were declared "State Youth Day." Each Saturday morning members of the Hitler Youth gathered to participate in sports, paramilitary exercises, and be indoctrinated in the Nazi philosophy. Walter was not a member of the Hitler Youth, and he didn't have to go to the Hitler Youth meetings, but he had to attend school and there he had a similar program. In the beginning there were about 40 to 50 boys, but as time went on, the group got smaller and smaller. There were about 12 boys left when Walter discussed with his father the possibility of joining the HJ (Hitler Youth). Walter didn't want to be an outsider anymore and he thought it would be easier for him to be accepted at a college. Bruno and Walter discussed it in detail, Walter's "pro" against Bruno's "no." After a time Bruno gave his permission and Walter joined the Hitler Youth. Maybe Bruno thought: A wrong unintentional word from Walter could bring him much harm.

There were four areas of training for the HJ. They were:

1. Sport: track and field, soccer, and handball with 11 men on each team;
2. Field Sport: training like army and battle attacks;
3. Handling guns: training in the use and maintenance of guns;
4. Nazi Doctrines: teachings and training on the philosophy of the party.

Walter enjoyed the sport and field sport activities. He became very good in using the small bore guns and he attended a school where he was taught to train others. The training included learning to teach Nazi doctrines. "Welt Anschauung" was the name. Walter passed all four areas, but because of his LDS affiliation, he was not permitted to teach.

Bruno found office work in 1935 with the "Winterhilfe," a relief program for the needy. It was very similar to the LDS Church "Welfare Program." People and companies donate items and the organization distributed the items to the needy.

The Nazis had also organized an "Eintopf" (a one pot meal) on Sunday. People were encouraged, on a designated Sunday each month, to prepare a simple meal and donated the money they saved to the poor. Boys would stand on the streets with a donation can and collect donations. Walter collected money at times, and from what he saw people gave freely. The brethren in the church said Hitler learned much from the LDS Church (Fast Sunday).

To help the poor, home-carving industry in the Ore Mountains of Germany, the boys sold beautiful, small carved items, fabricated in the home industry there, to hang on the Christmas trees. People liked these items and they sold them fast. They positioned themselves on the street corners and showed the beautiful carvings and sold those to the bypassing public. In the beginning all this was done to help the poor, but later in the war the money went to help finance Hitler's war machine.

Most people who worked at the "Winterhilfe" belonged to the Nazi party. Bruno worked there and was also asked to join the party. He was not sure if he should join or not. The mission president of the LDS church, who was from the USA, was in town visiting the branch. Bruno asked him if he should join the Nazi party. He didn't like the mission president's answer. Walter guessed Bruno expected a "yes" or "no." However the mission president told Bruno that he had received the Holy Ghost when he was confirmed a member of the church to guide him and help him make decisions and that he should inquire of the Lord. When Walter was older and his father told him the story, Walter loved it. Bruno truthfully filled out the application form from the party and gave it to his superior. A few days later he came into the office of his superior and saw his application lying on his superior's desk. Bruno saw a change had been made on his entry under "Religion." Someone had crossed out his answer and had written "Gott glaeubig" (believing in God).

"Who changed my application?" Bruno asked.

"I did." his superior replied.

"I didn't give you permission to do that."

"Herr Rohloff," his superior said, "with your answers you will not become a member of the party."

"What do I care?" Bruno said.

He then told his superior in uncompromising terms what he thought of the party and of changing an application. Of course, that was the end of his employment. He was back looking for a job.

Bruno found work, much more to his liking in a private company, where he worked for many years, until the end of the war. The company made ammunition, among other things.

Walter finished his ninth year of primary school. Before he could get into a technical college, he had to undergo a talent test. He was told where to apply for work and school. Everyone who graduated from primary school had to do that. It was a General and Manual test and after the test he was told where to work and school.. Apparently he did fairly well with the test because Walter applied for and was accepted into a very selective trade technical college. It was part of the trade technical college system in town, but was located in a factory. It had students who came mainly from outside of town and from all over Germany. It was a model vocational training college. The school had visitors from many nations who were interested in how the students were taught and trained to make tools for all kinds of production work. For two years Walter received training in a shop. The supervisor gave the students an about 4'' long piece of u-iron and the boys had to make it square, drill holes into it and thread the holes. They learned to work safely on machines, like drill presses, milling machines, lathes and other machines. For another year and a half Walter worked in the different departments of the company: electric, electronic and more. The last one was the developing department where he worked on developing machines to produce parts automatically. Of course the students had one day of instruction every week. Because of this training, Walter was never without a job in Germany or here in the USA.

On holidays some people decorated their homes
(1935)

Walter knew the director was a member of the Nazi party, but he didn't know about the rest of the instructors. All of the students had to be members of the Hitler Youth and at special occasions the students had to wear H.J. uniforms.

From the beginning Walter communicated well with the students in his class and later with all in the school. He represented them well when he was class or student body president and he was well respected by them. Walter never had difficulties with the students for being a member of the LDS church, but they liked to tease him for not smoking or drinking alcohol.

On political holidays, like Hitler’s birthday, he had to lead the students in their activities. Like a company of soldiers, he had to direct the students at flag ceremonies. In 1940, Walter was kicked out of the “Hitler Youth” for disrespect of the flag, but he still stayed on as student body president and he was still required to lead the student’s flag ceremonies. Walter stood in front of all the uniformed students in his civilian clothing and gave orders. The director confronted him and asked, “Why didn’t you wear your uniform?” Walter told him, he was not a member of the Hitler Youth any more. The director didn’t ask why Walter left the H.J. and Walter didn’t give more information. The director didn’t object and he was student body president until he graduated. The director wore the party badge on his jacket, but like so many, was probably only a member of the party to keep his job.

What made Walter change and dislike his membership in the H.J. (Hitler Youth) was the change in leadership. Adult leaders from the S.A. (Sturm Abteilung, a part of the Nazi party) had taken over

The German model trade technical college in
Neubrandenburg, Germany (1937)

the leadership in this youth program and were putting more emphasis on Nazi doctrine. Before it had been more sport, field sport and shooting the small bore rifles.

Walter remembered one outing when the boys walked around the beautiful, about 10km long and 2km wide Lake Tollensesee. They visited on the way the castle of the once very popular queen of Prussia Louise and slept in straw at a farm. While the boys were tired, Walter was fresh enough to go for water and food. He served the hungry and thirsty boys.

Another clear memory Walter had was of a bike ride to the vacation paradise, the Ruegen Island, in the Baltic Sea, about 100 miles north of his hometown. Crossing the sea on a long bridge and visiting the island with rocky cretaceous mountains was much fun for Walter and the boys. His father was not in favor of his membership in the Hitler Youth, but as he saw the enjoyment Walter had with these activities he helped in his preparation.

In 1937 Walter, 15 years old, had a long talk with his mother before he started college. He told his mother he was not interested in girls. She didn't believe him and told him it wouldn't be long and he would make the acquaintance of girls. Walter didn't believe her, but after a few months he looked at girls in a different way. When he was with friends he made the acquaintance of many girls and after some time he met Lori Berendt. They did many things together. Walter surely loved her. She was not LDS and had a different view of life than he had, even though his own view was not very well established. One day they had a disagreement, She told him he didn't love her and she broke off their friendship. Walter was heartbroken and very sad. He explained to his mother his problems and his mother made some recommendations. One was to get engaged. But Walter was not ready and willing to do that. Sometime later, when Walter was in the Army and on recovery furlough, he met her again. She wanted to restore their friendship, but Walter had no interest then. He had changed.

Walter always liked sports. In the days of depression when his father was out of work for seven long years, the kids would play soccer bare-footed. Their parents complained about the boys wearing their shoes to play soccer. They told the kids they couldn't afford to buy shoes. Since they were used to running around bare-footed all day long in the summer time they didn't mind kicking the ball with the bare feet.

For a time Walter practiced some boxing and later Greek-Roman style wrestling. Because of the war and Walter's work schedule it was just practice within the club. His mother didn't like him to wrestle. He came home tired and exhausted and she feared for his health. He wrestled against a German champion, who was much better than Walter, but he never got Walter lying on his shoulder. After graduation he played field-handball for a sport club, Turnverein Jahn. When they would have made the liege best team they would have played for the German championship. The team was not good enough to make it.

Walter's favorite uncle, Kurt Rohloff, got married on the 22nd of October, 1940, and Walter's family was invited. His parents couldn't go, but Walter and his sister Elfriede went. The wedding was celebrated on the bride's farm in Ferdinandshof, Pomerania. It was the first time he had attended a wedding. Walter had heard about the amount of food served at a wedding on a farm. He was very much impressed with the food served and enjoyed every minute. There were many young people of Elfriede and Walter's age, and they were all sitting at an extra table. The girl assigned to Walter had chosen to sit with the adults. Apparently Uncle Kurt had discussed with his brother Arnold the seating arrangement and Arnold had objected to Walter sitting with that girl. Kurt had not agreed with Arnold's wishes and followed the wishes of the mother of that girl. Walter didn't know what was going on. They had nice conversations and she arranged for them to be alone. Walter had the opportunity and could have kissed her, but he was not interested to build a short term friendship with her, he was looking for an eternal companion.

Having heard about the drinking that went on at these parties, Walter had gone to his uncle and told him he wouldn't drink alcohol and he asked his uncle to respect that. He told Walter he would.

It was the custom in Germany to toast for the health of the newlyweds. After they took their seats, alcohol was served, but Walter turned his glass upside down so it was not filled. Before the meal everybody stood up and raised their glass filled with alcohol and drank. Walter just raised his empty glass and wished the newlyweds well.

After everybody sat down Walter's uncle got up and raised his glass, which had been refilled and toasted toward Walter. Walter had no choice. He got up, lifted his empty glass and wished him well. All the guests at his table (he didn't know any one of them) objected and insisted Walter had to fill his glass. Walter didn't give in nor allow them to serve him alcohol. To make things right, he had his glass filled with milk and he drank to the health of the newlyweds. The laughter of the guests didn't bother Walter. He was sure the Word of Wisdom, which said alcohol and smoking were not good for men, was given by the Lord and he tried hard to keep it.

Walter had courage at the wedding, but later in the year when he graduated from college, he almost gave in. In the evening after the graduation ceremony they had a party. They even had a band playing and Walter's friend, Hermann Cziborra, was in the band. These parties were more or less drinking parties and Walter typically stayed away from them. However, he couldn't miss this one. During the day the graduates had visited a beer brewery and had seen how beer was made. At the end of the visit they had been given a case of beer to use at their party.

All evening Walter was teased and invited to drink. "Just take one sip. It won't do you any harm." After Walter heard it often enough, slowly he started to believe it. Walter raised his full glass with beer and brought it close to his lips. At that moment he looked over to his friend in the band. A waiter offered him a drink and he declined to take it. Walter put his glass of beer down and was ashamed. Here he was ready to drink beer, while across the room his friend whom he had taught not to drink alcohol, declined. It was a good lesson for Walter. He thanked the Lord for this impressive lesson.

Walter had never seen their branch of the church make more progress than under the leadership of Elder Cox. He was a missionary from Price, Utah, and had Native American blood in his veins. The branch grew and they needed more room. Elder Cox found just the right rooms close to the railroad station.

Walter thought the poor living conditions in Germany, with

every third man out of work, made people look for help and many turned to God. When Hitler came to power, people found work and turned from God and joined the Nazi organizations. Over time Walter could see how the living conditions changed. Close to where he was living a large factory and on top of the hills, in the small town of Trollenhagen an airport was built. The Autobahn was started, and near where Walter was living, new homes with affordable prices were offered. Even his father spoke about buying a home there.

Of course, most of what was built or done was to strengthen the armed forces. Men had to join the army and before they were drafted into the army, they had to serve for six month in a so called "Arbeitsdienst (work service)." Men and women working on government projects also were prepared for army duties. They worked with shovel and spade. They exercised after work with the spade like the army exercised with a gun.

Walter, as student body president, leads the way.
Students visiting the shipyards in Warnemuende.

On the streets Walter saw men dressed in uniforms: field gray from the armed forces and brown from the Nazi party. On

Sundays people went to their party meetings and by 1940 the churches were almost empty. The attendance in the LDS branch was shrinking too. Of course some men were in the armed services, but others had turned their backs on the church. They had what they needed to make a living and didn't need God any more. The teachings of the party were against God and the church, and the party encouraged people with word and print to turn away from God and Christ. The LDS branch lost the rooms in which they held church meetings, except for the classrooms. Then in 1942, during the war, they lost those rooms too. Soon after Walter joined the armed services and left the area, no regular meetings were held in that branch.

4

ESCAPING HITLER'S ARMED SS

Walter didn't remember the reason for him being at the railroad station when he saw Rudy Steudt. He was a member of the LDS Church, but Walter had not seen him lately. He looked good in his dark armed SS uniform. They talked about the past and then he talked about the much-praised armed SS unit. He told Walter never to join the armed SS (Schutz Staffel—protective squadron). As soon as he could, he would get out. He didn't want Walter to tell why, but he said it was not for him. Walter's father counseled him against the armed SS too, but Rudy was even more convincing. He didn't want to tell Walter why that if he joined he would regret it very much.

Many people probably agreed with Hitler when the old territories Germany had lost after the First World War were taken back by the German armed forces. Hitler lied and deceived not only the German nation but the leaders of other nations too. He talked about peace and prepared for war. He had brought bread and butter to the table and people started to believe him. His favorite words were; "Give me ten years' time and you won't recognize Germany anymore." How right he was. After 10 years he had Germany turned into rubble and ashes.

The leaders of other nations had started to get along with Hitler in Munich, but were betrayed when Hitler attacked Poland. Walter remembered that day very well. The employees were all ordered into the factory's large meeting hall. Walter took a place close to the entrance door and watched how the people came into the room; most were smiling. They were told they would hear a message from Hitler. Perhaps some people expected an attack on Poland. Hitler had tried to get back the Polish Corridor, which divided East-Prussia from the main body of Germany. Poland of course was not willing to give their only connection with the Baltic Sea away. The press had reported how much Poland had wronged Germany. Hitler spoke explaining that Polish soldiers had attacked the German radio station in Gleiwitz, Silesia, Germany. In response, German troops had attacked Poland earlier that morning. The room was quiet; no one knew this would be the beginning of World War II. At home Walter's father's face was serious. He would have liked to have his home town become part of Germany again, but he didn't like war. He said, "What will Poland's allies say and do about all of this?"

After graduation from the trade technical college in the fall of 1940 Walter stayed with the company of which the college was part. He worked in production because more and more men were taken out of production and placed in the armed services. His department had two groups and Walter was asked to supervise one of the two. In his group he had between twelve and fourteen women, some barely older than Walter, and all from out of town. He had to give the women work, set up their equipment and repair their equipment when they had problems. They were good looking women, mostly from Austria. Most liked him and would have loved to entertain him. Even when the women ruined items to get his attention, he didn't report them, but he didn't accept their invitations for a date either.

In the other group was a man who had a wife and five kids. He did his work well, but when he opened his mouth filthy jokes and songs came out. At first Walter thought it wouldn't affect him, but once, when he was helping a woman with her job, he realized he was humming a song of this fellow. Walter was shocked. He didn't want that. He had warned that fellow many times to quit his offensive jokes and songs. The man just smiled at him and told him he had no authority over him. He was right, he didn't, but Walter went to the boss and told him he would leave the department if this man didn't quit his offensive behavior or wasn't transferred. First their boss tried to mediate between them, but that fellow wouldn't change and Walter didn't give in. The man was transferred.

Germany attacked Poland from the west and later Russia attacked from the east. England and France declared war on Germany when Germany would not call back its troops. However they didn't declared war on Russia, who had also penetrated Poland's soil. The good relationship Germany had on paper with Russia didn't hold for long. They didn't trust one another. In 1941, German troops stormed into Russia. Germany already had armed forces in Denmark, Norway, Belgium, France, and in all the Balkan nations and now they were attacking that large and mighty Russia. Hitler must have been blind to reality.

Walter worked long hours. After his regular 8½ hours he worked in research developing new materials. He had to work many Sundays. Sometimes he didn't go home, but slept on the work bench. Walter made good money but couldn't buy anything with it. For all products you needed a ration card, and the cards were hard to get. On one payday, his money was less than he expected. After inquiring, he was told that because he was young and should be in the armed services, money had been taken out to finance the war. Walter didn't like that a bit and went over to the union leader. He of course, was a Nazi and favored this arrangement. Walter was straightforward and told him in no uncertain terms how he felt about them stealing his hard earned money. If there was money needed, he wanted to make the decision about how much he wanted to donate. Besides that, would he guarantee Walter wouldn't be drafted into the armed services tomorrow? Walter feared he would be picked up and put in jail, but he didn't hear anything about it again. He also got his money. Both the army and the armed SS wanted him. The army sent him a compulsory draft order and he gave it to his company. They called him essential and that took care of it.

Walter was notified that the armed-SS wanted him and he had to appear for a medical examination. At that time the difference between the Army and the armed-SS was that the Army could draft him, but he would have to sign up voluntarily for the armed-SS. They talked a long time to Walter and pressured him hard. They told him a good German would join the armed SS. He had to watch what he said. A wrong word could put him into prison. Walter knew they would like to have him. They liked tall and healthy men and Walter was over 6 feet tall and healthy. The problem was he didn't want to go. He fabricated a lie and told them he was going to join the Air Force. Hermann Goering, the field marshal was still favored by Hitler and the armed-SS couldn't touch recruits for the Air Force.

The second time Walter received draft orders from the armed-SS it was much more difficult and they pushed him hard. Walter stood by his lie. When they couldn't change his mind and he didn't sign the paper, they let him go.

The third time was different. Walter knew his old trick wouldn't work anymore. Before the medical examination they placed about 100 men into a room that held just that number. Walter sat on the last row and there was a pass-through in front of and along the back seats. The SS showed a movie and one of them gave a talk about the excellence of the armed-SS and why good Germans should join. After the talk they moved the tables so that only one man could pass to get out of the room.

Alongside the tables were armed-SS men who pressured the men to sign the paper to join. From his seat Walter could see that almost everyone signed the paper, some after a long discussion. Walter looked for a way to get out of the room. In the rear of the room on the end of the pass-through was a locked double door which led to the outside. Walter checked the door and it was in poor shape. He went back as far as he could on the pass-through, ran and threw himself, as hard as he could, against the door. The door broke open and he along with many others left the room as fast as they could.

It wasn't long before Walter got another compulsory draft paper from the Army. At this time he asked his company to let him go. They didn't understand why Walter wanted to go while everybody else tried to stay. His father couldn't understand it either. Bruno thought Walter's company had let him go. He wanted Walter to join his company and that he would take care of the order. Walter made it clear to his father there was something in him that wanted him to go. All who knew about Walter's decision called him a

"Dummkopf," but Walter felt it was time for him to join the armed forces and was tired of being home. All his friends were in the service and some had been killed in action. Their mothers looked at him as if Walter was a war dodger and Walter hated that. He was not afraid of the war, but Walter really didn't understand what that meant. While he was at home he worked hard. The company liked and appreciated his work and wanted to keep him. Years later Walter saw the hand of the Lord in this. Soon after Walter joint the army the armed-SS got the permission to do the compulsory draft and Walter wouldn't have had a choice and would have to join the armed-SS.

The war was now more than two years old and no end was in sight. After many German victorious battles in Russia, the winter 1941/42 brought a change. The German armies were surprised by the unusually early winter and the bitter cold. They were not prepared and had heavy casualties. Many froze to death or had frozen body parts. The Russians were well prepared and prevented the Germans from coming close to Moscow, the capital city. All over Germany, people were asked to donate blankets and coats to keep the troops warm. It came too late for many. Food had been rationed since the beginning (butter a long time before) the war and the rations became smaller and smaller. Money was plentiful, but it was almost useless. Ration cards were required for the food people wanted. There was a black market, but drastic penalties kept it small.

Air raids were not a problem at this time. The General of the Air Force, Herman Goering, had declared at the beginning of the war, "No enemy air force will penetrate German airspace or his name will be Meyer." After the Allies bombed Hamburg, people called him Herman Meyer.

Listening to enemy radio stations was forbidden, but people did it anyway. Heavy penalties were given to those who were caught. All reading material had been censored since Hitler came to power. One day there was a meeting on the hills behind Walter's house. The Nazi party started a big controlled fire to burn all books not in line with the concepts of their party. People were allowed to hear and to read only what the party approved.

On a beautiful morning, the 18thof February 1942, Walter reported with others for military duty at the railroad station in his home town of Neubrandenburg. From there they were transported to the city of Schwerin, where the "Infantry Regiment 89" was stationed. Since the train was not expected to leave before the afternoon the commanding officer gave the draftees furlough on their word of honor to be back in time. Walter liked that and visited with his girlfriend Elly Pilgrim at her work place. However, his feelings changed after the men arrived at Schwerin and the gates to the barracks were closed behind them. He felt as if he were in prison.

Walter's Opa, and Irene's Father, Wilhelm Boers

Before Walter left home, his father talked to him about army life and things he would have to face. Bruno encouraged him to stay firm in the gospel and gave Walter a pocket size New Testament. His father counseled him to make good use of it. While Walter said "thank you" to his father, in his mind he thought "I will leave this New Testament in my clothing when I mail the clothing back home." That's what he thought, and that's what he did. After they were issued uniforms, Walter placed his clothing in a box and left the New Testament in his jacket.

Walter didn't know why the mailing was delayed, but for several days the boxes with the clothing laid on top of their lockers.

5

WHAT IS THAT?

Every morning they had their uniform inspection and received instructions. One morning the drill instructor stood before them and Walter heard him say, “Rohloff”. “Yes, sir,” Walter said and ran to the front of the company. The drill instructor looked at him and said:”I read in your “Soldbuch” (pay book, also used as a passport) the entry under religion. I can’t understand that. What does it mean?”

If Walter had read it himself without context, he wouldn’t have known either. On the day Walter had to provide his personal information to the military he told the man, “I am a member of The Church of Jesus Christ of Latter-day Saints.” The clerk said, “There isn’t enough space.” So he wrote, “Jes. Chr.”

While the officer was questioning him, Walter felt very uncomfortable in front of so many men and his face turned red as he said, “It stands for The Church of Jesus Christ of Latter-day Saints.”

“What is that?” the officer asked.

Walter asked himself, “What is that?” In all his years of attending church and going along with what had been said, he had never been confronted with a question like that. Yes, he understood what he heard the most: The Word of Wisdom, not smoking and not drinking alcohol, but what the church teaches or to explain the difference in between the teaching of The Church of Jesus Christ of Latter Saint and other religions organization he never thought about and never hat to explain his religion. Walter prayed daily, but he had done very little thinking on his own. Walter hesitated and before he answered, the officer told Walter to return to his place. What a relief!

All morning during the drill, Walter couldn't get rid of the thought, "What is that?" Plenty of thought went through his mind. Walter realized all of a sudden how little he really knew about his religion. Why did he belong to this church? Why did he believed in Jesus Christ? What is the difference between Christ and other phylosophers like Nitsche who was often mentioned.

At noon, when he returned to their barracks, he went into the room he shared with many others. Walter took the box with his clothing down from the top of the locker, opened it, and took out the New Testament. Walter was eager to find a satisfactory answer to the question, "What is that?" From that time on Walter studied the only scripture he carried with him, the New Testament intensively to find a satisfactory answer to that question. Before he was drafted, his father had encouraged him to study the Book of Mormon. He agreed and read Helaman and the war stories but overlooked the spiritual sermons of King Benjamin and Alma and the teachings of Christ. Now he wanted to know what Christ did and taught.

The next day the boxes with clothing were gone. The Lord was good to Walter and his spirit was still sensitive to the Lord's prompting. Little did Walter know that this little question would make him, after intensive study, transform from a nominal member to a defender of Christ.

The drills were hard and strenuous, but Walter did well. Having been actively involved in sports and never having smoked or drank alcohol, he was well prepared. Soon the platoon leader called on him to continue the drill with the platoon while the platoon leader talked to the other non-commissioned officers. The platoon leader must have given a good report about Walter to the company leader, a captain, who called Walter into his office and asked him if he wanted to become an officer. Walter was surprised and asked the captain to give him a week to consider. Walter was a member of the infantry and one day he would be in the trenches fighting. He did not want to fight. He prayed daily to his Heavenly Father to prevent him from being in situations where he would have to kill. Now he prayed if he should become an officer. It seemed to be contrary to what he had asked the Lord before, not to kill. Walter needed an answer. He wrote his parents and explained what had happened and he asked for advice. His father felt it was not good enough to write; Bruno took the next train on the weekend and visited him.

Father and son spent a lovely day together. Bruno told Walter he was delighted and congratulated him on his progress. He felt it was all right for him to become an officer. Bruno said and talking about leaders from the Book of Mormon, "Mormon and Moroni were officers in the Nephite army even though they disliked the actions of the Nephites. This will be a lot of work for you. Accept the offer and study and work hard. No one gives you anything for free. Keep the Lord's commandments. Pray earnestly and stand up for what we believe. It will not be easy, but the Lord will be with you."

The next day Walter gave his affirmative answer. He didn't know at that time this training would keep him out of war action for a long time. He learned that besides him three other recruits had been chosen to become officers. The four were now partly removed from the rest of the company and had extra instruction, drills and duties. That meant they spent most of the day with the platoon they were assigned to, but their day started with going to the stables and cleaning a horse before the other recruits had to get up. They were always checked on how well they cleaned the horses. Most of the officers who checked their work were reasonable, but some complained and punished them with extra work. Then next, they spent the day with their platoon or in special training. Of course, the noncommissioned officers liked to show them they were still in charge and the recruits serving with them loved to tease them. Walter got along well with the other three candidates. They were the sons of well-to-do families and their fathers were all reserve officers in the army.

The candidates had to learn how to ride a horse. Walter's companions had lessons before and loved to ride a horse so they looked forward to the hour of instructions. For Walter it was a brand new experience. He had never been close to a horse, and would have gladly missed that hour.

There were guests present who watched their first training hour for their amusement. The instructor told the cadets they needed to get acquainted with their horses. They went under and around the horse. Never having been around horses, it was no fun for Walter. Then the instructor had them stand on the saddle and jump over the head of the horse. Hamann and Sims did alright. Jensen, one of the four, tried to step on the horse's head, but the horse moved his head away and Jensen fell like a stone to the ground. The guests laughed, but Jensen was hurt. When Walter's turn came, for him standing on the horses back was already an accomplishment. Looking down from the back made Walter nervous. To use the uplifted head of the horse as a step was tempting. It was good Jensen had tried it before him. Walter told himself, the three others had made it so he could do it too. He jumped and did alright.

Toward the end of the first instruction hour, the instructor put up a hurdle. The cadets were instructed to jump with the horse over the hurdle and while doing so raise their cap from their head and call out the name of the horse. They had no stirrups and no spurs on their boots and were sitting freely in the saddle. Jensen tried first. His horse did just what it wanted and went around the hurdle. Sims tried hard, but he couldn't get the horse over the hurdle. Next it was Hamann's turn. The instructor got mad and grabbed the whip. The horse saw the whip in the instructor's hand, went wild, and jumped over the hurdle. Hamann hung on to the horse for dear life.

For Walter sitting on the horse was already an accomplishment and he knew he would have problems. Walter decided he would do as instructed. He tried to get the horse moving, but it wouldn't go. During prior assignments going around the hall the horse had followed the others. Now that he needed it to move on his order it didn't respond. Walter tried everything he knew, but it didn‘t move. The instructor with the whip came close. The horse saw the whip, started to run toward the hurdle and jumped over. During the jump Walter did as he was instructed lifting his cap and calling the name of the horse. With a high arch he flew through the air and landed on the ground. The horse leaped for joy and the men watching laughed. Walter was lying on the ground in pain. Lucky for him it was nothing serious, but it surely didn't make him look forward to the next hour of instruction.

Walter's attitude toward the horse-back riding hour improved with every training hour, but he never developed a real love for horse-back riding. In a parade, marching into a town, the officers and cadets were sitting on a horse. Walter felt fairly good except when the drummer hit the kettle-drum and the horse became uneasy. Walter had a difficult time calming the horse down, but managed somehow. His illness and his hospital stay later was the end of his training.

The four reserve officer candidates had a great time together. Jensen was the only one whose family was living in the Garrison city. His mother wanted to give the cadets a treat so she invited the four cadets and four beautiful girls to a party. It was delightful. The food was good and they played games and laughed all afternoon. The lady of the house was a great hostess and enjoyed the party with her guests. Toward the end of the party, Grandma Jensen came and the cadets were introduced to her. The first to be introduced was Sims. After she asked him about his well-being she asked,

"What is your father's profession, Herr Sims?"

"My father is professor at the University of Rostock. Right now he is a captain in the army," was his answer.

"Very welcome, Herr Sims."

Then Hamann was introduced. She used the same approach as before. She asked, "What is your father doing for a living?"

"He is head of the department for construction and development in the state of Mecklenburg. Right now he is serving as a captain in the army," Hamann responded.

She was delighted.

Next was her grandson. Jensen of course didn't have to tell her what his father was doing. His father was director of the large post office in town and currently a major in the army.

Finally it was Walter's turn. He didn't have the credentials the others had. She started out the same way as she did with the others by asking,

"Herr Rohloff, what is your father doing?"

"My father is home and is an office worker," Walter said.

She stared at him incredulously as if she had wanted to say, "How did you come to this party?" Then without saying a word, she turned around and left. She didn't shake hands with Walter as she had done with the others nor did she welcome him.

The hostess was upset with grandma's behavior, and she tried to appease Walter. But he had run into these kinds of people before and it didn't bother him. He told the hostess what a great party it had been and thanked her for the invitation.

It was easy to get permission for weekend leave to travel home when the destination was within a 100km radius. It was much harder for a further distance. Walter applied for weekend leave and to his surprise he got permission, even though the distance to his hometown was more than the 100km. It was good to be home and visit with his parents. He had to be back at his garrison by Monday at 9 am. Somehow when he looked up for the arrival of his train in the time table he misread the time of his arrival as being before 9 am, but his arrival was at 9:30 am. After arriving at the garrison railroad station he tried to explain the oversight but no one believed him. It hurt him that his officers were thinking he was lying. The punishment was three days in prison with water and a little dry bread. It was a hungry three days.

Spending most of the time in the cell, he had plenty of time to think things over. They were permitted to leave the cell once a day for a 30 minute walk in the yard. In the yard they were not permitted to stand still or talk to anyone. Walter thought that since his officers thought he had taken things into his own hands, why not do so. He just had to make sure he wouldn't be caught. From then on Walter took weekend leaves with or without permission.

After that Walter felt he needed a few days off, he would go. He made plans about how to do that. He talked to Hamann whose hometown was within the 100km radius and on the way to Walter's place. Walter‘s father could bring his bike to Hamann's home and Walter would go from there by bike to his home. Bruno had no objections and they thought it would work out well. While Walter talked to his father about his intention, Bruno made him aware of the consequences. He cautioned, "Think about how things could end if you do what you plan and get caught." Walter threw all considerations to the wind and thought only of the adventure and good time he would have.

Going out with his comrades, Walter made the acquaintance of a young lady, Ursula Jones. Their relationship grew into a nice friendship. On one of their dates they talked about religion and Walter saw her understanding of God and the purpose of life was much different than his. She was a child well-trained in Nazi doctrine. Walter tried, but couldn't convince her to look into and investigate Walter's beliefs. Once Walter was really rude to her and mockingly said, "When your forefathers were monkeys, mine were not." She was hurt and Walter apologized. He liked her and loved to talk with her. He would visit her every time he was in town, but Walter had made up his mind; he would never approach her as more than a friend.

A couple of years later, on Walter's last time in town, he introduced Ursula to a comrade. After the first visit with her, he came to Walter and asked if it was true that he had never kissed Ursula. She had told him that. Walter told him, "Yes, she is a good friend of mine, but she is not the girl I want to marry." Ursula and her new friend got along fine, and would have married, but he was later killed in war action.

Part of the training of the cadets was with 7mm guns. The cadets had opportunities to practice directing and leading a crew.

Then came the day they practiced shooting with live munitions. The cadets competed with both the officers and non-commissioned officers in this drill. Targets were assigned to them and one unit after another brought their gun into position to destroy the assigned target.

Walter had his turn close to the end of the practice day. Up to that time only one group had destroyed their assigned target. Many officers were standing around and watching the men closely and critically. Being so close to the general and working under the critical eyes of the officers made Walter a little nervous. No one was permitted to interfere or criticize the groups. Walter was calm and in charge when he brought his crew into position. He could see the target through his field glasses. He gave the orders and he could see the first shot was too far. He also saw that he had the right direction. He reduced the distance, but the shot was too short. With the third shot Walter could see the debris flying through the air. He had a direct hit. He and his crew felt good about their accomplishment and reported to the general standing nearby, "Target destroyed." "Thank you," said the general, "very well done." Walter and his crew were delighted.

Then Walter's training had a setback. On the 27thof June, 1942, he was admitted to a military hospital in town. He had a fever and a sore throat, which was later diagnosed as diphtheria. He was taken to the quarantine station of the hospital. In the room where his bed would be, a male nurse was sitting on a table. He wanted all kinds of information from him. Walter felt tired and was in much pain. His sore throat made it hard for him to talk, and all he wanted was a bed and sleep. He could think and speak clearly even though his mind was in a delirium. The nurse asked him all kinds of medical and personal questions. When he asked about his religion, Walter told him he belonged to The Church of Jesus Christ of Latter-day Saints. One of the soldiers in bed lifted up his head and asked, "Are you a member of that church because you believe in the teaching of the church or because of your parents?"

The question was unexpected and came at an awkward time. Walter felt miserable but could think clearly and responded, "Because of my parents."

Walter went to bed, but was awake until a nurse came with a very large syringe and injected medication into his body. Then he slept well.

Every day Walter felt a little improvement. The hospital patients had nothing to do, so they talked about many things. One day they talked about religion and in the discussion Walter tried to explain his belief. The fellow soldier, who had asked him the question when he was admitted, spoke up and said to him,

> "How can you make us believe in the teachings of your church? You don't believe it yourself."
>
> "How can you say that?" Walter asked.
>
> He answered, "The day you were admitted, you claimed you were a member of that church. I asked you if you were a member because of your belief or, because of your parents. You answered: that you were a member because of your parents. Now, tell me what is true?"

A fist in his face couldn't have hit Walter harder. He had completely forgotten what happened the day in question, but now he remembered clearly. He was ashamed of himself and especially that he did not stand up for the Lord Jesus Christ. He was speechless. It took him awhile to gather his strength. Then Walter said,

> "I am sorry and I beg for your forgivingness. I didn't have the courage to stand up for what I believe. I am a member of The Church of Jesus Christ of Latter-day Saints, because I know it is true."

This was the end of this discussion, but others followed. Walter realized that his knowledge about the teachings of the church was not good enough; he needed to study more and be better informed. He wrote home and his father acted right away and sent him plenty of church literature. Until his release from the hospital on the 14th of August in 1942, Walter used his time wisely and studied the scriptures.

When Walter returned to the barracks the officer training had ended and his three companions had been transferred. His drill instructor was still there and requested that he join a new group of candidates. However before he joined that group, Walter got two weeks of recovery furlough.

While at home, Walter wanted to prepare himself for the strenuous drill ahead. Running around the block, he found he was dragging his legs, and when he drank any fluid the fluid came back out through his nose. The backflow of fluid through the nose disappeared after a week or so, but the dragging of his legs got worse with every day. He couldn't see anything wrong with his legs, except he couldn't move them well. He had no pain.

When Walter returned to the barracks and started the drill with the cadets, he had a hard time moving. His instructor took him aside and asked him what was wrong? Walter told him, "I don't know. Everything looks healthy but I have no control over my legs."

6

YOU WILL NEVER WALK

The instructor sent Walter to the clinic and a doctor checked him over. When the doctor sent him back, he gave Walter a sealed envelope with the instruction to give the envelope to his instructor. The instructor read the report, grasped Walter's arm and said, "The doctor says you are faking. Let's go and see him." As they went to the clinic, he had to help Walter because he couldn't keep up with him.

Walter crawled into, but walked out of the hospital. (Jan 1943)

The instructor had nothing nice to say to the doctor. He hollered at him the same way he did at the cadets during their training: "When you don't know what is wrong with the man, get him to another doctor. I know the man is sick and needs help." The instructor left Walter there and Walter was send to town to a hospital for further examinations.

Getting there was easier said than done. Traveling by bus to the hospital was all right, but getting up the stairs to the hospital was another problem. Walter's legs just didn't want to do it; he had to crawl. Being in Army uniform and crawling up the stairs was a humbling experience. Walter felt terribly helpless. A doctor examined him and this doctor did the examination completely differently than the first one. After the examination the doctor told him he had nerve paralysis. The doctor kept him in the hospital. Walter wrote home and told his family about his problems. On Sunday his father came and visited with him. He had sent Walter away as a young, sports loving man and now Walter could hardly move. His whole body had to be in motion to get his legs moving. Tears came in his father's eyes as he saw his boy.

> "Buby," he said, "The war is over for you. You will never walk."

Walter was transferred to another hospital. No one in this hospital had illnesses Walter was familiar with. Most of the men had epilepsy and looked healthy, except when they had a seizure. Others had problems similar to Walter's. Many lay in bed all day long. Walter tried to move around as much as possible. Every morning the nurse came around and gave the patients their medication and/or injections. On Walter's chart he could see what his shots contained: strychnine, pro strychnine & insulin. He didn't know how good or how harmful the medication was, nor did he know the side effects. He had no way to look it up in a book. Rumors were that the patients were being used as human guinea pigs. The doctors were trying out new medications on them.

As the time went by, Walter didn't like to wait for the nurse to come around and give him a shot. He went into the nurses' station to get his shot before she went out to give everyone their medication. That gave him time for a more positive conversation with the nurses than he had with the men in the large room. The men were very negative and Walter thought some didn't want to get healthy. They were afraid they would have to go back into the trenches on the front, and that was very likely. The situation for Germany was not good. In Russia, Germany was losing the battle for Stalingrad. With Stalingrad, Germany would be losing the 6th army. In the west an attack by the allies was very much expected.

Walter didn't want to go to the front and fight either, but he wanted to get healthy, and in his daily prayers he asked the Lord earnestly for help. One day the thought hit him, "why don't you try exercise?" Walter laughed to himself, just a few days before; he had slipped when he walked in the hallway. He fell and unfortunately his head hit a pail of water and he made a pool of water on the floor. He couldn't even get up alone. A nurse passing by helped him out of that embarrassing situation. The pails with water were standing in the hallways to extinguish incendiary bombs in case of an air attack.

Walter couldn't see much improvement in his condition, but he did a lot of thinking and praying about his illness. He surely didn't want to live a life dragging his feet. It took Walter a few days until he made up his mind what exercises to do and where. No one else did exercises, but he decided to try exercise even if he had to get his whole body in motion to move his legs forward. He chose the small backyard for his exercise. The backyard was surrounded by high buildings but had a small, about 25-foot long oval shaped lawn. He wanted to be where no one could see him. He was sure he would make a pitiable picture. Closely he checked that no one was around when he went down the stairs. It was more crawling than walking, but he was determined to try exercise. He "walked" around the lawn. After a week or two he could see a small improvement in his movements. That encouraged him to continue.

As the time went by, Walter added knee bends and other body movements to his exercise. Some of the female nurses crossed his place of exercise and laughed and positioned next to him and did the knee bends of course much faster than Walter. But not for long, and he did almost as well as they did. It didn't take long until the other patients discovered Walter's activity. They would lean out of the window and mock and laugh. By then, it didn't discourage Walter. He felt he was on the right track and went on. When the doctor saw his improvement was so much faster than anyone else's, he inquired and made everyone do exercises, but he left Walter alone. This didn't make Walter popular with the patients, for they didn't like to exercise. Walter entered the hospital on the 2ndof October 1942, and left on the 23rdof January 1943, with the medical statement k. v. (fit for active military service).

His unit gave him 14 days convalescent furlough. His parents were delighted when they saw Walter and how well he had recovered. They all were very grateful to the Lord that He heard and answered their prayers. The little branch of the Church in Neubrandenburg almost did not exist. After discussing with his parents the possibility of having church meetings in their home, Walter went visiting the members of the branch. Walter invited the branch members to attend church service in his parents' home. They had a good spiritual meeting and the ones in attendance decided to have church meetings every Sunday.

After returning to his unit, Walter found that none of his former comrades or leaders were there. He thought that was the end of his officer training; but then he was told he had to continue his training. Walter had nothing against that. He was glad that he didn't have to go to the front fighting in Russia. Walter couldn't see any good in the war. There was no officer training at his garrison. He was sent to the town of Gniezno (Gnesen) in the state of Poznan (Posen), about 220 mi east of Schwerin, close to his father's hometown of Hohensalza (Inowroclaw) to attend training there. The course was already in progress, but Walter had no problems catching up.

7

SCHNEIDEMUEHL

After arriving in Gniezno (Gnesen), Posen, and being there for a few days, Walter felt the need for a spiritual lift: He needed to find the nearest branch of the LDS church. Walter wrote home and his father sent him all the information for the LDS branch in Pila (Schneidemuehl) a town 80mi north. He also mentioned that a former member of his branch, Brother Philipp Bauer, was now living there. Having that name and address gave Walter the ability to request weekend leave to visit Philipp Bauer. Arriving in Schneidemuehl, he went first to see where the branch held its meetings. At the address he had, and looking for a place where the branch could meet, he saw only buildings with apartments. He looked inside of the building he had the address off, but he didn't see anything that looked like meeting rooms. As Walter came down the stairs he saw two young men entering the building. He asked those men for the meeting rooms of the church and they told him to go with them. The branch had their meeting place in the rear.

The branch had very nice rooms. Walter was favorably impressed with the number of members in attendance. Of course, the many young sisters caught his attention too. He noticed a young sister playing the harmonium. He later learned her name was Ruth Birth. It was district conference and they had a good spiritual meeting in which many young people participated. After the meeting Walter made the acquaintance of some of the youth and went home with Brother Bauer.

Brother Bauer was a generous host and he was the father of a large family. His oldest son Philipp was living here in Schneidemuehl with his family. Walter knew everyone in the family. Of course, he knew the younger ones near his age better than the others. He went to the Sunday morning meeting. Again he was astonished by how many of the young members participated in the program. At noon Brother and Sister Friedrich & Emma Birth had donated a meal for all who attended the conference. Walter was surprised with the generosity of the Birth family. This was 1942 and you could buy food only with food stamps. It was a good meal and after all had eaten, the youth went into a nearby park. Sitting under a canopy, Walter told quite a few made up stories about what Vati (he) had done. Walter shouldn't have given himself the name Vati (meaning Father), because from then on he was called Vati by young and old in the church.

Following the afternoon meeting Walter was invited to visit the Birth family and the young people who met there. He talked it over with Brother Bauer and he agreed. Walter spent his time at the Births' until he had to return to his garrison. It was a long way back and he had plenty of time to think about the experience he had. He was very impressed with what he saw and the way he was treated. When Walter found time in the next few days, he wrote a letter to the Birth family about how welcome he felt with the people of the branch and in the Birth family home. They wrote back inviting him to come back and visit with them any time he could get away from his duties. That was all Walter needed.

Walter carefully planned his next visit. He knew he couldn't get a weekend leave so soon, but he didn't want to wait. Walter decided he would go without a permit. It was clear to him, that if he was caught, it would mean an end to his training. The punishment would be certainly time in prison and maybe a transfer to a company with convicts. In his youthful optimism he threw all consideration out of the window and planned his next visit. On most weekends they had no activities going on and they could go and visit the city in which the unit was stationed.

Leaving the barracks was no problem. At the railroad station Walter bought a ticket to Schneidemuehl. To get to the platform to enter the train was the problem because he had to pass controls, one who checked his rail ticket and a military police (M.P.) man who would check his furlough permit. He didn't have a furlough permit so he couldn't pass. The station had a fence around and he jumped over the high barrier. When he entered the standing room only wagon, he met some of his comrades who of course had a furlough permit. Walter told his fellow cadets that he had no permit and asked them to watch for the Military Police. The M.P. would go from car to car and check for violators such as Walter. Then he checked the restroom to see if it was a pass through restroom that had a door from both sides, but it didn't.

His fellow cadets told him M.P. men were in the next compartment. To get out of the way Walter wanted to change compartments at the next station. To his surprise the M.P. man already had his hand on the door handle, ready to enter. Walter went out of the door on the other side of the train and jumped on the tracks and entered the next compartment from that side. At the next station the M.P. and Walter changed places again, except the M.P. man didn't know it. Safely and without any problems he reached the station in Pila (Schneidemuehl.)

It was dark and to protect the station against air-attacks, it was only sparsely lighted. Walter was standing on the platform and didn't know what to do next. He didn't know how to leave the station without running into an MP man. When his train went on, he could see on the main platform Military Police men standing, talking and looking over at him. Between him and the M.P. men were tracks. Walter saw one of the men starting to cross the tracks toward him. Walter turned in the opposite direction and ran over the many tracks toward a wooden fence. He threw his little suitcase over the fence and grabbed the top of the fence to swing over, but with a great noise the fence broke and fell down. He hustled over the fallen fence and ran. He didn't know how far the MP man followed him, but he outran him.

Walter had lost his orientation. This was only his second visit to Pila (Schneidemuehl), but after thinking a little he found the right direction. It was already past midnight when he reached the Birth family home. The home was dark and he didn't want to wake any one up. Walter turned and went back the way he came. On the way to the Births' family home Walter had passed some garden spots and he had seen some small sheds. He went over the fence of one of the gardens and found the shed door was unlocked. In the shed he found some boards and he placed the boards so that he could sleep on them. He slept very well until the morning. Before he left he restored everything the way he found it then went to the Births' home. Father Birth greeted him.

"Where do you come from?" he asked.

"From Gnesen," Walter said.

"There is no train coming from Gnesen at this time."

"I came around midnight and the house was dark. I didn't want to wake up anyone. In a garden spot I found a shed that I slept in."

"We will change that," Mother Birth said. "In the future you knock on our bedroom window and we will let you in."

"By the way," Father Birth said, having been a soldier himself during the First World War, "how did you get furlough again so soon. Do you have a permit?"

"No," Walter said, "I took furlough without permission."

With a big smile on his face, Father Birth said, "I like that."

Now that Walter knew the way he could use the railroad, and could make the trip with only minor complications; he knew he could see the Birth family often. He enjoyed his stay with the Birth family and their encouragement to see the family more was appreciated by him. From that day on he took every opportunity to visit

Schneidemuehl and the Birth family with and without permission. In the large family he felt welcome and he had a good relationship with every child in the family. There were still 10 children at home. Gerhard, the oldest, was in the army in Russia. Here Walter found people who not only knew, but lived the teachings of Jesus Christ. After every visit he took, he felt strengthened and was encouraged to stand up for his redeemer Jesus Christ against the atheistic ideology of the Nazi party. Walter, spiritually uplifted and looked for more.

These experiences in Pila (Schneidemuehl) and his father's teachings and letters had a great and good influence upon Walter. It gave him direction for his life. Walter felt, speaking figuratively, blessed and protected, being under the wings of the Almighty.

The Friedrich and Emma Birth Family
(1939)

As time passed, Walter got to know the Birth family better. During his visits they shared life stories with him regarding their conversion and experiences in the church. Father and Mother Birth were both converts to the church and Father Birth had come from a God-fearing family. He was very well acquainted with the Bible. He had visited different churches and found they were not in harmony with the teachings of the Bible; for a time he was actively involved in spiritualism. He prayed often to find the true Church of Jesus Christ. About summer 1922, Elder Gustav Weller knocked on his door and invited him to attend a Bible discussion so he agreed to attend. He told his lovely wife he thought it was a sect, the same as all the others, and he would show them what the Bible taught. When he returned from the meeting Mother Birth asked him,

"How did it go?"

"I found what I was looking for."

He was well read in the Bible. Elder Weller told him not much that he did not already know, but one teaching was new to him, the Word of Wisdom. This teaches abstinence from alcohol and tobacco. Father Birth had started to smoke while serving his country during the First World War years, and now he couldn't get rid of that habit. To make a little extra money to feed his growing family in those difficult days after WWI, he played in a band. He had played in an army band. He was very talented and played many instruments: trumpet, piano, cello but the violin was his favored instrument. For a year he attended all LDS church meetings, but his smoking habit kept him from becoming baptized a member of the church. He tried to break the habit, but without a cigarette he was unhappy and hard to get along with. He was in a dilemma. He knew the LDS church was true and he wanted to become a member of it. He also knew smoking was no good for him and that the Lord wanted him to abstain, but he was not able to break the habit.

He was so discouraged. One day he was playing cards with his smoking friends from the band and he realized he had already smoked 15 cigarettes. He was so upset and frustrated about doing what he knew he shouldn't, he dropped the cards, left his friends, and went into the forest. He knelt down in prayer and said, "Heavenly Father, you help me now or I die. I can't go on this way. I know smoking is no good for me, but I still keep doing it. I can't do it by myself. You need to help me". He stood up from prayer and had no desire to smoke from that time forward. For four more weeks he carried cigarettes in his pocket, but he had no desire to smoke. Now he was ready to be baptized and become a member of The Church of Jesus Christ of Latter-day Saints. Mother Birth had been waiting for him and both were baptized on the $19^{th}$of May 1923.

After Father Birth had been a member of the LDS church for a few months, he had a very interesting dream. In the dream he saw himself and he knew that he wanted to speak to Satan. He saw a large beautiful house where a tall man clad in a red cape stood in the entrance hall. He saw the person had no underwear under the cape. Father Birth said to the man,

"My name is Friedrich Birth and I would like to speak to the boss."

The man in the red cape answered, "Please wait a minute. The boss is busy."

Father waited and looked around. After a little time had passed, the door opened and many people came out. It was a group of everyday people. It was not a particular group; it seemed to be people from every walk of life. Father recognized many, among others, his brother and some Catholic priests. After all had passed, there came a tall, good looking man with a noble expression in his face. He was well dressed in a dark suit, white shirt and a black tie. He came to Father Birth and said:

"Mr. Birth, you wanted to talk to me."

"Yes," Father Birth said, "I wanted to give notice: I am now a member of The Church of Jesus Christ of Latter-day Saints." All of a sudden, he felt Satan becoming taller and he grew smaller. He felt a strong fear of destruction. In his despair he prayed

"Heavenly Father, I prayed to you to show me the truth. You

have heard my prayer. Now help me."

As he prayed he could feel that he became taller and Satan smaller until Satan disappeared. Father woke up and was wet from perspiration, as wet as if he came out of a bathtub.

Father Birth had another interesting dream some years later. In the dream he saw the personification of death who wanted to pick up Sister Schmeichel, a member of the LDS branch in Schneidemuehl, because she was destined to die. Father Birth didn't even know Sister Schmeichel was ill with an infection (puerperal fever), an illness that was deadly for many mothers, but he knew she had a baby girl. In his dream he saw that he should bless Sister Schmeichel, but the personification of death stood in front of him. Father could feel how the evil spirit got taller and taller and he got smaller and smaller. He prayed with all his strength to our Heavenly Father:

> "Father, I didn't give myself this priesthood, but Thou hast given me this priesthood to bless the sick and make them whole again, when it is thy will."

As he prayed he could see he got taller and the evil spirit got smaller until it disappeared. He woke up and heard the doorbell ringing. Mother Birth woke up when she heard the doorbell and Father told her,

> "Mama, go to the door; Brother Schmeichel is there. His wife is sick and he wants me to give her a blessing."

Brother Schmeichel was indeed at the door and he told her what she knew already. Seeing the inconvenience at the time of night, Brother Schmeichel said,

> "Why don't you come by tomorrow morning?"
> Father Birth said, "No, I will come right away."

He was wet from perspiration and had to dry and clean himself before he went. After he arrived at the Schmeichel home, Brother Schmeichel told him the doctor had told him, to be prepared for the worst; His wife might not see the next day. Father Birth gave her a blessing and promised her health and another child. Her health was restored and she had another child eight years later.

Not only their conversion story was of interest to Walter, but also how this large family made a living. About the year 1929 the Social-Democratic Government helped the people with building small homes in this settlement. With the encouragement of the boss of the company father Birth worked for, he applied for a larger home, and because of his large family he got permission. In 1931 in the worst years of the depression, he started his own business. After a difficult beginning and later with he help of his son Gerhard, he was now very busy. When his son Gerhard was drafted into the army, his son Nephi started to work with him. His daughter Irmgard also learned the glass business and took care of small repair orders and the art store father had in down town.

Mother Birth, with her cheese stand on the marketplace. Visiting with mother, her daughter Irmgard and two LDS Missionaries

Mother Birth started her own grocery store at the house. They added a room to their home for the store. The store did well and they harvested the fruit of their hard labor. Over the course of time, every able child helped in their mother's or father's business.

These stories of hard work ,and faith, and harmony in the family influenced and strengthened Walter's testimony. The time of Walter's visit went by fast, and soon it was time to return to his garrison the same way he came.

In Gnesen Walter missed the good relationship he had with his fellow cadets in Schwerin. Of course he was the new comer, the others had been together already for some time. Walter had no difficulties keeping up with the training, but somehow with the men he didn't harmonize as well as with the men he served with before. Most were the son's of well to do farmers and from the food they got from home they didn't share, but they shared with the son of a pharmacist who got good packets from home too and he shared with them. Walter didn't like the pharmacist's son. His vocabulary was dirty and girls were for him just sex objects to satisfy his sex drive. Walter didn't go with them to town in the evenings or weekends, but they didn't disclose his unauthorized travel to his friends in Schneidemuehl. One day the group decided to visit a brothel in town and they wanted Walter to go with them. After a long discussion, they tried to force Walter. Walter put his back against the wall and defended himself successful. They left without Walter.

8

IN THE TRENCHES

Walter's company came back from a field exercise. The men had to prepare for a physical and weapon inspection. Walter thought he was well prepared, but as the officer looked through the barrel of his gun, he saw dirt. Walter couldn't see any, but the officer could and he got three days in prison. Walter was punished for the second time with 3 days in a single cell. He had to live again on only water and a little bread. This was a prison for major offenders with high walls and fortified with barbwire. Walter was there with another candidate of the school. As they had their half hour walk in the prison yard, Walter could see that his comrade took it hard receiving this punishment. They weren't allowed to walk and talk together. Looking at him Walter thought, "Maybe he didn't eat his bread…"

Passing him by, Walter said, "How are you?"

"Terrible" he said.

Walter increased his walking speed and passed him again. Did you eat?" Walter asked.

"No" he said.

The next time Walter asked, “Do you have bread?”

“Yes.”

“May I have it?”

“Yes.”

Then Walter’s final question: “Where do you have it?”

“On the window sill,” was his answer.

Walter was one of the first entering the building when they were ordered to return to their cells. Walter ran up to the comrade’s cell first, took the bread and went back into his own cell. No one saw what he did. It was not enough, but it helped.

Walter successfully completed the course of instruction in Gnesen, and became a private first class (Gefreiter, 1st of June 1943). They had a little party. Officers and cadets celebrated and they had plenty of fun. One of the cadets had put a paper together where he mentioned the activities of some of the cadets. While talking about that, he told about Walter taking furlough without a permit and not being caught, but he didn’t mention a name. The officer next to Walter wanted to know who the cadet was. The cadets knew of Walter’s unauthorized activities, but none of the officers did. Walter was very careful and didn’t tell. So he was never caught.

By this time Walter had been in the armed services for more than 18 months and had not seen the front. He was drafted to serve as an infantryman serving in the trenches and attacking or killing the enemy attackers. His earnest daily prayer was that he wouldn’t have to kill. There was no desire in him to become a hero at the front. He was thankful to the Lord for keeping him away from war action. He did well in the training courses because he felt what he learned there could help him later, but he didn’t want to go to the front.

About 10 officer candidates of this training course were from the same regiment as Walter. Walter was asked to take the men back to their garrison. There they received all the equipment they needed to go to the front in Russia. Before leaving for Russia they each applied for a two week furlough, which was granted. Walter enjoyed being home, but after a few days he missed his new-found friends in Schneidemuehl. At first he hesitated to say anything because he saw how his parents enjoyed his presence, but then he asked and they let him go to Schneidemuehl to visit the Birth family. They agreed with heavy hearts, but they knew he was in good hands there.

Walter (left) on his way to the Russian front
(1943)

Making the trip was easier said than done. His permit allowed him to go to his hometown, but Schneidemuehl was much further to the east. He put on civilian clothing and hoped no one would stop him. In Stargard, in Pomerania, he had to transfer and had time to do some sightseeing. While he looked at the old defense installations, a policeman in civilian clothing stopped him and asked for identification. After looking at his permit the man told Walter he was very careless and could get into lots of trouble. But then he said, "Be very careful on the next train." A friend of his was a military policeman and controlled that train. When Walter was on the train he looked out for that man, but reached Schneidemuehl without any complications. He thoroughly enjoyed his time with the Birth family. He stopped at his family's home on his way back to his garrison and arrived at his garrison on time.

It was the 5th of August 1943, when the cadets left Schwerin. The ten officer candidates, under Walter's leadership, were on their way to the front deep in Russia. On the way they got a little insight into what has been happening there. The railroad tracks went through beautiful forests. For protection from attack for about 100 yards on both sides of the tracks, the trees were cut down. In some places they saw wreckage of railroad cars and locomotives which Russian partisans had blown off the tracks. To protect the men from the same fate their locomotive pushed some empty cars ahead of the train.

Partisan work in Russia

The ten cadets were in good spirits and didn't have any fear. They were greenhorns and really didn't know what war meant. He had always prayed to the Lord for protection. Pretty soon he would be in the trenches at the frontline. Walter asked the Lord to keep him away from situations where he would have to use his gun. Their ride went smoothly and after walking a few miles they reached their division's headquarters near the town of Loknja.

To become an officer, the cadets had to have war experience and had to learn and show leadership abilities. Walter was placed with the 3rd Company in the 89th Regiment. After it started to get dark, he walked with a few other soldiers to his new emplacement without any enemy encounter. His new home was a hole in the ground covered with big logs and plenty of dirt on the top. The "Bunker," as they called that place, was connected to the "Hauptkampflinie" (main front line or trench). The trench was about 20 feet away from his bunker. A squad of about six to eight men occupied a bunker. Walter was placed in a squad and introduced himself to everyone. One of the men was standing guard, looking over the no man's land and watching for enemy activities. The other men were inside the bunker playing cards.

As Walter's turn came he had to stand guard with a machine gun. About 40 yards in front of him was a barbwire entanglement. A few Russian dead bodies were hanging there from a past battle. In a far distance he could see something lying on the ground. In the daylight he saw it was a downed Russian airplane. He couldn't see the Russian line, but he saw the flash from their rifles. Walter and his comrades had strict orders not to use their guns, but to save their munitions. It was an uneasy feeling to stay alone in the dark and know enemy soldiers might be watching you and waiting to attack you.

At a later assignment, Walter heard the last cry from a soldier who was captured by Russian soldiers not far from him. They probably had crawled close to him for the attack. At another time the Russians used the famed "Stalin organ" (many rockets mounted on a carriage) and bombarded a place not far from Walter. With the "Stalin organ" they would shoot many rockets at the same time. It was a great spectacle. When the rockets hit the ground a great mushroom of fire appeared. It was pretty to see and while Walter was watching it, he got careless. He felt the touch of a hand on his back. He was startled, but it was not the hand of an enemy, it was his corporal. He had come up behind him. He reminded Walter of the danger and that Walter should protect himself. He told Walter that the Stalin organ is not very accurate, it makes lots of noise and seldom hits it target. While they were not bombarded, it still could stray over to hit them.

Walter (left) at a bunker entrance

The next morning after that bombardment, Walter went along the trench and visited the place where the rockets had hit. It damaged only a few places of their position. There he saw the first dead, and he made up his mind to be more careful in the future. The soldiers here were in trench warfare and had relatively little enemy contact, which Walter was grateful for. He could have been at other places where the war raged. Walter thanked the Lord for hearing his prayer and protecting him.

Even in this trench warfare they lost men and new men took their place. The tragedy was the old timers kept going strong, while the newcomers lost their lives. It takes time to learn to hear and act fast.

After being on the front for a relatively short time, Walter became a squad leader. He didn't think the men in his squad liked the idea of having him as their squad leader. He had the same rank as some of them; what probably troubled them the most was that he was a greenhorn with no war experience. As an officer aspirant he had to prove that he was able to lead. They were assigned a section and they had to build their own bunker. While the enemy could see their trenches, they couldn't see their bunkers. To dig the hole was not hard, but getting the hole covered so it would be shell-proof was. They went to the nearby forest and cut as many trees as they needed. As they carried the logs on their shoulders to the hole, Walter noticed that the men let him carry the heavy end. He didn't mind. He wasn't afraid of hard work. With every log they carried, the men came nearer to him, until everybody took a fair share of the load. Walter could feel more trust from the men toward him, and it helped them to make a good squad. While he was on the front they didn't have an attack. They had to watch out for artillery and gun fire and they returned the same to the enemy, but they never encountered a direct assault.

On the 9th of October 1943, Walter was released from duty in the trench and was told to attend another course of instruction. Only men from his division attended this course. The men who completed this course successfully would go to the academy. Before Walter entered this course he was promoted to a "Fahnenjunker Unterofficier" (Cadet, Corporal), an NCO (non-commissioned officer). The course was easy for him. Walter worked hard and did what he could to become an officer. After about 14 days, Walter took sick with a kind of yellow fever. It kept him in bed for a time. He had not fully recuperated when he returned to active duty. He still had medical problems when the course ended on the 30th of October 1943. Before they were released, the commanding officer called Walter into his office and showed Walter his report card. He told Walter, he was one of the six best men in this training course. About 10 men went on to the academy; all others went back to the front. Walter was put in charge to bring the men back to Germany.

One tragic happening occurred during this period. While he was ill and transferred to a nursing station another candidate took his bed in the bunker. (This man had told the other cadets if he didn't pass the test, he was afraid of war action, and would not go back to the front, he would rather kill himself.) Of course no one took him seriously. He didn't pass. He reported sick and was sent to a doctor. The doctor examined him and couldn't find anything wrong with him. When the cadets returned from a field exercise on one of the last days of their training, they found that man dead in the bunker. He had placed a gun against his head and pulled the trigger. The scene was awful. (No men liked to go back to the trenches, but taking his own life, the thought never hit Walter.)

For their return to Germany, they had to walk a long distance to the railroad station. After they boarded the train and traveled toward Germany, Walter had a great idea. He thought they could take a few days off, enjoy the days with their loved ones, and then report to their unit. The train that they had to take across Germany would pass through Schneidemuehl and Neubrandenburg, and stopping there was always tempting to Walter. Walter knew he would have plenty of convincing to do. No one wanted to lose the privilege to become an officer. No one had experience in taking unauthorized furlough. He talked it over with his fellow candidates anyway. He had plenty of time to form a plan because it was a long way from Loknja, in Russia to Schwerin in Germany (over 1000 miles). When they reached the first city in Germany (Tilsit), they had all come to an agreement. Walter gave everyone his own papers, and every one would stop at the place of their choice, and after three days they would meet at a café in Schwerin. Walter would be the first to leave the group. He trusted his fellow candidates that they would do as they had agreed. Walter spent two wonderful days with the Birth family in Schneidemuehl, and then went on to Neubrandenburg and spent a day with his parents. He enjoyed every minute of his self-made furlough.

Reinhold takes fresh water from a well in Lithuania

Walter arrived on time at the café they had designated to meet. Everyone was sitting around a table and received Walter with great hellos. When he asked his comrades how it was at home, it became gravely quiet. He was told no one had stopped and visited their home. They were too concerned about losing their rank and opportunity to become an officer. When they arrived in Schwerin they reported to the unit and reported one man missing. They received orders to wait until the one missing man arrived and then report. Now Walter was a little concerned. When they left the café Walter told the men to look sharp tomorrow morning and have their uniforms spic and span. They would report in the morning.

In the morning, they gathered in front of the captain's office. Walter had the men standing in line for inspection. He looked over everyone and every man looked good. Walter went inside the office and reported to the captain,

> "The officer candidates of the 12th Infantry Division have returned from the front and are ready to attend the academy in Thorn."
>
> Not realizing that Walter was the missing man he asked him, "Did the missing man arrive?"
>
> "Yes sir," Walter answered.

The captain came out into the hallway and looked the men over. He liked what he saw. He asked Walter what they wanted to do next. Walter didn't hesitate a minute. He knew exactly what he wanted to do next,

> "We look forward to representing our division at the academy but for now we would love to have two weeks furlough."
>
> The captain thought for a minute, and then he said, "I have nothing against it. Go over to the battalion commander, and if he agrees, it is fine with me."

After he released the cadets and went into his office, the men hugged Walter and were all excited that they might get furlough. They went over to the commander's office, where Walter did just the same as he had done before. Walter went inside the office and reported to the commander. The commander came out to inspect the men. He was impressed with the young fellows. He asked many questions: How the division was doing, how the morale was and many others. He knew that our division was engaged in trench warfare and that the divisions to our south were in hard fought battles and retreating. Then he asked Walter what they wanted to do next. He gave him the same answer he had given the captain.

> "We look forward to representing our division at the academy but for now, we would love to have two weeks furlough."

> "That is fine with me," the commander said. "Come by this afternoon and I will sign your permits."

Walter thought his train would leave in the early afternoon and the next train in the evening. He didn't want to wait that long.

> "Sir," Walter said, "how about me running over and doing it now?"

> "Go ahead" the commander said and added, "When you can."

The commander knew how slow the process was to get the permits ready, but Walter was determined to get it done fast. The commander released the men, Walter went to the office.

The commander was right. When Walter told the office staff the cadets would like to have it done right away, they said it can't be done. Walter didn't take no for an answer and explained to them that he had plenty of experience and could help. When he was in the hospital, he had lots of time on his hands and he had volunteered to help in the hospital office. He knew what was needed and how to do it. He had a little convincing to do, but then they showed him what they wanted and Walter did it. After the office staff and Walter had the permits ready, Walter had the furlough permits signed by the captain. Then he hurried over to the commander and had him sign. The commander was not a little surprised when he saw Walter, but he signed and wished the cadets well. The men were excited when

Walter gave everyone their furlough permit. They hurried to the railroad station.

Arriving home, Walter knocked at the door at home and his mother opened. When she saw Walter her face turned pale and she asked,

"What did you do now?"

"Nothing wrong." Walter told her and showed her his furlough permit.

She couldn't believe it. He had just left the night before and here he was back. This furlough was to the Birth family, but Neubrandenburg was on his way to Schneidemuehl and he could leave the train without breaking rules and regulations.

After 14 days furlough, the cadets prepared in Schwerin for the academy. At the end of November 1943 they left their garrison in Schwerin a few days before the beginning of training and instructions at the academy in Thorn. His comrades wanted to be a few days early at the academy, but Walter was not interested in spending more time there than he had to. On their way to Thorn they passed Walter's favored city Schneidemuehl and he used the opportunity. He left his comrades and they went on to Thorn, while Walter visited with the Birth family. He missed Nephi Birth, who had been drafted in September 1943 into the army, but Edith Birth had returned from a mission for The Church of Jesus Christ of Latter-day Saints in Berlin. (1943)

Walter had met Edith once before. At that time, she was a missionary for the LDS church and was on her way back to Berlin from a district conference and she had received permission to stop at home for a visit. Now she was permanently at home and helped her mother in her grocery business because Father Birth was often away from home with his glass company. He had to replace glass in different towns after the glass was destroyed in an enemy air attack. Walter got along well with Edith. They studied the scriptures, exchanged thoughts and did other activities together. Her heart belonged to a young man who was serving in the armed services,

Helmut Kinder. Walter enjoyed his stay and would have loved to stay longer, but had to leave.

Four sister missionaries with East-German mission leaders
Edith 2nd row 5th from right, Bruno 3rd from right 3rd row
(1943)

9

A RELIGIOUS ORIGINAL

Walter was really surprised by how many men were standing in line to be admitted to the academy. He had arrived at the last minute because he was in no hurry. All the men waiting had the rank of corporal or sergeant. It was a large number of men who wanted to be admitted to the academy. Walter could see the need for the master sergeant to help. Because of Walter's past experience with those men, he would have liked to get out of the way of the master sergeant, but it was Walter's turn and he called his name.

He asked all kinds of personal questions which Walter truthfully answered. Then he asked the always interesting question,

"Your religion?"

"I am a member of The Church of Jesus Christ of Latter-day Saints."

"Let's write Lutheran."

"No," Walter said, "I am not a Lutheran."

"Well," he said, "then let's write Catholic."

Looking back, Walter now thinks the master sergeant, knowing the rules, had been trying to tell him that he would never become an officer as a member of the LDS church, but at that moment Walter was only irritated.

"I am not a Catholic, I am a member of The Church of Jesus Christ of Latter-day Saints, and listen: you write what I tell you, will you?"

He looked at Walter in astonishment. Walter guessed that nobody had ever told him that. He, the mighty master sergeant, the right hand man of the commander and Walter, a little corporal, a nobody in the army.

"I have to write what you tell me, but you will get to know me well."

"I have no objections," Walter answered; and yes, he got to know him well.

On the campus were large brick buildings, the living quarters for about 120 men and the instructors. The rooms in the buildings were large. It had room for lockers, bunk beds and a table large enough for a squad, about ten men. The men were instructed in how to train men for the battle field, how to care and use a gun, how to teach discipline and prepare men for parades, how to teach the duties of a soldier and many more items. In all activities they had to take charge and show their ability to lead.

About the third day Walter was ordered to come to the commander's office. The commander standing a few feet from the secretary's desk was a tall, good looking man with plenty of decorations on his chest and a Ritter Kreuz (knight cross, one of the high decorations given. Only the knight cross with sword was higher, given mainly to officers), presented for exceptional bravery in the battle field, was hanging on a band around his neck. After Walter saluted and introduced himself, the major asked some questions like how his mother and father were doing and other similar questions. Walter knew the major wouldn't have called him to his office to ask him these questions. Walter thought he knew what the major wanted and he was right. Then he asked the question Walter had expected, "I can't understand the answer on religion in your sold book (pay book used as a passport)." The answer in Walter's sold book under religion was written as "Jes. Chr."

"It stands for The Church of Jesus Christ of Latter-day Saints," Walter said.

"I've never heard of that church," he told Walter.

"Herr Major, you have heard of this church, you just have never heard the correct name. You have heard of the Mormons, haven't you?"

"You are a Mormon?" he asked as he took two steps back.

"Yes sir, I am a Mormon."

This was really an eye-opener for Walter. How can someone know that this is Christ's church when they know the name of the church only by the name of Mormon? LDS memers know that the Book of Mormon is another witness of Christ, but for non-Mormon's that doesn't sound like Christ's church. Walter had decided to always use the revealed name of the church and Mormons only for explanation purpose.

They talked about the church and about church doctrine. Walter asked him if he would like to know more about the church and if he would like to read some church literature. He said he wanted to. Walter hurried down to his room and brought back three books: the Book of Mormon, the Program of the Church, and one other book. When Walter presented him with the books, the major told him he would read the books and he would discuss Walter's case with the Herren of the school (the commander of the academy and the section heads). He also told Walter he couldn't guarantee he could remain at the academy. He would let him know. Walter saluted and left. This conversation came for Walter not unanticipated. He wanted everyone to know that he was a Mormon and a strong believer in Jesus Christ.

Everyone at the academy took the training seriously. The cadets were not informed how the soldiers on the front were faring, but they were glad they were at the academy. The information they did receive came from the newspaper and rumors. Not one of the cadets attending the academy was really interested in returning to the fighting units. Losing battles were being fought in Russia, Italy and Africa. The instructors told them glorious stories about Germany winning the war. If they really believed what they told them Walter didn't know, but certainly he and many of the other candidates didn't believe in a victorious outcome.

About two weeks after the meeting with his commander, Walter was called back into the major's office. This time the major was sitting at his desk. He told Walter he had read the books he had given him. Then he told Walter he had discussed his case with the "Herren" and they all agreed that Walter could remain at the academy but they would keep an eye on him. He didn't explain what they meant by "keeping an eye on Walter." but he started to tell Walter the advantages Walter would have when Walter left the Mormons and became a Nazi.

When he saw and heard Walter's negative stand toward his proposal, he told Walter his religion had changed its doctrine. Walter asked him what doctrine had changed. He told Walter "Vielweiberei" (a negative word for polygamy).

Walter had always liked a discussion. When the major said this, he bent forward, placing his hands on the desk and looked straight into the major's eyes, saying, "Vielweiberei, Herr Major, is what you see around here. Men who are married are going out and having sex with other women. Mormons who had more than one wife were married to them and honored their marriage covenant." He didn't like Walter's behavior and what he alleged: "Rohloff," he said, and that reminded Walter he was speaking to a major and he, Walter was a corporal (Unterofficier). Walter stood at attention. "Here are your books." Walter saluted again and left. The major was always fair with Walter in his informal relationship; what he thought of Walter, he later showed on his report card. Walter had no loyalty to the Nazi party and didn't consider changing. Every week the major taught at least one lesson on Nazi doctrine and one on the duties of a German soldier.

In the first weeks of their course Walter saw the charts of those in the course before his still hanging on the wall. To his surprise he saw the name of the son of his branch president on the charts. Walter wondered how it came that he was the first Mormon at the academy. Later he learned the young man had turned his back on the church. Walter met him after he returned home from the war. In their conversation the young man quoted from the book Doctrine & Covenants to show Walter that he still remembered what he had learned in his youth, but laughed at Walter's invitation to return to church activity.

Walter never felt alone. He knew exactly the way he wanted to go with the encouragement from his father and the blessings of the Lord. Walter was a little surprised about his father encouraging him to become an officer in the army. His father hated every day he spent in the armed services during his service before and during World War One. He encouraged Walter in his letters to do his best and to stand up for Jesus Christ and the teachings of the church. Walter agreed with him. The only thing they didn't agree upon was Walter's taking furlough without permission. Walter liked and enjoyed it and he felt he needed it. Walter didn't like the military to tell him what he had to do in his spare time.

At one time his room was on the ground floor. Walter had gone visiting the Birth family but had no permit for his adventure. When he returned, Walter couldn't enter the building without getting caught. Luckily, the men had left the window unlocked so Walter opened the window and went in. When he turned the light on, he saw there was a letter from home lying on his bed. He opened the letter and his eyes fell on his father's statement, "Don't take furlough without permission." Walter had just violated his counsel. Walter had no regret and smiled a little and remembered the uplifting time he had in Schneidemuehl.

The drill was hard, but Walter expected that and he didn't

mind. He didn't see anything wrong with him learning the skills. Besides, it was time away from war action and he thanked the Lord. He never heard anyone saying that he was eager to get into war action, but heard them say how glad they were to be here, away from the war. The cadets learned to take charge and also how to instruct. Until late in the night they would sit and study. During their study time, when Walter felt he was well prepared, he would take out his church literature and prepare, not for war, but for bringing peace by preparing for a mission.

During one of the preparation hours Walter was sitting at the head of the table with his back toward the entrance door. He had finished his preparation for the next day and had spread out on the table his church literature, and was studying the scriptures. So far no officer had checked what the cadets where doing during their study time. On this day however, the door opened and the master sergeant came in and stood at Walter's side looking over his shoulder for a while.

What book are you reading?"

"The Bible," Walter said.

"Let me see the other men first and then I will talk to you."

He talked and checked on the others, one after another, and then he returned to Walter. Walter knew the master sergeant didn't believe in a living God and in the teachings of Christ and that his chances to change the master sergeant's belief were slim. You could get by in the military and be accepted in claiming you believe in God, but believing in Jesus Christ was another story. How could a Jew be the Redeemer of mankind? That was unacceptable for a Nazi. Walter and the master sergeant talked for about half an hour. He listened attentively and asked many questions which Walter answered. Then he looked Walter straight in his eyes and said,

"I can't prevent you from doing this, but I want to tell you, you and I have nothing in common anymore."

"We didn't have anything in common before," Walter thought.

Cadets didn't have to give lessons on politics, but on army functions. The commander took care of politics and he was the instructor, on what cadets had to teach about army functions. He expected the cadets to be prepared and to present the lesson. Apparently the master sergeant had reported his experience with Walter to the major, and the major called on Walter to present the lesson. Walter was well prepared and gave the lesson. After the lesson the major asked everyone in the class to evaluate Walter's presentation. It was always done after anyone's presentation. No one of the cadets had a negative judgment, but to Walter's delight, the major's judgment was, "Very good Rohloff." This was the only time the master sergeant attended this hour of instruction.

While the days were full of activities, the weekends were boring. Walter took every opportunity to visit, with and without permission, the Birth family and the LDS branch in Schneidemuehl. In one of these visits Edith showed Walter a picture of her sister-in-law, Helga. She was the wife of her oldest brother Gerhard. Gerhard was in the army, and had been wounded in Russia and taken to a hospital in Koenigsberg. At a district conference of the LDS church, the youth visited the wounded LDS soldiers in the hospital. Helga and Gerhard got acquainted and married 11th of February 1942. A few days after they were married, Gerhard had to return to Russia and was killed in war action in the battle of Ssytschewo, Staraja, Russia on the 1st of April 1942. Edith gave Walter the address of Helga and Walter wrote her.

After a few letters Helga invited him to visit her in Tilsit. Walter applied for a permit for weekend furlough, and after he had not heard anything by Wednesday, Walter thought the furlough was granted. At the roll-call on Thursday night the master sergeant, gave out furlough permits to some of the cadets who had requested furlough. Walter expected to get his permit. The master sergeant let Walter wait, but at the end of the roll-call, he called his name.

"Rohloff see."

Walter looked at him and he could see the master sergeant held over his head his permit, signed by the commander. Everyone could see it.

"Can you see it is signed by the commander?"

"Yes sir, I can see. It is signed," Walter said.

"Do you think you can go?"

"Yes, Sir" Walter said.

"No," he said, "You can't,"

and he tore the permit apart. In front of all the men he had put Walter down. Walter was mad, but he tried not to show it. Instead Walter smiled. Walter thought that this action was his reply, for the way Walter's lack of respect when he entered this academy.

This humiliation was on Walter's mind all day Friday. He thought of going without a permit, but he felt it was too far away about 5 hrs with a train, too dangerous, and getting caught because he would have to leave the academy about noon and would arrive in Tilsit in the dark. Besides that, he had to change trains in Insterburg and that train in Insterburg was a D-Zug, a fast moving train. A person could walk from one car to the other which was good for the traveling public, but not good for Walter. There was no way Walter could hide or get around the military police. Another negative point was: that Walter didn't know the railroad station, nor did he know the town. The field exercise on Saturday lasted usually until noon, making it too late for him to make the train in time. Walter wrote Helga that he wouldn't come, but he still didn't give up hope for some kind of opportunity to go. Nevertheless, on Friday night Walter asked a fellow candidate to lend him his small suitcase.

"You didn't get a permit. Why do you want my suitcase?" he asked.

"Oh, I might go anyhow," Walter replied.

"We will all be punished when they catch you."

"Do not worry. You know it has not happened in the past and it won't happen in the future," Walter assured him. He gave Walter his little suitcase and Walter started packing, not knowing how to proceed.

On Saturday morning they went out for field drill, a long distance from their barracks. Only a few of their officers were with them. The others were preparing for their weekend furlough. No one was interested in doing anything. About mid- morning, they were all standing together in formation, when the conducting officer said,

"Everyone, who has a furlough permit come forward."

Quite a few men came forward, and he dismissed them, and wished them well. Walter observed what was going on, but before he had made up his mind to go or not, all the men had left. Walter went forward anyhow.

"What do you want?" Walter was asked by the officer.

He answered, "To take furlough."

He didn't ask Walter if he had a permit, but he asked, "Why didn't you come out right away?"

"I didn't think you would let the men go," Walter answered.

"You are late now," he said. "Take a bike and hurry."

He didn't have to say that twice. Walter arrived at the barracks before anyone else. This made it possible for him to get to the train on time.

But Walter had one more problem he had to solve. The office of the master sergeant was just above his room. From Walter's point of view he was the only one of his instructors who knew Walter had no permit for furlough. Walter made sure the sergeant did not hear nor see him when he returned the bike and cleaned himself in the bathroom. Walter hurried and watched carefully so as not to run into the master sergeant. When Walter arrived at the railroad station in Thorn-Podgorz and looked at the big clock at the entrance he saw he had only two minutes until the train left. At the ticket window many people were waiting to be served. Walter had no time left to wait in line.

Walter went to a ticket machine and bought a ticket to get on the Bahnsteig (platform). No time was left to jump the fence. He had to go through the gate. Walter showed his ticket to the attendant and he punched it. Then he showed it to the MP man, but the man wanted to see his furlough permit. Walter told him he had none. The MP man told him he couldn't pass the gate. "That is what you think," Walter said to him and ran down the stairs through the tunnel, and up the stairs to his platform. The MP man followed him. Not too far away Walter could see his train started to move. Walter ran after the train that had increased its speed. Walter reached the last car. A man helped him first by taking his suitcase, and then he helped Walter into the car. It took all of Walter's strength. Safely on board and breathing hard Walter, not thinking what consequences his action could have, turned around and waved goodbye to the gasping MP man.

This train was a slow passenger train stopping in many small towns. The car Walter entered transported mail to the different stations. Some men were sitting and sorting mail. Walter started right away to help the men with their work. As he helped, he told them from where he came and what he planned to do. By doing this, he gave himself away and they could easily turn him over to the MP at the next station. They didn't. Walter realized by now, the MP man had reported to his superior what happened, and they would look for him and check the train intensively. Through the mailmen he was informed, what was going on at the different railroad stations. The mail car was not visited by the MP. Apparently the MP men were not informed that Walter entered the last car. Walter was not concerned, not worried and felt save being with the mailmen. After some time passed he was informed by the mailmen, that they didn't see any MP any more. Walter went out on the platform and bought a ticket for his trip from Thorn to Tilsit. To get a ticket, he had to tell the ticket agent his story. Now she knew why there had been so many MP men on her train. She couldn't believe that so many MP men didn't catch him. Walter told her, he was just taking weekend furlough without a permit, but he was not deserting the army; he would return to his unit. Walter didn't tell her to what unit he belonged or in what car he was riding. Of course she didn't like what Walter did and could report him being a passenger of her train at any station but apparently she didn't.

In Insterburg Walter transferred to a faster-moving passenger train. This train would stop only in Tilsit. The cars had a passageway and many compartments. One MP man would be inside the compartment and check the permits and another would be with him, but standing in the passageway; nobody could pass him. Carefully, Walter observed the movements of the MP on the railway station's platform. He saw the MP men entering the last car of the train when the train started to leave. They went from one car to the next and Walter went just one car ahead of them. When they reached the car just behind the locomotive, Walter looked for a way to hide. He opened the car door to see if he could stand on the footboard, but it was very cold on this January day. He stayed inside and saw the MP reaching the middle of his car, while the train arrived in Tilsit. He was very relieved and pleased, to leave the train without hindrance.

While the passengers were leaving, Walter stood on the platform and looked for a way to leave without going through the guarded gate. At this dimly lighted station he thought, he saw an open gate in between a large and a small building, away from the main platform. He didn't use the tunnel, but crossed the tracks to the main platform. Walter was wrong, the gate was locked. Without hesitation,

Walter threw his little suitcase over the gate and jumped over. Was he shocked, when he straightened up, and saw a policeman standing on his side! The police man probably was as surprised as Walter. Quickly Walter grasped his suitcase and mingled with the large group of people in front of the railroad station.

Walter moved away a short distance from the station, and looked feverishly through his notes for Helga's address. He found the address for the LDS church meeting place, but not Helga's. In despair he walked through the streets. He looked around, but didn't see anything that sounded familiar. He walked back to the railroad station with the intention of asking for a hotel room. Walter wanted to walk into the army information office, but at the last minute he changed his mind, realizing they would ask him for his permit when he asked for a hotel room.

Aimlessly, Walter walked the streets, hoping to meet someone who knew Helga. It was already after 11 pm and he didn't see anyone walking. Walter was now on the outskirts of the town. He entered a few of the apartment buildings, but he didn't see any light and didn't want to wake anybody up. Then in one of the buildings, he thought he saw light in one apartment. He rang the bell and a sleepy woman opened the door. Walter apologized and asked her for Helga, but she didn't know Helga. Rightfully she reproached Walter for getting her up. When the bell rang, she thought, it was her husband coming home on furlough. After they talked a little while she said she would like to help him, but she didn't know how. As Walter left the building and was on the street, she opened the window and told him, that there were unfinished barracks close by and she gave him the directions.

Walter followed the directions the lady had given him, and after a short walk in the moonlight he saw the barracks. As he came close he could see there were no windows and no doors mounted in the building, but it had a roof and the walls were up. Inside, Walter found rolls of fiberglass, about 3 or 4 feet wide. Part of a roll he placed on the floor to lay on, and the rest he used to cover him. It worked out great. It gave him all he needed to protect him from the bitter cold. Walter slept warm and well until the sun came up. After restoring everything the way it was when he came, he looked for water to wash and shave. Every puddle was frozen, but Walter saw a river in the distance. He walked to the river and touched the water. It was ice cold. He took his clothing off (except for his pants) moved some ice out of the way and washed himself. It was refreshing, but shaving was catastrophic. Walter thought his face looked worse after shaving, than it did before.

It bothered him somewhat to attend church meetings purely shaven, but he had no choice. He walked back to the town and found the meeting place. The LDS church members met in a small room in an apartment house. Walter was early but found a brother there who fed the stove to make the room warm for the meetings. To pass the time, he helped the brother with his preparation. Helga arrived a little after the meeting had started. She didn't recognize or expect Walter because he had written her that his request for furlough was turned down. After the meeting Walter introduced himself and they went to her Aunt Lusche's home. Before the meal Helga shaved Walter with such a soft touch, that he decided he would take her service any time. To Walter's great surprise he met Ruth Birth. She had vacation time and had a boyfriend here. All the young folks came and all had a great time together.

Even the best time has to end. All the youth walked to the railroad station, the youth of the branch the normal way and Walter by the way the boys had explored for him. A railroad crossing close to the station made it easy to enter the platform in the dark. While they were standing and talking they saw trains arriving on both sides of the platform Helga asked Walter which one of the trains he would take. Walter pointed at a "Fronturlauber," a train that carried soldiers with furlough permits from the front to their destination. This train was always under heavy control by the MP. Two of these MP men were walking up and down in front of the train. Realizing the danger of Walter getting caught, Helga turned pale. Ruth laughed and told Helga not to worry: that Walter had visited Schneidemuehl many times without a furlough permit. What Ruth didn't know was the train to Schneidemuehl was a slow moving train of individual cars and stopped on every small station so it was easy for Walter to move out of sight by moving from one car to another. The train Walter was using now was fast and stopped only in Insterburg and at his destination Thorn, just like the last train he used when he came. Walter was a little worried how he would master not being caught by the Military Police.

The passenger car Walter entered had just been added to the train. In one of the compartments he took a corner place where he could sit and sleep. Walter placed his coat there to reserve the seat for himself. He opened a window and talked to Helga and Ruth and the boys, but his main attention was on the two MP men and where they would enter the train. They entered the train the same way Walter did. They used the last door of the last car. When the train started moving Walter waved good bye to everyone and then checked the restroom for a hiding place, but it was no good. He walked to the end of the next to the last car and waited. Walter didn't know what to do. He considered standing outside the car on the footboard, but it was too cold and because of the window in the door he could be seen. Waiting until he arrived in Insterburg and then changing cars was another option, but Walter didn't like it either.

When he couldn't think of any other options, he decided to take a risk. As the MP arrived at about the middle of that car, he did something he never had done before. One of the MP men stood in the passage way and the other in the compartment and checked the permits of the soldiers. Walter hesitated for a long time because passing the man in the hallway was very risky since he could ask him for a permit, but Walter couldn't think of any other way. As the MP man in the passage way turned his back toward Walter, Walter walked toward the man and put his hand on the MP mans shoulder and said, "Excuse me, comrade." His voice was clear and didn't flicker. He moved and let Walter pass without saying a word. The MP man could see Walter walk but Walter's walk didn't show any agitation, and Walter went to his reserved seat and fell asleep.

In his sleep it seemed to Walter that he heard the conductor calling the name of his destination. Waking up and looking through the window he saw it was his destination. Many soldiers had already left the train. Walter had to hurry to jump the fence before anyone left the station and saw him getting over the fence. He had some difficulty getting over the fence because it was much higher than he had expected. He had just made the jump over the fence when the first soldier left the station. Walter hurried to his barracks and entered without a problem. Carefully he opened the door to his room, because he didn't want to wake anyone up. As he entered the room everyone was awake and sitting up in bed, as if they were expecting him.

"How was your trip?" they asked.

"Good, but I will tell you later. Let me get some sleep."

It was shortly before 5am and there was not much time to sleep, since they had to be up at 6am.

While preparing for the drills, Walter told them his story and they told him theirs. Apparently the military police were looking for a missing man at any garrison in Thorn. All the candidates were called for a roll call. They were instructed to report anyone who left the garrison without permission. Walter's roommates knew if they didn't tell and he got caught, they would be punished and their career would end. They debated but remembered that Walter had done this successful many times before, so they didn't say a word and hoped Walter would do all right. Walter saw the master sergeant during the day, saluted him smilingly and thought about the great time he had in Tilsit.

Walter saw Helga in Tilsit once more toward the end of his stay at the academy. Walter wrote her almost daily and she him. He was enthused, to say the least, about Helga. He surely looked forward to meeting her again. Traveling was not as exciting as the first trip. He had a permit to go and visit, and he knew where to go. Helga invited him into her single, nicely furnished room. Someone had rented her this room, which was part of a larger apartment. Helga had not made other arrangements, but wanted Walter to stay with her. They had a good time together. After a while she was sitting on his lap. They talked and kissed. Later Helga made Walter's sleeping arrangement on the couch and she slept in her bed. She mentioned how nice it was that they could sleep in one room, but not in one bed.

The next day Helga had to go to work and Walter stayed in her room. There was only one problem: a cleaning lady would come and clean the apartment and her room. No one was to know that Walter was in her room. Helga solved that problem by placing Walter in her bed, and then piling all of the bed stuff Walter has been sleeping in, over him. As she left for work, she reminded Walter with a smile, not to cough or to blow his nose while the lady was there cleaning the room.

It took a while until the cleaning lady came. Walter would have liked to sleep, but he was afraid he would unknowingly make a wrong move while the cleaning lady was there. He could hear her moving around after she arrived, but she didn't notice the strange visitor under the pile of bed stuff on the bed.

Walter had plenty of time on his hands. As it was his habit in the past, in the evenings he would look over all he had done and said on the past day. He did that now. He surely had enjoyed the evening with Helga, but when he recalled what they had talked about and what they had done, he asked himself, if Helga was the woman he wanted to marry. He thought he loved her, but the last conversation with his father came into his mind. Enthused he had talked with him about Helga, but his father's answer was, "Why do you want to take her away from her husband? She belongs to Gerhard."

This and many other things went through his mind. Walter realized his actions might have given Helga the impression that he was thinking of marriage. In reality, he was not ready yet to take this important step. He wanted to keep Helga as a friend, and his father's words were heavy on his mind. He loved the Birth family and doing something they didn't approve of was on his mind. He had never met Gerhard, but had heard much about him. He had prayed and prayed about what to do.

Walter came to the conclusion that he couldn't go back to his unit as if everything were fine and then write to Helga. He felt he had an obligation and that he owed Helga an explanation. Walter went and bought a beautiful bouquet of flowers and then went to say goodbye.

When she saw him, Helga smiled, but when she saw the flowers her face turned pale. "What went wrong?" she asked.

Walter thanked her for the beautiful time and asked her if they could continue to be friends. It was not an easy thing for both of them, but he felt it was the right thing to do. Their ways crossed in the future many times and they are friends to this day.

Walter made good progress in his training to become an officer in the German army. Most of his instructors helped him to be successful. All cadets were grateful to be at the academy and not somewhere on the battlefields because things didn't look good for Germany. In Russia, the army retreated in many places. Goebbels, Germany's propaganda minister said, "The army is straightening out the front line to have better positions." Germany had fought a losing battle at Stalingrad and the losing battle in Africa was almost over. Rumors had it that Germany's allies were no help. At the first confrontation with the enemy, they left their positions and ran. At home, the outlook too was bleak. The air raids had increased and some factories were moved underground. The workload was laid on the shoulders of women and older men. Walter's mother had to go to work at the same factory where his father worked. She hated it, but couldn't change it.

At the academy everyone who completed the training successfully would become an officer. About four weeks before the end of their training the cadets were notified that the best men from every group would be promoted two or three weeks before the rest. Walter's group and Walter counted on his early promotion, but it didn't happen. What went wrong? Not one of the officers knew of his unapproved excursion to Schneidemuehl or Tilsit. Otherwise, Walter was an exemplary cadet. Walter had prepared himself very well for all activities. Every one of the instructors treated him fairly including the major; of course, Walter couldn't read their minds. The only exception was the master sergeant. He might not have forgotten how Walter rebuked him when Walter was interviewed by him, at the time he entered the academy. No one talked about his religion in his presence, but outside his presence, he later found out, they did. Walter was disappointed to say the least, and felt he might not leave the academy with a promotion.

Receiving mail was an important part of the military life. Walter's mother seldom wrote, but his father stayed in close contact. Walter still has many of his letters today. They gave him encouragement and helped him to do what was right. His father knew the scriptures well and encouraged him to study the word of God.

Walter's days at the academy came to an end on the 15th of March 1944. His feelings had not betrayed him; he was not promoted to a second lieutenant. He was not told why, but others knew more than he did. On the last day a sergeant came and asked for Walter. He introduced himself as a Lutheran minister, and he wanted to get acquainted with him. He was older than Walter and looked more like a sportsman, with his well-built, athletic body. He shook hands with Walter and said,

> "I wanted to get acquainted with you. I understand you didn't become an officer because you are an active Mormon. I don't think well of the Mormons, but I respect you for standing up for what you believe."

Not thinking well of the Mormons was, in Walter's opinion, because he never looked for what the Mormon Church stood for. They didn't know the name of the church. That was one of the easons why Walter insisted when he entered the institution that they had to write down the real name of the church. He wanted to make sure they knew Walter believed in Christ as the Son of God.

The minister left as fast as he had arrived. Apparently he was an active Lutheran and shared with Walter the same fate. Later Walter wondered how the minister knew he was a Mormon. The instructing officers must have talked to him. It looked like most of the institution staff knew about his affiliation with the LDS church and that pleased Walter.

Not being promoted was not as easy to take as Walter had thought. Walter watched when his comrades changed from their old uniform into the good looking one of an officer. Their friendly teasing didn't bother him, but then came the realization that he now had to salute these men, and it did bother him. Walter had helped the former cadets on their way, but that was forgotten now.

The men who came from Schwerin returned from the academy in the middle of March 1944, to their garrison in Schwerin. Before joining the fighting unit in Russia all men received two weeks' furlough. Walter spent his time with his parents and with the Birth family. His father congratulated him for standing up for their belief. He encouraged Walter to stay firm in the future. Walter enjoyed the love and sympathy his parents and the Birth family had for him. He still carried some disappointment, but being with these families helped him to overcome it and encouraged him to do what is right, by standing up for Jesus Christ.

After returning to his garrison he received orders to join the fighting units in Russia. Two other men who had been at the academy and didn't pass, accompanied him. Their unit was stationed deep in Russia near the town of Mogilev. To reach Mogilev by train they had to pass Schneidemuehl. One of his comrade's parents lived in Schneidemuehl so they stopped there and took three days unauthorized furlough.

The fellow who stayed with his parents called Walter one day. Walter had given him, at his request, the envelope Walter was to deliver to their commander at the front. The comrade had used steam to open the envelope. He told Walter that his own report card was not good. Then he read the grades on Walter's report card and they were all good and very good ratings. There was a footnote under Walter's report which read,

> "Religious original (Sonderling), belonging to the Mormon sect- politically not bearable (tragbar)."

Now Walter knew for sure why he hadn't become an officer. Walter felt good. It gave him a great lift because he had accomplished what his father and he wanted: that the Nazis should show their true intention. They showed Walter he wasn't welcome to become an officer, but he was good enough to fight and get killed for them.

10

ALCOHOL IS NOT FOR MEN

Without any difficulties the three men reached their regiment and reported to the commander. He first invited Walter's two comrades into his shelter. Walter stood outside the door and could hear what was going on inside. It sounded like a thunderstorm. The commander told the two men they were a disgrace to his regiment. For quite some time he raised his voice. When he released the men they looked like something had hit them.

Like moles the men were hiding in the trenches. In this area at that time in Russia the trenches were many miles long. In between the German and the Russian trenches is the no man's land. (1944)

That didn't make Walter feel good either. The commander ordered Walter in and Walter expected the same treatment. After the commander read Walter's report card he looked at Walter and said,

"There is nothing we can do. You have your belief and we have ours."

Then to Walter's surprise, he continued "Do you have a wish?"
It caught Walter unprepared; he had never heard that soldiers were asked what they wanted. After thinking for a minute Walter asked if he could return to his old company, the 3rd. The Major told him he couldn't do that, but he would send him to his old battalion, the 7thcompany. Walter had no objection.

That same day under the cover of darkness Walter went with the men who had to bring food and supplies to the main battle line. There he reported to the platoon leader. The platoon leader kept Walter in his shelter and asked Walter where he came from. The platoon leader poked fun at Walter for not successfully completing the academy. It hurt Walter and the hurt never left him while he was under that man's command.

The next day a squad with shelter (a hole in the ground covered with tree trunks} was assigned to Walter. All shelters were the hiding place for a squad and protected them from enemy fire. The shelters were placed just a little below the top of the mountain with a view over the valley. The shelter of the platoon leader was behind the top of the mountain chain. There was no trench connecting the platoon leader's shelter with the main trench. The platoon leader could move freely, but the squads had no contact with him during the daytime. As far as Walter could see, the main trench went below the top of the mountain chain for a long distance. The shelters were just a little above the main defense line and connected with it. The men could oversee the territory well up to the enemy line. Of course the enemy could see the German men as well and bombarded them daily with gun, mortar and artillery fire. The Germans had great respect for the Russian sharp shooters. During the day every squad had one man watching for enemy activity in the no-man's land. The territory a squad had to protect was far too large for the few men. A major attack would find little resistance.

In one of the first days at the front, Walter was ordered to see the commander, a captain. As he entered the shelter he could see it was poorly built. It had water standing on the floor and boards over the water, a very unhealthy condition. You couldn't stand up because the ceiling was so low. He had logs to sit on and he invited Walter to sit across from him. He explained to Walter that he had read his report card from the academy. For him it was not clear how a man with Walter's abilities and talents could turn his back on the opportunities offered. He reminded Walter how much better he could serve his homeland if he were an officer. He couldn't understand how Walter could worship a God no one has seen. He could comprehend someone worshiping the moon or the sun, but to hold in awe something unseen was impossible for him to believe. He invited Walter to look at how Germany had changed and progressed under Hitler's leadership. He painted a rosy picture of how Germany would look when the war was won. He encouraged Walter to leave his church and join the progressive forces. Walter told him he appreciated him taking time out and talking to him about his belief. Walter then explained to him what he believed and why. The officer had a little temper and any time Walter contradicted him he would raise himself from his seat and hit the ceiling. The face he made after he hit the ceiling was so funny Walter had a hard time suppressing his laughter. They had a long discussion, but the officer was not willing to change and neither was Walter. He dismissed him and Walter never heard from him again.

North of their position the front had collapsed and needed to be reinforced. Walter's unit was taken out of its position and ordered to fill the gap in the frontline. That sounds easy but it was hard work. They had to carry their own equipment and had to help the horses pull the wagons. Not one of the men was permitted to sit on one of the wagons. They had to walk all day. The dirt roads were in terrible condition. Because it was late spring, the road was full of water filled holes. The ground was soft and muddy and at times the wagon would sink almost up to the axle in mud. It was a relief when they reached their destination. After the day on the road all the men were exhausted. The only good thing was there were no artillery shellings and no air attacks while they marched after dark into their new position.

There was no water in the trenches. That was a relief until they saw that the trenches were filled with the corpses of dead soldiers. The field in front of them and the area called "no-man's land" were full of dead men and even in the barbwire entanglement there were dead bodies hanging. It was a horrifying picture. Walter shuddered and realized that these men on either side were just numbers. They were told they fought and gave their lives for their Fatherland, while in reality they fought for the megalomania of a dictator.

In the daylight they could see there were plenty of alcohol bottles lying around. At first, Walter thought the German leaders had given the men alcohol for a party, but then Walter remembered alcohol was often served to make the men careless and do what they wouldn't do when they were sober. They buried as many dead bodies as they possibly could. On bodies where they found identification, they sent the identification back through their supply line. The men covered up the trenches that were filled with bodies and dug new trenches. They had to be very careful because the Russians had excellent sharpshooters. Because of them, they didn't dare to touch the dead lying on the field in the no man's land or in the barbwire entanglement. It took a while to get used to knowing the men in the entanglement were dead bodies and not new attackers. The smell from the dead bodies was terrible, especially when the wind came from the east.

They didn't have enough men to cover the whole area assigned to them. Besides this, it was also the dividing line between two divisions. While their platoon covered a large area, there were no German soldiers for about 100 yards in between them and the other division. At night the officers who checked on the guards covered that empty area and made contact with the other division. The men at the last station of either division were very nervous because they knew that during an attack they hardly had a chance to survive.

For those who checked on the guards at night it was always risky to cover that area. Most non-commissioned officers who had to control that area took other men along, but Walter went alone. He knew anyone who would cross his way would be an enemy. Thankfully he never came in contact with any enemies there, but he was once nearly killed approaching the other division. He knew everyone in that group, so when the guard called at his approach for the password he said just as he had done many times before, "Its Walter." This particular time he heard the guard take the safety off on his rifle. Walter was surprised and dropped to the ground. After the guard had fired in his direction Walter said the password. The guard's group had heard the shot and every man came out of the shelter to see what was going on. They introduced themselves and Walter found out that the old division who has been stationed there had been replaced with a new one who didn't know "Walter."

This new division was made up of men who had served before in the air force, but the once glorious air force didn't exist anymore. Not only ground personal, but also pilots now served with the infantry. With little training and no infantry war experience they were afraid. They were told to be alert because enemy men would crawl close to them and attack. In one such incident Walter had heard the sound made by a man when the enemy's hands closed his throat. An awful sound and you wonder if Russians in front of you, were lying in the dark to get you. The enemy didn't kill that man but tried to obtained important information from him. Walter wondered if the Russians knew how few men the Germans had placed here in that middle section of the German east front. Walter later learned the German high command had taken out men and equipment from the middle section and placed some men in France against the Allied offensive and others into the southern section of their front. The Germans did expect an attack in the south, playing, knowingly or unknowingly, into the hands of the Russians. (Many high ranking officers hated Hitler and worked against him.)

There was never a quiet moment on the front. Even though their munitions were restricted and they were told not to shoot, there were always shots fired at an imaginary target. The squads had spare munitions in their shelter that they didn't report. They knew the position of their enemy well because of the light given off by every shot. It showed the position of the gunner and the men directed their shots in that direction. Of course the same was true for the Russians. They surely knew the Germans' position. To fool the Russians, the Germans' made it look as if they had more men than they had in reality. Walter designed and made rifle holders. They placed guns which would hold five shots on these holders. A string connected this gun with a man on guard. He would pull the string and fire a shot once in a while. The passing patrol would reload the gun. Walter doesn't know if they really fooled the Russians, but there was a nice side-effect for him. While the other men had to dig trenches or work on other projects, Walter worked on these rifle holders or had spare time. In this spare time he studied church literature his father had mailed him.

Walter's workshop in the trench

His father tore the book The Articles of Faith apart and sent

Walter pages with his letters. This way Walter gained a good knowledge of the teachings of the church.

When there was no major fighting going on or when there were no work assignments one man would stand guard and most of the others played cards for money. Drinking alcohol was a problem. It was freely given when an attack was expected or when the Germans planned to attack. If the Russians had known that at times Walter was the only sober soldier in the trench while the others were sleeping off their drunkenness, they might have overrun their battalion.

At times they had a nice "treat." The Russians placed large speakers in their trenches and would play good German folk music or the "Don Kosacken choir," a Russian choir very much liked in Germany, would sing. Of course they didn't do it to entertain the Germans. They had a message for the men in between about every song which invited soldiers to leave their position and come over. They told them how good they would have it over there. What surprised Walter the most was how well they knew who they were, where their garrison was and the problems they had, but Walter never saw any one accepting their invitation.

The middle section of the Russian front was quiet while the Allies started their attack in France and also built a base for further attacks there.

In Italy, the German troops had left Rome without fighting, but were resisting strong Allied attacks north of Rome. As Walter learned later, on the Russian front Germany was expecting an attack at the southern section of the front and moved all available troops there, even taking more men out of the sparsely occupied middle section.

For Walter and the men around him one day was the same as the one before. They were glad they were not in the middle of a battle. In early June Walter was ordered to appear before the battalion commander. Arriving at his shelter, Walter notified the clerk of his arrival. The commander came outside and made Walter stand at attention while he read from a letter, "The cadet corporal Walter Rohloff is, as of this day, dismissed as a cadet and from further officer training. Reason: Walter Rohloff is a religious original

(Sonderling), belonging to the Mormon sect, politically not bearable (tragbar)." (By order: B1.B. from 2.6.44 ziff.7.) He told Walter he was sorry and dismissed him.

Cadet Corporal Walter Rohloff

Maybe Walter should have felt bad about his dismissal as an officer aspirant, but he didn't. Walter was not dismissed because he was not able to be an officer; he was dismissed because of his religion. Walter felt very good about that. Now, for the first time he officially heard why he hadn't become an officer. On the way back to his unit he passed a small forest. Walter went inside the forest and on his knees he thanked the Lord for being with him always and giving him the strength to stand up for Him. Walter could have easily become an officer. All he would have to do was tell them he believed in God, but not mention Jesus Christ. That would have made all the difference. Jesus Christ was the hated name. Their question was,

"How can a Jew be God's Son?" They often asked Walter how he could believe in the mission of Jesus Christ. They thought maybe he was a philosopher, but the Son of God?

Walter took the shoulder stripes off his uniform which identified him as a cadet. He thought this was the end of his striving to become an officer, but it was not. A few days later he was called into his company leader's shelter. Apparently all the officers were informed of his treatment and wanted to help him. The company leader told Walter there was a way to become an officer if he would take over the leadership of a company of convicts (120 men). By showing his ability to lead, the army would have no choice but to make him an officer. That would be the last thing Walter wanted to do. The company leader didn't realize how little Walter cared to become an officer. Walter never had seen a unit of convicts (Strafkompany), but he assumed many of the men would be political prisoners. Walter thanked the company leader for his effort to help him and then Walter begged him not to recommend him.

Apparently he didn't recommend Walter because Walter never heard a thing about this again.

The shelter Walter occupied with his squad was well built. When the artillery of the enemy bombarded the trenches, the shelter shook, but it held. After building this shelter he had told the men to build their beds to their liking; Walter didn't care how it looked. Walter had made himself a nice bed and he slept well in it. He didn't like to sleep with his boots on and would take them off when possible, which was against orders. Day and night they had one man in the trench watching the Russians and the no-man's land. At night there was one man awake in the shelter to wake up another man to relieve the outside guard after two hours. One night the guard stood for more than three hours, when the man who took care of his relief fell asleep. The guard on duty couldn't leave his position. He rang the alarm and every man jumped out of bed to get into his assigned position. In the dark, Walter had a tough time getting his boots on. They hurt and when he took the boots off he saw he had mixed up the right and left boots. From that time on Walter slept with his boots on.

Soldbuch
zugleich Personalausweis
Nr.
(Dienstgrad)
(neuer Dienstgrad)
ab
Walter Rohloff
(Vor- und Zuname)
Blutgruppe A

The first page in Walter's Army passport.

It was the early afternoon on the 20th of June 1944. Walter was alone in his shelter, lying on his bed. Walter must have been sleepy or sleeping because like a dream he saw that his unit was going to be attacked, and that he was wounded and taken back to Germany. He woke up and went outside the shelter. He looked over to the Russian lines, but didn't see anything suspicious.

Walter thought, "Nonsense." But then he got thinking a little more and he felt, "Maybe the Lord wants to tell you something." Walter went back into the shelter and took his books out of the hole. The hole was formed in the dirt wall like shelves and made it easy for him to reach for the books. He placed his tiny New Testament in the little breast pocket in his jacket and the "Doctrine and Covenants" and the pages of the book, "The Articles of Faith," his father had mailed him with his letters in the large pockets.

The next day he had the last tour before dawn to check the guards in the main battle line and to make contact with the neighboring division. When daylight came and he had satisfied himself that everything was all right, he went to the shelter of his platoon leader to give his report. This shelter was on the other side of the hills, a short distance from the main battle line. It was quiet and Walter had nothing of real importance to report. His platoon leader was talking on the phone to another platoon leader. While Walter was waiting to get his platoon leader's attention he heard a raised voice out of the telephone, "Ivan im Graben (Russians in the trenches)."

Without saying a word Walter hurried out of the shelter to join his men, the place he should be. Outside, the picture had changed. It was not quiet any more. The Russians rained heavy artillery and mortar fire in between the platoon leader's shelter and the main battle line. This sealed off the front line; no help could come from the rear. Walter had no choice; he had to cross through the fire line to reach his men. He listened carefully to the flying grenades. In between the salvos he kept running and before the grenades exploded he was on the ground flat on his belly. He reached the defense line unharmed. He informed the agitated men what had happened and positioned them to resist an attack. It was almost over when, after a salvo missed the trench, Walter raised his head to see if there were enemies in front of them. A late grenade hit the ground and exploded in front of Walter. Fragments hit his face on the forehead and below the lower lip. It didn't penetrate his skull and he never lost consciousness.

After the attack calmed down, Walter went to the company

leader's shelter for first aid. A medical orderly treated his wounds and told him the wounds were not life-threatening but an infection would be. The medic wanted to send him back to a nearby hospital in Mogilev. Walter was not sure what he wanted to do. His company leader told him he could stay or go, it was Walter's decision. Walter disregarded his platoon leader's pleading to stay and he chose to go to the hospital. He had to take along a badly wounded man in a wagon pulled by a horse. Without any interference they reached their baggage unit (Tross) while it was still daylight. From there they were transported to the hospital. The hospital was very busy and had no place for Walter. Walter left the badly wounded man in the hospital and went to a convalescent home (Erholungsheim) nearby.

Unknown to them and to the German military leaders, the Russians had placed in the middle section of the front an army three and a half times larger than the German army. The Germans expected an attack in the south, but the Russians prepared an attack on the middle section of the German Army. The good Lord held His hands over Walter. He was wounded on 21st of June and on the 22nd of June the Russians started their major offensive. They broke through the weak German defenses and the Germans retreated in a wild escape and not in orderly retreat. In four weeks the Russian army advanced over 400 miles, close to the Polish capital, Warsaw. On the Weichsel River, the Germans were able to give organized resistance to the tired Russian army. In this Russian attack Walter's unit was completely demolished.

In the convalescent home, a chess tournament was planned on Sunday, the 22nd of June. Walter always enjoyed a good chess game. He would have liked to play a game, but in the past he had always tried to have a spiritual hour on Sunday by studying the scriptures or attending a church of any denomination. In all the years before or after this time he was never close to a LDS church. Even when he attended church in Thorn and Gnesen he had to travel many hours by train. Walter debated with himself whether to play chess or to keep the Sabbath day holy by finding a church. Because it was very dangerous and forbidden to walk alone along the streets in an enemy town, Walter asked his fellow comrades to go with him but no one was interested. So he went alone.

Mogilev (Mahlyow) a town in Belarus on the Dnepr River with a population of about 160,000. Walter had no idea where a soldier's church of any denomination might be, but he thought it might be along a well traveled highway. After walking the streets for a while he found the place he was looking for. Walter walked in and saw a few soldiers and a minister getting ready for the service. The details of the service are forgotten, but the theme was: "And we know that all that happens to us is working for our good, if we love God (Rom.8:28)." This scripture never left him and he remembered it well in the upcoming difficult times.

Walter's interest in playing chess was gone when he returned. He felt spiritually uplifted and contemplated what he had heard in the service. Walter had a great desire to serve the Lord and up to that hour, the Lord had been with him always. It was only a few days since he had been wounded, but the wounds didn't bother him. Wanting to meditate he went to bed early. During the night a toothache woke him up. Looking for help, Walter found the place in an uproar.

Upon asking a member of the staff, he learned the Russians had broken through German lines near the place he was wounded and were moving in their direction. This was a typical attack plan. A few days before, the Russians had been able to penetrate the German line with a few men: They had found a weak place, so they started a major attack at that point. The attack came in the completely unprepared middle section.

Getting up the morning of the 23rd of June, in the convalescent home and looking around the house, it looked like a beehive. Items were packed and material and men were moved to the railroad station. The staff was able to take almost all personnel and patients with them except for a few who were able to move on their own. Eleven men had no space on the train and Walter was one of them. Ten of the men argued with the hospital staff and begged them to take them along, but Walter thought on the scripture from the day before and was willing to remain. He was asked to take the ten men and return to the hospital.

11

A STEP AHEAD OF THE RUSSIAN ARMY

They returned to the hospital. There they were greeted with the same confusion found at the convalescent home. It took a while to find someone in charge. The officer was very helpful, but had room on the train for only five of them. Walter was one of the six who were left behind. That was not encouraging, but Walter again thought about the scripture from Sunday and that made him feel better.

Those left behind were instructed to see the city commander of Mogilev. The commander's office was in a beautiful villa on the highway. They were informed the commander was not present and would not return before 4 pm. When the commander arrived his message was short and clear: Mogilev would be declared a fortress on June 23, at 6 pm and would be defended up to the last man. At 6 pm no one could leave the town and no one could enter. He told the men they could do whatever they wanted, leave before 6 pm or stay and fight to either be killed or become a prisoner of war. He couldn't help them in any way. Walter was not interested in dying in this town or becoming a prisoner of war.

In walking from the villa to the street, Walter thought about what to do next and about what he had heard the day before; "For the believer in God everything would be to his best." Walking along deep in his thoughts, Walter heard someone calling his name. A large truck had passed and someone from the truck had called his name. Walter yelled as loud as he could, "Stop!"

Walter couldn't believe it, but the truck stopped. Talking to the driver he found out he were part of his unit and had to go back for material. He took him along as they drove westward. He told Walter what had happened on the front and what little of his unit was left. They drove until they crossed the River Berezina. (This is the same river at which the French conqueror Napoleon lost the battle and the war.) On the drive Walter saw not only Germans fleeing before the Russian army, but also Russians moving westward to get away from their own army. Long columns of civilians walked the road carrying their belongings or had a horse with a small wagon. These people feared their own army and history shows their fear was justified. As Walter saw these people he thought of his own folks at home and hoped it would never happen to them. Passing by railroad tracks he saw railcars loaded with tanks and heavy army equipment that should be with the fighting units on the front. It seemed that someone in high command hated Hitler and sabotaged the action. Walter found a place to sleep in a large hall filled with soldiers. He thanked the Lord for his marvelous help and remembered the message on Sunday. He felt secure and he slept well.

The next morning Walter went over to the nearby highway crossing. Usually military police would patrol these places to catch the soldiers fleeing from the front. They would organize these men into new army units and send them back to the front. Not here. A military policeman was stopping every vehicle that tried to pass him and placed soldiers waiting for transportation into the vehicles. Walter joined the group, but the MP man made Walter wait until all the other men were gone. Waiting was not to Walter's liking. Walter argued with the MP man, but to no avail. He had to wait and it was for his good, as he later saw. A van came by and the MP man placed Walter in the van. Walter couldn't have asked for a better transportation. It was not an ordinary van, it was specially fabricated to transport and sort mail. It was comfortable and it had plenty of food, which was very important to Walter. Walter asked the men if he could help them sort the mail. They taught Walter how to do the work and he was in business. It was just too bad these people didn't go all the way to the city of Minsk. Walter's intention was to go into a hospital in the large town of Minsk. Walter transferred a couple of times to different vehicles until he reached the outskirts of Minsk.

The truck he was in carried many soldiers and was stopped by the military police. Everyone but Walter had to leave the truck. He was kept there because he was the only one who had an injury tag that stated that he was wounded in war action and needed hospital treatment. The truck with only Walter on it was permitted to go on. Before the truck arrived at the hospital the truck driver stopped, leaned out of the window and asked Walter:

"Should I take you to the hospital or to the railroad station?"

This was an unexpected question. It made Walter think for a minute and he said,

"To the railroad station, please."

Walter was very tired. In one of the many barracks close to the railroad station Walter found an upper bed and fell asleep. He doesn't know how long he had slept when he thought he heard a voice shouting, "Everyone who wants to go to Germany, get to the railroad station and into the waiting train." That woke him up. Seeing the commotion he knew it was real and not a dream. Walter had nothing to carry but himself so he was quickly at the railroad station and in the train. He found a window seat, but because he was so tired, chose to climb into the suitcase net above the seats and instantly fell asleep.

He didn't hear the railroad car fill nor did he hear any one complaining about him sleeping in the suitcase net. Neither was he aware how everyone was checked by the MP, which surely happened. Apparently no one could wake him up or they saw Walter's injury tag and left him alone. Walter woke up while the train was moving and was on its way to the town of Vilnius in Lithuania, a long distance away from Minsk. The train continued on to Warsaw, the Polish capitol.

Right at the railroad station in Warsaw the clerks took information from the soldiers. They asked Walter who he was and what kind of injury he had. The clerk didn't even look at him while he wrote down the information. Walter was then transferred to a hospital. His wounds were healed by now, with the fragments still inside. There in the hospital Walter met a comrade who had been on the staff of the convalescent home in Mogilev. What he told Walter was not good news. He was one of the few who escaped when their train was attacked by Russian tanks. The soldiers who were healthy enough tried to escape, but were mowed down by the Russian tanks. Walter was thankful to the Lord that he didn't get a ride with the train. The good Lord kept his hands over him. "All that happens to us will work for our good, if we love God."

Walter was not kept in a hospital in Warsaw for long. A hospital train was prepared and he was transported into Germany. What a blessing. Some days after Walter left (1st of August,1944) there was an uprising of the Polish Underground Army. They surprised the Germans and conquered a large part of Warsaw. This Polish rule was short lived. Their hate was strong against all Germans. They killed all Germans in their conquered area. It was reported that the wounded German soldiers in the hospital were thrown out of the windows and nurses were butchered. The Russian army did or didn't want to arrive in time to help their Polish comrades.

Walter's train arrived in Kirchhain, near Cottbus on the 7th of July 1944. After their arrival they were examined. Walter's wounds had healed and there was no risk of infection anymore. There was no room in the hospital for Walter so he was placed in a gymnasium filled with beds and patients. There was no privacy but there was a bed to sleep. Here Walter took the time to write to his parents. The high command had notified his parents that Walter was missing in action. To give his parents a little more hope of him being alive they mentioned it might be possible that he was a Russian prisoner of war. Knowing Walter was stationed in Russia and hearing in the news what was going on, they had feared for his well being. Their thoughts and prayers were always with him. How happy they were when they received Walter's letter. The scripture reading, "When we love God, all things will be for our best;" had been on Walter's mind all the way through his travel back to Germany. Now that he was in his country, he remembered his dream when far away in Russia. Walter marveled how everything he saw in the dream had come about. He was very grateful to the Lord for hearing his prayer.

His parents informed him where the nearest branch of the church was. Walter applied for weekend furlough to the city of Cottbus, but his application was rejected. There was not much to do in the city of Kirchhain. The city was known for the many tanneries which were located there and made the city smell. For these reasons Walter didn't explore the surroundings of the city. What Walter wanted was to visit the LDS branch in the city of Cottbus, so Walter made plans to go without a permit. He found out there were no men from the military police stationed in Kirchhain at the railroad station. However leaving the gymnasium was a problem because the doors were locked and the windows were high off the floor. He decided to try it anyway.

Early on Sunday morning while everybody was deeply asleep, Walter moved a table under the window, placed a smaller table on top of it and a chair on the top of both tables. Now he could reach and climb through the window. Without any difficulties he reached the railroad station and bought a ticket to and from Cottbus. Having never been in Cottbus he inquired of the passengers how the station was built, and after admitting he had no permit for furlough, how he could leave the station without being caught by the MPs. One lady spoke up and told him there were no MP men on platform 4, only an inspector of the railroad. That was the place he would go.

After he arrived in Cottbus he went to platform 4. Many people left the station through this gate. Because there was no MP men at the exit, no member of the armed forces were permitted using this exit. Walter knew this, but he also thought, it would be difficult for the controller to leave his place and get after Walter. Only one man could pass by the inspector in his booth since it had a long waiting line. When it was Walter's turn to give the inspector his ticket, the inspector told him he couldn't leave the station through this gate, he had to use the main gate. Walter told him he couldn't leave the station through the main gate because he had no furlough permit and the MP men would be standing there and would arrest him.

When the inspector heard this, he told Walter in no uncertain terms he had to go through the main gate. Walter smiled at him, placed his ticket on the counter and walked through the gate.

The meeting house of the church was close to the railroad station in the Lausitzerstrasse. Walter was early and took the opportunity to talk to the members who also arrived early. The district president, Brother Fritz Lehnig, was there and Walter talked to him. He asked Walter among other things if he was married. When Walter told him, "No," Brother Lehnig invited him to take a good look at the girls of this branch. Walter really didn't need this invitation. After Sunday School Walter talked to Brother Lehnig's daughter, Jenny, and to the branch members. The meeting was uplifting, just what Walter needed, and he felt right at home among the members of the church.

Walter was invited to lunch by the Guido Schroeder family. As they walked along the main street, Walter was saluted and had to salute as it was an order in the armed services. Walter used the army salute while the others all used the Hitler salute. Walter felt there was something wrong, and he asked Brother Schroeder to take a less populated street. What Walter didn't know was that on the day before, 20thof July 1944, a Colonel Stauffenberg had planted a bomb in Hitler's headquarters. But Hitler had not been killed. The war was lost at this time and many lives would have been spared if the assassination had been successful. To show their solidarity with Hitler, the army high command had ordered all members of the armed forces to use the Hitler salute. All connected with this attempted assassination were looked for and later killed.

Walter enjoyed the meal and the large Schroeder family very much. In the evening the sacrament meeting was held. After sacrament meeting, Walter went home with the Eckert family and their daughter Gerda, took him to the railroad station. Not knowing the layout of the railroad station and not able to use the gate, Walter decided to jump the fence which ran along both sides of the road leading to the main entrance. The fence was not the problem; the problem was the many soldiers who stood along the fence kissing their girls and saying goodbye. Walter said goodbye to Gerda and excused himself to one of the soldiers who had his girl in his arms. Walter explained his problem to the soldier, and went over the fence. As expected, the soldier was a little irritated, but he and his girl made room for Walter. Walter took the train back and soon, without any problems, he was back in the gymnasium (the gymnasium was open till midnight) and in bed.

In the morning, one of the male nurses came by and told Walter he was reported missing yesterday and he would have to appear before the captain. Walter cleaned and polished his uniform extremely well to make a good impression. At the appointed hour Walter reported to the captain. He was an elderly gentleman, nice and friendly. He had Walter stand in attention and read the report to Walter. Walter was looked for and missing and not found at 9am, also at noon and also at 3pm in the afternoon. The captain asked Walter what he had to say about the report. Walter told him the report was correct, that he was not in the building at the given times. The captain looked surprised. Walter thought he didn't expect him to acknowledge the accuracy of the report, he probably expected a denial. The next question Walter couldn't answer,

"Where have you been?"

Walter knew there was a minor penalty for leaving the hospital without permission, but there was a major penalty (like three days imprisonment) for leaving the city. Walter said,

> "I can't tell you. If I tell you, you'll have to punish me. But I would like to say I didn't do anything wrong. I just took a weekend leave without permission."

Walter couldn't tell how the captain felt or what went through his mind. He took Walter's passbook (Soldbuch) and turned the pages over for a little while and then he asked Walter,

"What does the entry mean under religion?"

Every time someone looked through Walter's Soldbuch, he or she would ask Walter about the meaning of the entry "Jes. Ch." Walter liked that it gave him an opportunity to explain his faith. Walter told the captain that the name of the church was The Church of Jesus Christ of Latter Day Saints, better known as "Mormons."

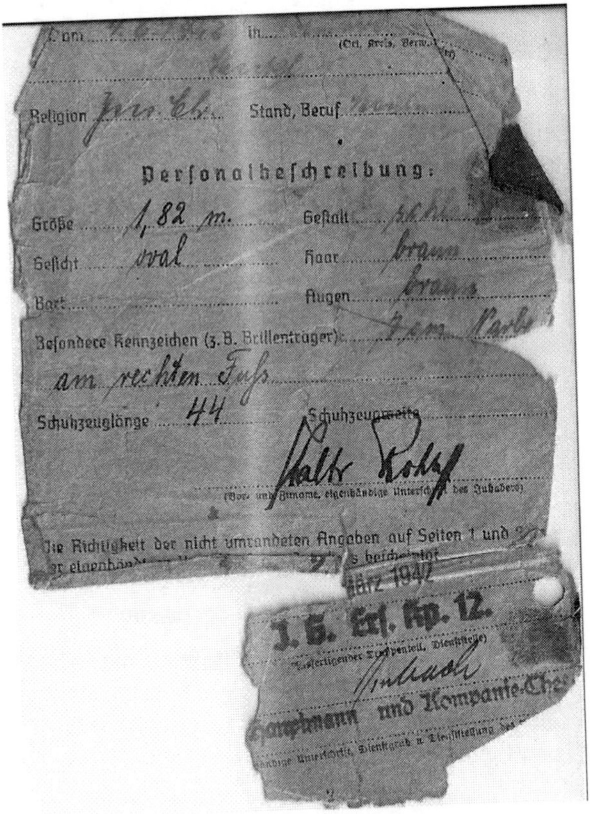

Religion Jes. Ch. Stand, Beruf

Personalbeschreibung:

Größe 1,82 m. Gestalt

Gesicht oval Haar braun

Bart Augen braun

Besondere Kennzeichen (z.B. Brillenträger):

am rechten Fuß

Schuhzeuglänge 44 Schuhzeugweite

Walter Rohloff

(Vor- und Zuname, eigenhändige Unterschrift des Inhabers)

Die Richtigkeit der nicht umrandeten Angaben auf Seiten 1 und 2

März 1942

J. E. Ers. Kp. 12.

(ausfertigender Truppenteil, Dienststelle)

Hauptmann und Kompanie-Chef

Pages from Walter's Soldbuch (Passport)
Look at religion

"Do you believe in the teachings of that church?" he asked Walter.

"Yes," Walter said.

“I wonder what your minister would be saying about your past actions.”

Well, Walter couldn’t tell him that he had just seen his minister, so Walter told him he had not broken any laws, only some rules and he didn’t think his minister objected. Then he asked Walter questions about the teachings of the church, which Walter gladly answered. After a friendly discussion he released him with the words that he wouldn’t punish him at this time, but if he did it again, he would have to punish him.

Walter promised he would not have to do that. The next time Walter got a weekend furlough permit. After being in the hospital for three weeks, on the 8th of August, the doctor looked at Walter’s wounds and decided he would take the fragment out of his forehead. It was done with local anesthesia. Walter could hear the doctor working on the bones but didn’t feel anything. Walter was decorated with the Purple Heart in black (Verwundeten Abzeichen. Black is the lowest class decoration for being wounded once or twice. Silver and Gold were the higher classes.)

After returning to his garrison city Schwerin Walter received a week of recovery furlough. He took furlough to Schneidemuehl and visited with the Birth family first. Father Birth was very busy. He had many out of town orders to replace glass in bombarded buildings. Irmgard, who was trained in the glass business, was in charge of their business in Schneidemuehl. Ruth went to work at the city office and Edith helped her mother in the grocery store. After work Edith and her mother would glue the collected food stamps on paper sheets in preparation to deliver those stamps to the government. Father Birth came by and something must have irritated him about Edith’s work because he scolded her. While Edith reacted with a smile, it hurt Walter, but he kept quiet. In the morning Edith and Walter studied the scriptures together. Walter enjoyed being with this large family. On his way back to his garrison in Schwerin, he stopped for a few days at his parents’ place. On the 16th of August, he reported back for duty.

As Walter looked back on what had happened to him in the

last two months, he was most grateful to the Lord for hearing and answering his prayers. Walter had absolutely no interest in injuring or killing anyone. He felt he had truly been protected under the Lord's wings.

While in Schwerin, Walter heard a new 12th division was being formed near the town of Dirschau in West-Prussia. There was no enthusiasm by the men to go back to war. No good news was available, German armies were retreating in all places. The Allies were close to Germany's western border. In Italy the Italian army had joined the Allied forces, and the Russian army was close to the Polish capitol of Warsaw.

Of course Goebbels, Hitler's propaganda minister, was singing a different tune. He claimed Germany had a miracle weapon. If he meant the new jet airplanes, they were good. Walter had seen them flying In Schneidemuehl. But where would Germany get the fuel? There was hardly any gas in Germany and the gas in Romania had been lost to the Russians. Maybe he meant the V-1? But the rocket was not effective. The V-2, the father of the rockets which are used today, could have made a difference but it was far too late to have an impact on the war.

Yes, Germany had worked on the development of the atom bomb, but for the betterment of the world, the Allied air force destroyed the laboratories and factories. Even for the men in the trenches, better weapons were developed, but they were a bone of contention between the army which couldn't get any and the SS which got what they wanted. Old men were drafted into the service and youth, 17 and 18 years old, formed a new SS unit: The Hitler youth division. Walter's father was drafted into the "Volkssturm," when he was 53 years old. Women had taken the place of men in the factories. During the day they worked hard and at night many didn't get the rest they needed because of the air raids. Some factories in Germany had been placed underground, in caves. The food and clothes were purchased with stamps, but the allotment got smaller and smaller. How long could the war still go on?

12

CANNON-FODDER

With others, Walter was transferred from Schwerin to Dirschau in West-Prussia, near Danzig. Here the 12th division, which had been destroyed in the battle of Mogilew, Russia, was restored and all the units were given their old traditional names; however, the officers and men were all new. The equipment and 98k rifles were old and used. A panje wagon, a wagon that was used much by the Russian farmers and pulled by one horse, would carry their equipment. They had one machine gun, but no artillery or other heavy guns. All this was loaded on a train and they went westward near the city of Aachen, on Germany's west border. The men received no training and had no practice or preparation whatsoever. They hardly knew each other. Walter didn't know where the men had come from or if they could even use a rifle. The train moved slowly westward, crossing Germany for several days before they reached their destination during the night.

Unloading went fast and without any problems. The company then walked a few hours and stopped. They were told to build a ring to protect them from every side (einigeln). This order made Walter suspicious. He went over to his company leader and asked him why they had to protect themselves on all sides. The company leader told Walter there were no German soldiers around here and their assignment was to show resistance. Walter didn't feel good hearing this. It made him realize they were to be used as cannon fodder, or as the officer said, to show resistance. They would have to attack without any support. They had no mortar guns, no artillery, no tanks—just a gun for every man and one machine gun.

In the morning the company moved close to Schevenhuette, a town lying on the top of a hill. They could clearly see the Allied tanks and to reach the town they had to cross an open field. They organized themselves at the foot of the hill in the forest. They attacked. The Allies were smart enough to let them come halfway up the hill before they started shooting. Their rifles were no match against the enemy tanks and they retreated as fast as possible back into the forest. They had lost about half of their men. They regrouped and at noon they attacked another nearby village. This time the Allies smothered their attack as soon as it started. As they regrouped, they saw they had lost two-thirds of their men. Still, they attacked one more village in the evening. Returning from the skirmishes there were now in the company only 11 men out of the 80 men who started the day. In the turmoil of the day Walter had forgotten it was the 17thof September, his mother's birthday. What a day! Walter was tired, but otherwise unharmed.

New men came the next day and took the place of the men who had been lost. Still, they had no heavy equipment, only a few more machine guns. That evening they moved into a new position. They had barely dug their foxholes when, to their surprise, they were attacked. Heavy artillery and mortar fire fell on their defense line. When the attack by the infantry came they resisted, but not for long. Walter saw only tanks, no men. They had to retreat. They tried to move back into their former position between the salvos, but one grenade exploded nearby while Walter was moving. A splinter hit his helmet which he hadn't tied to his head and the helmet flew off. Walter was not wounded, just momentarily blinded by the light of the explosion. The soldiers didn't retreat much, but instead built a new defense line.

Those still alive in the original group were taken back behind the front and given time to recuperate. The company was brought back to its former strength. Even though they were not under enemy artillery and mortar fire, there were plenty of Allied airplanes in the air waiting to make their lives miserable. Walter didn't see any German airplanes.

During the recuperation period they got acquainted with the new men. Than under cover of darkness they had to move back to the front line. In the daylight Walter saw it was a terrible place, right at the foot of a hill in some underbrush. The enemy was on top of the hill. Walter didn't see any men in the pine forest, but he saw tanks. It was a beautiful day. The sun smiled down on them and the front was calm. Walter felt comfortable in his foxhole. He moved some of the dirt in front of him to the side and smoothed the dirt out. Next he spread out a clean white handkerchief and placed his food on the top. Standing in the foxhole, he wanted to eat in style. Someone on the Allied side apparently didn't like that. The shot he fired hit the dirt, ruining his food and dining. Had he placed his shot a little higher it would have killed Walter. What a fool he was!

After a few days two German panther tanks were moving into position to help in the attack. The tanks were camouflaged with bushes. Did they think the enemy was blind? As the attack started Walter saw the two mighty "bushes" moving forward. He heard two cannon shots and that was the end of their help. Walter had no time to think about this because he had plenty of problems himself. To his right was a little village and from an upper window of a two story building, a machine gun kept Walter and his men under fire. The gun made it hard for them to progress. Walter didn't hear nor did he see his man's machine gun firing.

Walter did not like to get out of his foxhole since he made a great target for the enemy's machine gunner, but in all the shooting and noise from the gun and artillery fire, Walter took the risk of getting hit and crawled on his belly over to the machine gunner and asked him why he was not shooting. He signaled that he couldn't shoot, he had no ammunition. Walter crawled over to the guy who was supposed to bring munitions to the gunner. He was sitting in his hole, his head down to the floor and his behind up. Walter was mad and hit his behind. As he looked up Walter saw his pale, fearful, jittery face. Walter felt sorry for him, but this didn't help their situation. Walter told him to get munitions to the gunner. He did that, but it didn't help. During the enemy's counter attack Walter's group lost their position and had to fall back about a hundred feet.

On another day, the new company leader wanted to make a counter attack to regain the territory they had lost so he organized a group of men. He told Walter to go with him, but Walter declined. Walter told him he couldn't see risking men's lives with an unprepared attack, putting guns against tanks. He told Walter he would put him before a military court for disobedience. Walter told him that would be fine with him. To do this the officer would have to return from his undertaking and Walter doubted that would happen. Walter never saw him or the men he had taken again. Their new defense line was not to Walter's liking either. They tried to dig foxholes but the ground water started almost under the turf even though they were on a hill. They did what they could to protect hemselves.

During the night the battalion commander came and wanted to make a counter attack to get back their old position. The officers talked it over with Walter. (Walter was a non commissioned officer, all higher in rank were killed), who voiced his opposition, but decorations on your shoulder counted more than common sense. The commander decided to infiltrate the enemy line where their front line made a 90 degree angle. It was a clear, beautiful night and the moon was bright. They could see well, but so could the enemy. They walked one behind another, Walter right behind the commander. They came to an open space. The commander wanted to cross the open space, but Walter wanted to go along in the dark under the trees. Walter explained his concern. The commander didn't listen and walked right on. Walter kept standing in the dark while the men passed him by. Too bad, Walter was right. They almost reached the middle of the clearing when hell broke loose. Walter saw rifle fire coming from many sides. In the moonlight the men made an easy target. A man walking in front of Walter was hit in the leg. Walter gave him first aid and told him to raise his hands and he would be treated well. Walter made it back to his former position, gathered the men and built a new defense. He didn't see the commander again, but he heard later that the commander was decorated for this fiasco with the knight's cross.

Speaking of decorations, Walter was decorated with the Iron Cross second class on the 17th of October 1944. The presenting officer asked Walter,

"Now, are you proud to receive this decoration?"

"I would have enjoyed two weeks furlough more."

He surely didn't like Walter's answer.

They were still sleeping in their holes when the morning broke. Looking around Walter couldn't see much of interest. The little village behind them seemed to be quiet and sleepy. Then Walter thought he heard the noise of tank movement down in the valley where the enemy had their positions. It didn't take long until he saw tanks coming up the hill toward them. What now? They had no weapons to defend themselves against tanks. Walter was afraid and didn't know what to do. The shallow holes didn't offer much protection either. There was no help in sight and the tanks came closer and closer.

Walter prayed. He always prayed, but this time it was different. It was a cry to the Lord for help. Walter surely didn't want to be crushed under the weight of a tank. Helpless, he sat in his crater as the tanks came closer. When the tanks were about fifty yards away from the men, Walter heard noises behind him. To his relief, he saw a Volkswagen-swim wagon (a vehicle that can go on the road or in the water and stay on top of the water) pulling a 7mm gun behind, it crossed the field and came to a stop behind them. The gun turned and in almost no time the crew had the gun firing. The first shot was a hit and a tank started burning. They hit another tank and the rest of the tanks rolled back and went out of sight. What a relief! Walter's thanks went up to his Heavenly Father for sparing his life and the lives of his comrades.

The loss of men and material in these battles had been very heavy. Walter and his unit were pulled out of the battle line and another unit took control of their position. Those in Walter's unit who were left were placed in a school in the town of Eschweiler in the Eifel Mountains. Once again unprepared and untrained men took the place of the men they had lost. In the few days or hours they had, they tried to train and prepare these men. Walter had target practice with his platoon. Every one of them had five shots. The whole platoon of about 30 men had a total of five hits. When Walter checked the results later, it was depressing. The whole platoon of about 30 men had a total of five hits, three hits were Walter's and the other two hits were done by his runner. It was bad for the unit, but even worse for the individual men. Unprepared and unqualified, they had to go to war.

The people who used to live in Eschweiler, as in all the towns near the battle zone, had to leave their homes for their own protection. Those who didn't leave on their own were forced by the military police to leave. Walter was glad he had nothing to do with that. One morning Walter walked through the village and saw an elderly woman walking around her home, lovingly touching the walls and crying. Maybe she felt she wouldn't see her home again. How many people in this ugly war had the same experience?

Apparently not everyone had left the village. Some were hiding and were not detected. Walter's platoon was in the middle of receiving instructions in the school building when artillery bombardment started. Walter thought they were the only people in town. While they went into the basement for their protection, he heard someone crying loudly. He hurried over to that house and found an elderly woman buried in the rubble of that house. As the men were getting her out of the rubble, she called for her husband. The soldiers started looking for him. They found him dead, buried in the rubble. Walter asked her why she hadn't left. "It is our home," she said. Probably everything they owned was invested in this house. Walter thought of his loved ones at home and hoped nothing like that would happen to them. After the bombardment they looked for other civilians, but didn't find any.

They were quickly transferred to the nearby city of Stolberg and they built their defenses in the suburb of that town. However, they didn't see any enemy in the short time they were there. The enemy probably knew where they were because they bombarded with artillery fire. During the day the men hid in the basements of the buildings and had only a few men watching outside. But by night everyone had to be outside in foxholes, by orders two in every hole. (Stolberg was in Germany and Walter assumed many soldiers left alone as guards, left for home.)In the darkness an attack was harder to recognize and with all men out, easier to oppose. Moving from one place to the other was terribly noisy. The nails on the bottom of the boots let everyone know where they were walking on the pavement. Every hour Walter checked every guard position.

They had found in one of the basement storage areas the ingredients to make "Schmalzkuchen" (a pancake dropped and fried in lard—similar to a doughnut). While Walter cooked he had one man at a time come in and eat since the cake tasted much better fresh. When no one else came in, Walter went out to see what was going on. The last man who had been with him had returned to his foxhole, but didn't find his partner there. He found the gun of the man standing in the hole but not the man. All men looked for the missing man, but without success. Of course the enemy could have captured him, but they would have taken the gun also. They were in German territory and it could be he went over to the enemy or he tried to reach his home. The hard thing for Walter was he had to report a man missing without a shot being fired. That could cost him his head or at least land Walter in prison. They had a young lieutenant as their company leader and he didn't get along well with Walter. Walter was pretty stubborn and did things more or less his way. The company constantly had new officers, replacing the ones who were wounded or killed in action. When Walter reported a man was missing, his commander told him he would report the incident, and he would be court-martialed. The same night Walter got a new commander, a first lieutenant. He told Walter not to worry about this, nothing would happen. He was wrong.

They were taken out of the fighting line and again new men replaced the ones they had lost. Usually they got a few days' rest, but not this time. A few of the men from different units (including

Walter) didn't get any rest. A new battalion was built and the men thought they would have to go right back to the front. The men walking with Walter to the meeting place were very disappointed and complained, but Walter had learned a long time ago that everything would be for his betterment. He tried to influence the others to wait and see but they kept on complaining. After they were organized they heard they would not go back to the front, but they would be deployed to protect a dam holding a reservoir of water in the beautiful Eifel Mountains. Their commander asked Walter to be his adjutant.

They had a few restful days, but one morning Walter heard a lot of noise in the air. Outside, looking at the sky, he saw through the clouds many large airplanes circling over the dam. It was clear to Walter the airplanes had come to bomb the dam. Walter went inside the house, reported to the commander, and told him he was going to the bomb shelter. His commander laughed and called him "Angsthase" (chicken hearted). Walter told him he could do whatever he wanted, and Walter left for the shelter. The shelter was a closed tunnel into the mountain.

As Walter opened the heavy door a bomb exploded nearby. A man flew past Walter from the pressure of the bomb. Walter looked closer at the man who was in such a hurry to get into the shelter. To his surprise, he looked right into the face of his commander.

"Boy," Walter said, "Are you in a hurry?"

He almost misjudged the situation. After the airplanes had unloaded their bombs and the air was clear they returned to their house. It was flat and their car was buried in the rubble. The roof of the car was bent, but otherwise it looked okay. Most of the bombs had missed the dam and it was still holding back the water. The fruit cellar of the house was still in good condition and so was the food. It looked mighty tempting and Walter would have loved to take the food out. There was only one problem—lying on the only stairway into the cellar was a three foot long bomb. Walter felt that trying to pass by the bomb to get the fruit was not worth risking his life.

The few men left from the 89th infantry regiment had to

return to their unit. They removed the rubble from the car, straightened out some bends and to their delight the motor still functioned. They crawled into the car and sat under the badly bent roof. The position they were sitting in was extremely uncomfortable, but they felt it was better than walking all the way. Arriving back with their unit, they found the men they left behind had been reorganized and sent to the front. By now they had lost many men and needed reinforcement. Walter and the men were ordered to immediately march toward the front. They were given new men to join them, but didn't even have time to get acquainted with these men.

They took a position in the basement of a house where the front made a 90 degree bend. The basement was fine, but everything above was rubble. Nothing was standing upright, but it gave them protection. On one side the enemy was about 150 yards away from them and on the other about 800. No enemy could be seen at the distant position, but the nearer enemy position had four tanks. There were two homes in between Walter's men and the enemy. Every so often the enemy changed crews and four new tanks moved into position and the former tanks moved out of sight. If the enemy had known they had no armament for fighting tanks, they could have moved straight forward and Walter and his platoon couldn't have resisted them. Walter felt helpless and hoped the war would end soon.

Walter and his crew always looked for something to enrich their menu. Walter thought he heard chickens in the empty house next to the enemy. Walter asked his messenger if he was willing to go with him to find out if he had heard correctly. At daylight they notified the men on guard duty of their intention. The two went quickly through the one house and moved into the house only 20 yards away from the enemy position. Yes, there were chickens, Walter collected the eggs and put them into his pockets. His runner killed some chickens while Walter stood guard for their protection. They worked fast and on their way back they made it through the other house, but while they were crossing the open area to their house and trenches, they were detected. Because of rifle fire they had to crawl back into their trenches. When in the trench, Walter tried to pull out the eggs; he had scrambled eggs with shells in his pockets. It was not easy to clean the pockets, but they enjoyed the chicken.

Many mornings fog covered the no-man's land. Once in a while there was an opening in the fog and they could see the tanks. One time, Walter couldn't believe his eyes; he saw a large calf grazing about half way between their trench and the enemy. He alerted some men and Walter shot the calf. With the help of the men and the fog they carried the calf in. They cleaned the calf out and hung it up in the basement. After a couple of days hanging, every man enjoyed the meat. In the nights before, the visiting commander had seen the calf hanging and had brought a knife to help himself to the meat. It was a great, well-liked addition to their daily ration. Of course they couldn't do any cooking during the day; they had to do that at night, when the enemy couldn't see the smoke.

Walter didn't know what got into his men. They had received a gewehr granate geraet (a grenade thrower on top of a rifle) which was supposed to be able to cut through the wall of a tank. Walter heard some noise outside and when Walter checked the men, they had against his orders, tried out to shoot at the tanks with this thrower. They missed, but woke up the tank crew, who started shooting back. Then, the enemy artillery entered the battle and the German artillery started to hit the enemy trenches. The men were glad they had a lot of rubble on top of their basement that protected the men from shell splinter. In the end, when the shooting calmed down, Walter anticipated an attack. He wanted the men to take their positions in the trench, but of the 30 men, only his messenger went out with Walter. The others, with their eyes full of fear didn't go out, not even the squad leaders. The squad leaders told Walter, he couldn't tell them anything, because they had the same rank (corporal) as Walter, but Walter was the platoon leader. Walter could have reported the men to the commander, but he knew the harsh punishment for not following orders and didn't report the men. Everyone was glad that no attack came and no one was hurt. The allies kept the heads down of the Germans mainly through mortar and artillery bombardments, guided from men in helicopters who could see deep into the land behind the German front line. It was almost laughable because around noon and at six o'clock in the evening there was never any bombardment and the German soldiers could move freely. Walter thought it must be their mealtime at those hours. They seemed to have unlimited munitions while the Germans had to report every shot they fired.

13

DO AS YOU HAVE BEEN TOLD

One morning Walter was asked by his commander to go and make quarters for their unit with the civilians in the nearby villages. The outfit needed to be restored to what their leaders called "full strength" in men and equipment. Full strength existed only on paper. In reality, it was perhaps half the original size. He gave Walter all information he needed and Walter left.

Walking along the highway Walter went through a little forest. There he saw many gasoline barrels and many SS men running around. Two SS men walked toward him on the road. Walter could see they were officers and he had to salute them. There was not much love lost between the SS and the army. Walter didn't know what came over him, but as he passed them he looked the other way without saluting. After they had passed him one of the officers turned and confronted Walter asking why he had not saluted the SS officers?

Walter replied, "How should I know who is an officer in the SS?" The markings of their ranks were different from the ones in the army. The not-so-friendly discussion ended when the SS officer reached for his pistol. Walter was faster than him, but it didn't help. In no time Walter was surrounded by SS men and had to go with them to their commander's office. For the first time in his life Walter saw a nicely furnished motor home which the commander used as his office. To Walter's surprise, the commander was one of the same men he hadn't saluted on the highway. He had no nice words to say to Walter and gave Walter a long lecture. His words left Walter cold.

Then he called on two men to take Walter to the nearby military police. He knew he was in trouble. Walter had heard about this court of justice and what their judgment was. On his walk Walter had seen men hanging from the trees. This officer wanted to see Walter hanging or placed in a company of convicts, but again, the good Lord kept his hands over Walter.

Without his weapons and walking between the two men, they reached the highway. Walter saw in the near distance an army unit marching toward them. As they approached the men, they saw it was a worn out, poorly dressed unit with old equipment and horses pulling flatbed wagons. What a difference between the SS unit which had the finest equipment and this poorly furnished unit.

Someone called Walter's name. As Walter turned toward the caller he saw it was his company leader, a lieutenant. He asked Walter what he was doing here and why he was not doing his assignment. Walter told him he had not saluted an SS officer and the two men were taking him to a nearby military police station. The lieutenant told Walter to take his place with his platoon and he would give the two men as many SS men as they wanted who would not salute him. He and his unit had to pass the SS camp on their way. Walter hurried to his platoon knowing very well his company leader's word wouldn't mean anything should he meet the SS commander.

Because Walter didn't show up in time at the meeting place for the men to make quarters for their unit, others made quarters for his unit. After a few days, Walter got a completely new platoon. Walter didn't know anyone. Most of the men came from the defunct air force. No one had experience at the front and only a few had ever used a rifle. Under a clear sky in daylight the battalion marched single file on the road to the front, hiding under the trees because the sky was full of enemy airplanes. Once in a while a German jet flew over them and at that time they didn't see any enemy airplanes. They had to walk through a village and when they reached the middle of the small village their forward progress stopped. Walter sent his runner to the commander to ask if they could march forward and leave the village, but his request was denied.

Walter looked for shelter for him and his men. Some of the

men wanted to go into the basement of the house near where they were standing. Walter didn't like the house, but he didn't know why. Instead he had the men break open the house across the street. Most of the men went into different homes. Walter told the men to stay in contact with him. All this commotion must have gotten the attention of the airplanes above them. They had barely entered the basement of the house when Walter heard the first dive bomber attack. The first bomb fell, and hit the house they had just been standing by. A big crater and plenty of rubble was all that was left.

The next airplane came and the bomb fell in front of the home they occupied. A big crater was in the street and the home became a pile of rubble but the basement where they were hiding was still intact. Walter heard the third plane diving and that bomb fell to the side of the house and opened a side of the basement wall. What was left of the house now collapsed and some of the men were wounded by splinters. Walter was standing with his back toward the diving airplanes leaning against the wall. Walter thought, "This is the end," as he heard the fourth plane coming. At that moment Walter saw his life rolling before his eyes like a movie. He saw the things he had done wrong and those he could have done better. Walter prayed and cried unto the Lord,

> "Lord, give me a little more time. I promise I will serve Thee until the end of my days."

No bomb fell. Only machine gun fire hit the ground. After they felt it was safe, the men left the basement. Now Walter could see why the fourth plane had not bombed the building; the building was a pile of rubble. They had a hard time getting out from under all the debris. No one would have believed there was still someone alive under all that junk.

They were placed in what Walter thought a reserve position. In case the enemy broke through the front line, they were there to stop their forward progress. They found well prepared trenches and in some places built-in 8.8mm cannons with the barrel just a little above the ground. Walter placed the men so that they could defend this position. The trenches went right in front of a barn and Walter decided he would make his quarters there. Walter's runner, the medic, and Walter would take turns keeping in contact with the unit.

It was morning when Walter woke up and his two men were still sleeping. Walter went right into the trench to see how his platoon was doing. He didn't find any one. He and the other two must have been so deeply asleep that they didn't hear the commotion when his platoon left. Later Walter learned that orders were given from man to man to move to a new position. Because they were outside the trench no one contacted them. Walter looked around and he found three older men by the 8.8 cannon. Their emplacement was a little in front but connected with the main trench. Walter asked the men if they knew how to use the cannon. "No," they answered.

The enemy artillery had started shelling the line and behind them by now. While Walter talked with the men, he had not given any attention to what was going on in front of them. As he looked now he could see the enemy coming towards them in line and with tanks. Walter and his men had a good position; if they had someone who knew how to use the cannon they could have defended their position, even though it was a much larger group of men who came against them. The 8.8 cannons were very effective against tanks. Because no one knew how to use the cannon and there was no munitions, Walter and his men didn't even discuss how to defend their position. They were just interested in getting out of this situation without anyone getting wounded or killed. For them the war was lost and it was time to make an end. The enemy had sealed off their way back to their baggage unit with artillery salvos. The noise from the exploding artillery shells made communication impossible. They decided to try to make it back anyhow. Walter was the only one who had any combat experience and heard the grenades coming. Walter told the men to watch him. If he would lie down, they should too. When he started running they should do likewise. It worked. They all made it back to their baggage unit. Of the men who had gone with them into the trenches, they never saw or heard from again.

New men came and new units where formed. New men meant mainly teenagers and old men. Some men were Walter's father's age. (Walter didn't know that his father had already been drafted into the service.) While the teens moved easily and carelessly, the old men had a hard time moving. Many were hard of hearing—a big handicap on the front. While this reinforcement was going on, Walter was given comfortable quarters to recuperate in. It was just for a short time, but it was nice. Shortly before they returned to the trenches Walter was given a platoon. In his company, but not in his platoon, he made friends with two fine gentlemen. One was a high school teacher from Berlin. He was higher in rank than Walter and also a platoon leader. The other was an opera singer from the Schwerin opera, blessed with a beautiful voice. He had the same rank as Walter, but had no leadership responsibilities. Without any difficulties they arrived at their assigned front position, relieving the waiting men. While they were in this position they had no major attacks, just the usual exchanges of gunfire, skirmishes, and casualties. After they were there for a few weeks Walter was told by his company leader they would be taken out and transferred to another position. He told Walter to go and meet others at the regiment's bunker and make quarters for their unit. When Walter arrived at regiment headquarters the other men had already left. The commander told Walter he could follow the others, and make quarters for his unite or return to his unit and the others would make the quarters for them.

When Walter left the bunker he was ready to return to his unit, but he heard his inner voice saying very clearly, "Tue wie dir gesagt wurde." (Do as you have been told.) This voice was as clear as if someone had spoken to him. From this location Walter could look over to the front and into the no man's land. All was quiet. He hesitated, but then he followed his inner voice and went on to make quarters for his unit. Walter found a comfortable place for himself and went to bed. They expected their units to arrive the next day.

When Walter slept it was always a deep sleep and hard to wake him up. But this night, Walter woke up because of noise from outside and from the vibration of the house. He went outside and looked toward the front. It was lighted as far as Walter could see. Countless enemy airplanes were flying over the front and dropping bombs. The artillery from both sides was in full action. It was a complete surprise major attack. Later Walter learned another unit had just moved into his unit's position and his unit had just left the trenches when the attack came. For Walter's unit the attack couldn't be at a worse time. The changing of a unit always brought confusion and being attacked while doing so left men unprotected. Now Walter knew why the good Lord had warned him to find quarters and he was so glad he had listened to the Lord's counsel. Walter thanked the Lord from the depths of his heart. This was the second time the Lord had protected him from a major attack: The battle in the Hurtgen Forest was in full swing. For over a week Walter waited for orders to return to his unit. He reported daily to his superior but was told to stay where he was, which he didn't mind.

Walter was well rested by the time the call came to return to his unit. When he reached the battle zone he was concerned about how to make it through the artillery bombardment. Allied helicopters were circling over and near the German line and directing the enemy artillery. Walter walked along the road and used the trees as cover. As he came close to where the artillery was placing their salvos, he saw a medic waving his Red Cross flag, walking in the open field in full sight of everyone. The artillery stopped firing and let him pass.

Walter walked along with the medic, but under the trees near the road and out of sight of the enemy. He made it safely to his regiment headquarters. In the dark, he went on to the front to his unit. Walter's unit was now called a battalion even though it didn't have enough men for a company. All the men who used to belong to this battalion were grouped together in this much smaller unit. A battalion had about four times the man power as they had now.

His former company leader was now the commander of this unit and made Walter his adjutant. Their assignment was to prevent the enemy from crossing over the elevated railway. At the place where the road crossed the railway was a signal house. They used the little house as their headquarters and prepared it also to hold wounded soldiers. All of their men were lying in front of the railway crossing in a half circle prepared to defend the crossing. They had only rifles, not even a machine gun and no anti-tank guns. It was a terrible, helpless feeling, knowing they could be attacked by tanks and had nothing to defend themselves with. The thought of being crushed under the wheels of a tank made Walter shiver. He had no time to dwell on these thoughts; he had to prepare himself and the men for the next day. Walter got acquainted with their defensive line and made adjustments as needed.

In the evening Walter's friend, the opera singer, came and visited with him. He looked pale, sick and nervous. In his eyes Walter saw uneasiness and fear. He told Walter he was sick and he said he was going to die the next day. Physically, Walter couldn't see anything wrong with him. All the men were nervous and irritable and they all knew they had a hectic day ahead. No one was sure if he would get out of this alive. Walter tried to give him peace of mind and asked the medic to check him over. The medic checked him over but could not find anything wrong with him. Walter tried in vain to improve his thinking. He had no choice but to send his friend back to his foxhole.

Nervousness and irritability had Walter's schoolteacher friend and others thinking that they should give all the men alcohol which they had plenty of, but Walter was very much against it. He had seen in the past how carless men became under the influence of alcohol.

Walter felt a clear head was very important for their correct behavior and reaction to the coming attacks. Walter was alone in speaking for abstinence. The commander was neutral in this argument and ordered Walter to give the men alcohol. Walter had no choice and did as he was ordered.

As the sun came up, Walter checked every man in his emplacement. Only a few had a foxhole for their protection, the schoolteacher didn't. Walter reminded him that he had a family at home and needed to protect himself. He told Walter it was none of his business and that he knew what he was doing. He reminded Walter that he was higher in rank than Walter. He was drunk. When he was sober, he was very reasonable and careful. It was the last time Walter saw him.

After Walter returned from his inspection, the artillery

bombardment got stronger. It was an indication that the attack would be coming soon. As Walter looked around he saw four men carrying a wounded man in a tarp. Walking over Walter saw it was the opera singer. A grenade had cut off his legs, one leg above and the other below the knee. A medic had covered the wounds. In extreme pain he looked at Walter and Walter thought his eyes said, “Didn’t I tell you?”

Walter with his runner and medic

It pained Walter’s heart. There was nothing Walter could do for him except send him to a hospital. With only rifles they were not able to fight against heavy guns and tanks. They were fodder for the guns of Hitler's enemies. Every man was needed here, but Walter sent the four soldiers with their wounded man back to the hospital and the four were very willing to go. Walter learned later that the opera singer was killed by gun fire from a tank.

While all this was going on, they were continually under artillery fire. It was a constant down to the ground for protection then up. They had already filled the little signal building with wounded men to protect the men from grenade splitter. As if they didn't have enough problems already, their own artillery started shelling them. Maybe the German artillery thought they had given up defending the crossing. While Walter could hear the enemy's grenade coming, he couldn't hear the grenades from their own artillery. Because of that, their own grenades were more deadly than the others. Walter saw Allied tanks breaking through the undergrowth and saw the little building getting hit, the rubble burying the wounded soldiers. In this confusion Walter saw one other of his soldiers lying close to the path he had to cross to get out of the way of the tanks. Walter saw no enemy soldiers, just tanks. Only a short distance from them stood a tank which shot everyone who crossed the path. The soldier and Walter jumped up almost at the same time, Walter a little later than the other man. Walter saw the man crossing with him was hit, but Walter kept running zigzag. He could see twigs hit, but the machine gun fire missed him.

After Walter was out of sight of the tank, he came into artillery fire. Walter was now so nervous he would lay down even when the shots were not close. By the time he reached their baggage unit, Walter looked so exhausted the men didn't even recognize him. The battalion strength was 200 men in the beginning of this battle, but only eleven men made it through. Walter heard from his office staff that preparations were made to decorate the men with the Iron Cross 1st Class and other decorations. But Walter told the office staff he would much rather have furlough. He didn't know that the high command had forbidden any furlough permits except for bravery. The commander called Walter into his office and presented him with a furlough permit and wished him well. Walter didn't know if anyone else got furlough. The sad thing was when Walter returned he didn't find any one he knew with his unit.

Walter left on his furlough, went to the next railroad station and he was on his way home. He kept wondering what would have happened if he hadn't listened to his inner voice when it said, "Do as you have been told." Yes, the Lord could have helped him get through all of these scrapes, but answering his daily prayer to not kill anyone would have been hard to keep. From the very first day that Walter was a soldier, his prayers contained the request that he didn't want to kill and up to that day he had not had to shoot at a single person, well he didn't see any men, just tanks.

Walter's furlough went from the 12thof December 1944 to the 3rdof January 1945. As usual Walter stayed not only with his parents in Neubrandenburg, but also went to the Birth family in Schneidemuehl. Neither place had been touched by the war. There were not many who believed the war could be won. There was talk on the radio and in the press about the "Wunderwaffe" (miracle weapon). No one knew what was meant by Wunderwaffe. No one saw the production of new weapons. The Allies bombed away anything that could give them problems. Most people had given up and looked forward to the day when the war would be over. Only the Nazi party members hoped that Goebbels' propaganda was true.

Walter's father, 54 years old, now belonged to the Volkssturm, an old folk's army unit who carried rifles and were drilled on how to use them. Youngsters in their teens, were trained to use anti-aircraft guns. Young ladies served as nurses' helpers or in the communication service. The women had to take the place of men in the factories. Walter's mother had to go to work at the same place his father worked. His mother hated every day she had to go.

A portion of the factory where Walter used to work had a section which was fenced in. Women who were brought against their will from Russia and Poland and incarcerated in a nearby concentration camp worked there. All women wore an "R" or "P" on their clothing. Walter saw that the female guards didn't treat these women nicely. Walter didn't know if the factory still made parts for airplanes. He didn't think so, because since Romania was occupied by

Russian troops, Germany had very little gasoline for the airplanes. Many factories were moved underground or into caves.

At Schneidemuehl they prepared to defend the town. Christel Birth, who was sixteen years old, had to dig trenches with many other young people. Father Birth, fifty two years old, was in the Volkssturm and when Walter was there, he was in the army barracks in training. Every effort was made by the Nazis to defend the town. The Russian armies had reached the Vistula River and would soon enter German territory.

Walter celebrated Christmas with the Birth family. None of them had any Idea how fast everything would change; soon they would all leave Schneidemuehl and never return.

Not only were the Allies surprised, but Walter was surprised too, when he heard the news on the radio the morning of 16th of December 1944 that Germany had launched an attack on the western front. He was sure his unit was involved in the action because the attack was in the vicinity where his unit was stationed. Knowing the poor equipment his unit had, he assumed the other army units also had poor armament, except for the SS. There was no way, after the first days, that the attack would be successful. It was cloudy and the Allied Air Force couldn't take part in the battle, but as the clouds lifted the Allies stopped the German attack.

Walter can't describe how grateful he was to be home and not involved in this foolish undertaking. He would have been in the middle of the attack and he would have to use his gun to kill. The Lord knew of his deep desire not to kill and had sent Walter on furlough. It surely didn't make Walter eager to return to his unit. He hoped that after Hitler lost this battle he would end the war. How wrong he was. It seemed as if Hitler was out to destroy Germany; if he couldn't live any more, Germany shouldn't either.

When the day of Walter's departure to return to duty came, his father and mother accompanied him to the railroad station in Neubrandenburg. They all felt that terrible things were ahead of them. The German defense had further deteriorated in the East. In the West the Allies had started successful counter attacks.

Father told Walter, "Apparently Hitler wants to sacrifice us all. Should we make it through these difficult days alive, but end up in different places, let us contact the LDS mission home to notify them where we are. Stay close to the Lord." Then he quoted from the scriptures, "For everyone who loves the Lord, everything will be to his best." Walter had the feeling they all would see hard times, but would come through alive.

One of Walter's farewells at the railroad station

Walter was in no hurry to reach his army unit. In Berlin he had to wait for train connections to the west. He went to the military police, explained his delay and had the MP man mark his furlough permit with a date stamp (official acknowledgement). At every railroad station where Walter had a delay he had a stamp placed on his furlough permit. Walter needed these stamps to explain his delay for his late arrival from furlough. Over time, his permit was full of stamps. At night Walter slept in public bunkers or at the railroad stations. Walter was questioned only once on the way about why he was behind schedule? Walter was blunt and asked the MP man if he couldn't read. By this time there was no open place on Walter's furlough permit. It had stamps all over. Walter was sitting on a bench and the MP man was standing behind him. Walter couldn't see what he was doing, but he heard; he was turning Walter's paper over and over. The MP man was shaking his head, but he returned Walter's permit to him. These official stamps were not placed in any kind of order. Making the way Walter had traveled and the time it took was difficult to identify. The notation—Furlough for Bravery—on the upper corner of his permit probably helped too. The MP man wouldn't want to step on the toes of someone who had clout and they might be punished with a transfer to the front. Who wanted to die when they all felt the war would soon be over?

walking – walking – walking Walter carries his and also the gun of another comrade

14

ABOUT 10 HOURS TO LIVE

On the 11th of January 1945, Walter arrived at his unit. He was notified he had had an appointment with a military court on the 7th of January, but that date had passed. Walter remembered some months back when he had an officer who was transferred from their unit, had told him he would bring him before a military court. A soldier from Walter's unit disappeared while being on guard duty. His new officer then told Walter, not to worry, that nothing would happen. He was wrong, but the Almighty who kept his hands over Walter, helped Walter by delaying his arrival. With all the confusion the unit had, Walter didn't hear anything more about that. Walter didn't think anyone was expecting him or anyone knew that he had furlough because all who knew him were either dead, wounded, or POW.

As Walter arrived at his unit, at least his unit by name, he didn't know anyone. The men were clearing the rooms they had occupied because the SS had kicked them out and the army officers were powerless to stop it. They slept in the hallways of that building. Walter asked himself why he should risk his life so that these men could continue to kick him around and he didn't think he was alone with this thinking. What was especially disgusting to Walter was the way the SS handled the civilian population in Luxembourg. They took the last food away from those people. When Walter was standing alone in the middle of a group of SS men and tried to intervene, one of the men pointed his gun at him and said to him, "Just say one more word and I will blow your head off." Standing alone, Walter felt helpless and kept his mouth shut. Walter knew the man could do what he said and no one would care or report. In the state of confusion no one would do anything about it.

The unit Walter belonged to now was comprised of stray soldiers. A gun was placed into their hands and up to the front they went. No one asked if he could handle a gun or if he had any training. The men were from all age groups, from teens to men in their forties. When the men reached the front, many ran over to the enemy and became POWs. The troops were instructed to shoot anyone who ran, but Walter never saw anyone following that order. They all thought the war couldn't go on and would soon be over, but they were very wrong.

One day in March, 1945, Walter was placed with others behind an elevated highway. An attack was expected and they were told to stop the attack. Walter asked the commanding officer about digging foxholes to protect themselves from grenade splatter. He told Walter it was not needed. Not needed? That man either didn't know warfare or didn't care for the men's lives. Lying unprotected at the side of an elevated highway during an attack, was almost suicide because there was no protection against shell splinters. Walter covered his rank markings by wearing an unmarked coat. He intended to get away from that place before an attack came. In the darkness of the night Walter did what he had planned and was on his way walking five miles to Bad Godesberg on the Rhine River. Walter was once quartered in the home of a Mrs. Sommer and Walter returned to her home. For a couple of days he helped her to get food and then on the 8th of March, he went down to the river. He had no intention of becoming a prisoner of war and wanted to find a way to cross the river. Walter was sure the war would be over when the Allies reached the Rhine River. Looking back Walter doesn't know how he could think that. Walter knew Hitler had mentioned in his book, "Mein Kampf", and in many talks, that the high command in 1918, should not have ended the First World War, but should have kept fighting. Walter should have known Hitler would go on fighting until Germany was destroyed.

As Walter walked through the streets people told him to give up fighting and go home. Of course he had given up fighting, but going home was another thing. The good woman where he was staying had given him a large sandwich and on the way to the river Walter ate it. Not much was going on at or on the river. A motorboat was on the river side with the motor running. Walter went and talked to the driver. The driver told Walter the General wanted to go to the other side and would use the boat. He also told Walter he could come along. They talked and waited, but about noon they received the news that the general would not go to the other side of the river, but would stay and become a prisoner of war.

Just the thought of becoming a prisoner of war made Walter uneasy. In his mind, he couldn't see himself raising his hands and being kicked around. Walter decided to cross the river on his own. He didn't know how close the Allies were, but he didn't think there could be a good reason that the General didn't want to go to the other side of the river because the Allies were already at other places near the river. Walter could hear shooting, but didn't think it was close enough to give him problems. This was foolish thinking. He should have known the generals knew the situation much better than he did.

Surprisingly, he found a paddle boat on the riverside with a paddle. What a blessing; he could steer the boat with his feet. Walter had never used a paddle boat, but he had seen people using one. He didn't think either of the danger or of the strong current. He took his belt off and put it with his gun into the boat.

When he sat in the boat he felt comfortable. As Walter pushed away from the riverbank the boat seemed easy to handle and steering with his feet worked. Walter was on his way to cross the river. He was about 40 feet away from the riverbank when a bullet passed him. Now he realized the danger he was in. Should a bullet hit him or the boat below the waterline it would mean death for him. In his winter clothing and with the big boots he had on his feet and the cold water he wouldn't have a chance to survive. He had not taken into consideration that the boat would be drifting down the river and Allied forces could have reached some places on the river. For only a second Walter considered turning back, but he dismissed that thought right away.

It would be too difficult. He made himself as small as possible and said a short prayer, “Lord, help me.”

Walter paddled for his life. It surely was not a good feeling to be the target for some soldiers practicing. The passing bullets sounded terrible in his ears. He didn’t think of the danger, he only thought to get away. The current was strong and the boat drifted. Walter tried hard to get to the other side. The effort reaching the other side took all his attention. Luckily no bullets hit him or the boat. As he came close to the opposite side of the river, the shooting stopped. But a few feet from the river side the cord to his steering broke and the boat went back out against the current. What now? He didn’t know what to do. He had no control over the boat. Then he felt the underside of the boat hit something. At that moment he remembered that in school he had learned that dams were placed in the river to reduce the flow and keep the groundwater level up. He got out of the boat and felt the top of the dam only a few inches under the water.

He grasped his gun and turned toward the riverside when a single gunshot hit him. He fell forward on to his knees and his knees hit the dam. Had he fallen to the side he would have drowned in the deep water. Once again the good Lord held his hands over him, allowing him to get to a side of the river where he could get on land. In many places along the river the bank couldn’t be reached from the water level but here it could. He pushed himself up from the dam, crawled up the banks and through the underbrush. Walter was out of breath and felt weak. German soldiers helped him along. He started to feel pain. With the help of the soldiers they opened his clothing and they saw blood coming out of his abdomen. The shot had gone all the way through his body. “You need help right away,” said one of the soldiers. They gave him two first aid packs. Walter held one pack in front of his body at the exit of the bullet and the other pack at his back at the entrance of the bullet. He realized he needed to be on the operating table in less than ten hours or it would be the end of his life. Two of the men helped him to a highway that before the war had been very busy.

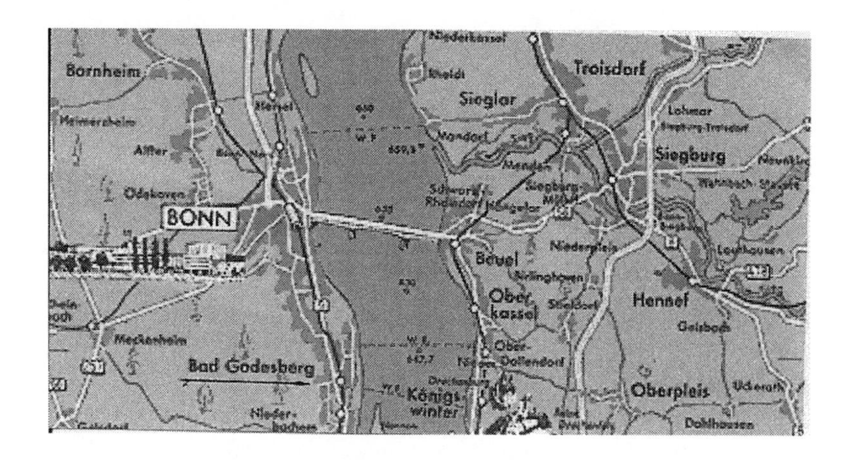

The Rhine River by Bad Godesberg

Now it was very unusual to see a vehicle of any kind on the highway because the Allies controlled the traffic on the road from the other side of the river or from the air. It was really a miracle for a vehicle to appear just at that time. Miraculously they waited just a few minutes before they heard the sound of a motor. Not a motor bike, but a volkswagen-swim-wagon came by and was stopped by Walter's many helpers who blocked the road. It was a dispatch rider who had orders to bring a written message to the commander of a Rhine bridge. A messenger usually used a motor bike, not a car. Walter had never seen an army messenger in a car, but here he was. The men asked him to take Walter to a first aid station, but he declined. Walter's helpers wouldn't take "no" for an answer and they were pretty forceful until he agreed to take Walter

He was a wild driver. He was worried about the delay this detour caused him in getting his message to the commander. The road was rough and Walter's wounds hurt him terribly, but Walter didn't say a word. He knew too well his time on earth was limited or over if they didn't reach a hospital fast. After about 30 minutes the dispatch rider found an aid station. He pulled Walter out of the car and dropped him on the lawn. He didn't report to anyone Walter's arrival; he just dropped him and left.

Many wounded soldiers were lying there. It was a beautiful

day, the sun was shining and it was warm, but Walter was lying in pain. He couldn't see a nurse. Walter didn't like to move his body to look for one because every movement hurt. No one there knew Walter needed help, but the Lord knew. After a while a man came around and brought drinking water to the men on the lawn. When he reached Walter, Walter told the man he didn't think he should take a drink. The man asked, "Why". Walter told him of his condition. He asked Walter what time he was wounded and Walter told him. The man said, "You need help right away," and he left. It took a long time before he returned; at least it felt that way to Walter. The man returned with a doctor, who examined Walter and dressed his wounds. When he was finished they placed Walter in an ambulance with three other men and they traveled farther into the mountains.

It was dark when they reached a convent by Siegburg. The ambulance driver got out, entered the building, and came back with a doctor. The doctor took one look and said to the driver, "We can't take these men." He turned and started back. The driver caught up with him, stopped him and they started arguing. Walter had a window view and could hear and see what was going on. Both were standing under the light so Walter could see the men well. The doctor argued that they were already under artillery bombardment and had no electricity. He started a couple of times toward the building, but the driver told him he would stay there arguing until morning. The driver told him he had to take at least one man who needed help right away. Walter was grateful that the driver stood up for him. He knew all too well that there was not much time left to help him. Walter prayed to the Lord that if it was His will that he should live, that he would make it possible for him to get help. After a while the argument ended. Men came and got Walter out of the ambulance and took him into the building. The lights in the room came from stable lanterns. Nuns took care of Walter. While one of the nuns was shaving Walter in preparation for an operation, she asked him many questions. One, of course, was to what church he belonged. Walter told her, "The Church of Jesus Christ of Latter-day Saints." She had never heard of that church but she knew who the Mormons were. Walter thought she was asking because they wanted to bury him with the correct service.

Verwundete
und andere chirurgisch zu Behandelnde.

Nichttransportfähig: zwei rote Streifen
Transportfähig: ein roter Streifen
Marschfähig: kein roter Streifen

Name: Roteloff
Dienstgrad: Uffz. / I. Wiede
Truppenteil: 10697 D

Verletzung: 9.00 Uhr
Bauchschuß

Knochenverletzung?
Sonstiges Leiden:

Erhielt an starkwirkenden Arzneien
innerlich? | Gabe | Zeit
Eingespritzt?
Wundstarrkrampfserum?

Verwundete
und andere chirurgisch zu Behandelnde

Trägt elastische Binde (Schlauch)?
Seit Uhr vorm./nachm.
Wo?

Sonstige Hilfeleistung:
Verb.-Päckchen
(Zeit)

Nächste Wundversorgung usw. erforderlich:
(Art, Zeit)

Besonders zu achten auf:

Wird (sitzend, liegend) entsendet nach:
zu Verbandsplatz / sammel / Lazarett Nr.

Name des Arztes:
Dienstgrad:
Truppenteil: Oberarzt

Ausgestellt am Uhr vorm./nach
8. III. 45

Accompanying note Walter carried when he was wounded.
This tack was given to Walter on the first aid station and he had to carry it till he arrived in the hospital

Laying there, waiting for the operation, knowing very well that this could be his last hour on earth. Walter knew he didn't want to be buried, he wanted to live. He thanked the Lord for His help. He felt peaceful. A nurse came and gave him an injection and Walter fell asleep.

When he woke up, he was lying in a large room filled with wounded soldiers. The pain Walter felt was almost unbearable. He was groaning and crying. A medic came to calm Walter down. The medic spoke kindly to Walter and asked him about his parents, if he had a girlfriend and many more things. While doing that he gently stroke with his hand over Walter's hair. It felt comforting. Abruptly the medic left Walter and so did all the others they went into the basement. An air attack was in progress. Walter was alone in the large room. He could hear the airplanes and could hear the explosion of the bombs. Thankfully no bomb hit the building, but some hits were close by. The glass in the windows broke and the dust moved into the room. The building was shaking but Walter was apathetic lying there. His pain was so overpowering that nothing else concerned him. When the air attack was over the medic came back and gave him morphine.

When Walter woke up he was in a basement room with no windows. Seven other badly wounded men were also in the room. Across from Walter a Catholic priest was giving one man the last rites. Later he did the same to the other man who was lying next to the first. The next morning both men were dead and were carried out. Walter found out the man next to him had also been shot through the abdomen. When Walter was later examined he was told it was a miracle that he was still alive. The shot had opened his large intestines. His abdominal cavity must have been a mess, the cavity full of digested food. The cleaning out must have taken a long time. Filling his stomach with that huge sandwich while walking to the river was the worst thing he could have done before receiving this injury.

Every day Walter felt a little bit better. He was always hungry because his diet was milk. He loved to drink milk, but only milk was not enough. The only way the men could tell the time of day was by the activities taking place with the nurses and medics. One day around noon, the nurse came and placed a nice meal on their bedside tables. It smelled so good and Walter was tempted to eat. He hadn't eaten a good meal for some time. The fellow next to Walter ate right away, but Walter was careful.

"Did the doctor give permission for me to eat this?" Walter asked her. She didn't know. "Would you please go and ask the doctor?" She went to ask and left the meal on the bedside table. What a temptation! Walter was so hungry and the meal smelled so good. The waiting was very difficult, but Walter didn't eat. The nurse came back in what seemed to him a long time and without saying a word took the meal. She gave him milk with a little semolina. When Walter woke up in the morning the man next to him was dead.

On the 16thof March, Walter was transferred from Siegburg to Lindlar. He began feeling much better while in Lindlar. His meals were improved to milk soups, but he was still not permitted to eat solid food. Walter disagreed with the doctor about the food he got. Walter thought he was healthy enough to eat solid food but the doctor didn't think so. Up to this point Walter had followed his orders but this nearly changed.

On the first evening in Lindlar all the men received "Schmaltz" (lard) sandwiches. Since his childhood Walter had liked Schmaltz sandwiches. If the Schmaltz sandwich was well spiced and with apples there was nothing better. The men enjoyed the sandwiches and Walter had his improved milk soup. That night Walter's problem was that the men had not eaten all of the sandwiches and they left the leftovers on the table. All night long Walter smelled the sandwiches and for a long time he lay in bed debating whether to take one or not. One couldn't do any harm he rationalized, but he fell asleep and didn't eat a sandwich.

They left Lindlar on the 23rdof March, and were transported by truck to Luedenscheid-Barklo. Walter had recuperated well; only the exit wound was open and hadn't healed completely. He could walk around and got permission to leave the hospital and go to town. In a movie theater, Walter sat next to a girl named Ruth and talked to her. In the following days they met often. She introduced Walter to the Catholic faith. Her families were strong Catholic Church members and didn't like her to meet with him. Walter and Ruth talked a lot about religion and Walter attended the Catholic Church service with her. After the service Walter would compare what they had seen and heard with the Bible. They talked about baptism, of being buried in water and coming up a new person and also living a life in harmony with Christ (Rom 4:3-5). Apparently she discussed what they talked about with her Aunt Alla who raised her and with whom she was living. Ruth told Walter her aunt didn't like him, but her aunt was very friendly to Walter when he met her.

On the 13thof April, the American Army entered the city and

Walter became a prisoner of war. Ruth was a brave woman and would go to the fence and talk with Walter. The fence was patrolled by the US Army. The last time Walter saw her was when US Army soldiers took her away from the fence. Walter was transferred on the 5th of May, 1945, to a hospital in Altena.

In the Altena hospital German doctors looked at his wounds and told him he was all right. Walter didn't think so, because it was two months ago that he was wounded and the wound was still open and there was pus. Walter thought the doctors wanted to get rid of him so they would have more to eat. The food ration was the same regardless how many prisoners were in the hospital so less men in the hospital meant more food for the doctors. Walter was transferred on the 8th of May, to a prisoner of war gathering place in an aluminum factory.

This was the day Germany made peace with the world. It was great to see the street lights shining again. During the day the POWs were kept in a fenced-off area. Being in Germany people would walk by and some would stand and watch what was going on. Some even talked to the American soldiers and told them to let the men go home because the war was over. At night the soldiers didn't like the prisoners to be outside of the factory in the fenced-off area because the fence was not high enough to keep a prisoner from climbing over it in the dark. Walter's guess was the guards didn't want to stay up all night and watch the POWs. All of the prisoners were forced to stay inside the factory. It was full of POWs, some even standing on top of aluminum parts. Walter didn't want to spend a miserable night in the factory, so he dragged his feet. Walter resisted going into the factory. He was pushed and hit and he fell to the ground. The soldiers grabbed his arms and legs and dragged him over to the factory door. He squirmed and wriggled to get loose. At the door they couldn't swing him in; the factory was too full. Disappointed, they left him and all the others who wanted to be outside. The prisoners slept well outdoors.

The POWs were transported to different places until they landed in an old camp for Russian prisoners of war in Paderborn. It was so full of bedbugs that no one could sleep inside. The camp was in terrible condition. Walter was hungry and found some beans. He and some others cooked the beans, but the beans were still hard as stones. By now Germany was divided into four zones of occupation: the Russian, the American, the British and the French zones. Paderborn was in the British zone and British soldiers had taken over the camp. Walter was undernourished. At first Walter couldn't eat because of his shot through his abdomen and then they didn't get much to eat in the hospital or camp. He was always looking for something to eat. He looked for work, but couldn't find any. Walter had been standing with other men at the gate, but none of the English men wanted him. One day a comrade, Henry Rehfeldt, who was lying in the same room with Walter, told him the English needed a man in the kitchen. If Walter would go with him in the morning he might get the job. Walter had absolutely no experience in cooking, but he went.

When the British cook saw Walter he said Walter couldn't do the job because he was not strong enough, but he didn't send him back to the camp. He told Walter he would feed him and build him up. It was the 3rd of June 1945, a day before Walter's twenty third birthday. The cook allowed Walter to eat as much as he wanted. He ate so many pancakes the cook thought he would get diarrhea, but he didn't. Slowly Walter got his strength back. He worked from early in the morning until late in the evening. When he had his work done he helped the baker, the man who got Walter the job. He was from the same state in Germany as Walter and they got along well. Walter worked as a helper and not as a baker or cook. He didn't mind what kind of work it was as long it kept him busy and he had enough to eat.

For a time, the two watched much uneaten food being thrown away. They didn't like to see that waste because there was so much hunger in the camp. They asked for permission to take the uneaten food into the camp. They received permission. After work in the evening they took the food to their room and shared it with quit a few men. This was a great addition to the daily ration for the prisoners.

15

BURIED ALIVE

The POWs had "interfaith" meetings and Walter attended their meetings. The sermons were presented by Lutheran ministers and they always had uplifting messages. Then the English started to send the POWs home and the Lutheran ministers were some of the first. The group was looking for new leaders and Walter offered his services, but when they heard he was a Mormon, they looked for someone else. Walter was disappointed, but it didn't come unexpected. He knew the negative attitude Germans had against the Mormons. A Catholic priest took over and there was no gospel message, only the mass was read.

At work Walter had met a man, Klaus Wiggess, who was of the Lutheran faith. Walter and Klaus had long discussions. Klaus had two friends who belonged to different faiths and the four decided to hold their own meetings. They got a tent from somewhere and put it up and used it for meeting and sleeping purposes. Many men in the camp now worked in cleaning the town Paderborn and one of them found a Bible and gave it to Walter. Walter made good use of it and studied whenever he had time. The four men of different faiths, a Lutheran, a Baptist, a free Christian and a Mormon, studied the book of Hebrews in the New Testament together. They prayed together, they sang beautiful gospel hymns and folk songs together and they had great discussions together. It was too bad Walter only had the book Doctrine and Covenants with him, which they didn't recognize as the word of God. But it helped Walter to explain that God spoke not only at sundry times as mentioned in the book of Hebrews, but also in modern times. Walter told them he believed in a God who spoke yesterday, today and In the future. Walter's intensive study of the scriptures during the war years served him well and he learned to explain his faith to others. His good friends, their families living in West Germany were sent home.

There was great excitement in the camp as one group after another went home. But the groups were all from West Germany. Then rumors had it that the POWs from the eastern part of Germany would be going home too in August 1945. The rumors were right. In August the POWs were loaded in railroad cattle cars, some were open and some were closed in. But as they saw the place names on the railroad stations the train went through, they realized they were traveling in the wrong direction and their prisoner of war time was not over. Realizing this Walter regretted that he had not taken the offer of one of his comrades to change his address and go to his home with him on the Rhine River. It would have been possible then but now it was too late. Walter thought about escape, but the doors were well locked from the outside. They traveled through Germany, then through Holland, and they stopped in Belgium.

Walter had been unaware of the great hatred the people in Belgium held for the Germans. Often when they passed under a bridge, people on top of the bridge would throw rocks at the POWs in the open cars. Thankfully, the car Walter was in was covered and he was protected. Their car had a little opening in the upper corner that permitted some of them to look at a station and to the other platforms. At one railroad station Walter took a look through the opening. There were many people standing on the other platform and looking over at their train. They were drawing their hand back and forth across their throats and yelling, "Dirty Germans." There were not just a few people; everyone on the packed platform made this sign and yelled. Walter was shocked to see the hate those people had for Germans. It was sobering as they realized this was the nation they had to stay and work in.

Walter didn't know where in Belgium they were unloaded by the British. Long before the British soldiers reached their car, they heard the racket and the shouting of the British soldiers. Every one of the POWs was nervous and fearful and moved closer to the door. Not knowing the language, what they heard sounded terrible. Without thinking Walter made up his mind to use the confusion to try to escape. He hid in the corner of the car on the open door side and tried to be as small as he possibly could.

As the British opened the door, the German prisoners hurried through the door, pushing each other. Walter almost succeeded in his attempt to stay in the car. Before the guard closed the door he looked to one side and then to the other. He saw Walter standing in the corner. All hell broke loose. Walter walked over to the door and saw the British soldiers lined up on both sides holding their swagger control sticks ready to hit Walter. Walter moved his rucksack over his head and told himself, "Don't fall," as he jumped from the railcar. He went almost to his knees under the blows of the soldiers, but he didn't fall. He made it through the line. If he had fallen they might have killed him. When Walter checked his rucksack later everything was broken, but the rucksack had protected him. He himself made it through this ordeal almost untouched. The next day the British commander excused his soldiers, saying:

> "The men didn't know what they were doing. They were drunk."

The camp was large. It was divided into 12 divisions. Walter's division was made up of about 2, 000 men. The food was poor and there was very little of it. There was a little fence that kept them away from the camp leadership and kitchen. Some prisoners, who had nothing else to do, stood by the fence and counted the incoming food. They would tell the other prisoners after a meal how much more they should be getting. To pass time the prisoners exchanged recipes of what they would cook when they got home. They used the restroom very little, but they had plenty of toilet paper. As Walter was studying the Bible he used the toilet paper to make his notes. They all slept in tents. Walter had brought a large pillow from the hospital, but he slept on newspaper and gave his pillow to an old man who didn't live far from his hometown and who had family. Walter felt sorry for him. He told Walter when they were released and home Walter should come by his home and he would have food for Walter.

It is hard to believe, but drinking water was hard to come by. Apparently their camp was on the end of the 12 camps' water pipe. Around midnight the water would reach their camp. Someone would watch and wake everybody up with the word "water." All the men would try to get there first, because often those who arrived last found no water. Walter's older companion who didn't sleep as well as Walter, would take care that they had enough water. Cleanliness suffered. Sometimes they had an elevated water hose with many holes on the lower side as a shower. They always had their afternoon tea. Some of the men also dried the leaves of the tee and smoked the stinky stuff.

Classes were organized on a variety of subjects. Teachers were lucky because they got a little more food. Walter took some classes which he thought would help him later at home and work. However, most of the classes were not well attended. Walter had made an hourly plan of what he would do each day. Having no clock, he would follow it as well as he possibly could. Some time before Walter had started working on a Doctrine & Covenants concordance. Now he spent plenty of time on it. He had an old D&C, which had been translated into German by Elder Eyring. Walter never finished the concordance. When he got home he found out the Eyring translation was out of circulation. While it brought no monetary profit, it increased his knowledge considerably. Walter also set aside a lot of time for Bible study. He studied it intensively and made sketches and charts from it. He wanted to prepare himself for serving a mission.

To improve his physical condition, Walter played soccer and walked around the camp. In the evening he liked to play a round of chess. By far most of the men sat around and talked, doing nothing constructive, but some talented men were busy making toys or other things from tin cans. The guards were their best customers. They loved what these handy men did and showed their toys to others.

These handy men got some food or cigarettes for their fine works of art.

There wasn't a blade of grass in the camp. Some men would even go into the six foot space in between the high, guarded fence and the parallel line fence that was about one foot high searching for grass. Entering this area was strictly prohibited, but there was no grass in there. Some men went behind the line which was around the kitchen. Hunger hurts. There was a hole in the ground where the old, empty tin cans were placed. Walter saw men jumping into the hole to find what was left in the cans. The worst thing for Walter to see was men standing under the guard tower and waiting for the guard to drop his cigarette butts. When he did, the men would fight for it.

Walter thought their rations were intentionally kept small. At noon they got a watery soup, sometimes with something in it. Walter thought it was the weeds out of a garden. Sometimes it was called bean soup. When they got bean soup Walter waited to be one of the last men, but he still didn't find many beans in the soup. In the evening they got a two pound loaf of bread for all the 10 to 12 men in their tent. The poor fellow who divided the loaf of bread had all eyes carefully watching what he did. There were always some who complained. In December, 1945, Walter too started to think his piece of bread was smaller than the others. He didn't like that. Hunger had made him weak. When they had to dig out a hole under their tent to have more protection from the weather, it was hard for him to move the dirt.

In the camp the prisoners had no radio or newspaper to keep them up-to-date. Rumors informed them what was going on outside of their camp. Walter knew his hometown was in the Russian zone. The Allies had released all POWs living in their zone but kept all POWs whose hometown was in the Russian zone. The Russian hadn't released any POWs. Walter thought it over and came to the conclusion their stay in Belgium would be for some years. He could stay in the camp and stay hungry or he could go to work and have something decent to eat. Work was, after all, why the Allies brought them to Belgium and kept them hungry to make the POWs willing to work in the coal mines. It was the only work option for the POWs.

Walter had never worked in a mine, but he thought it wouldn't be too bad. Rumors had it that the mines were old, in poor condition and could be kept open only because the prisoners were cheap laborers. Walter ignored the rumors as untrue and applied for work.

The men who wanted to work were transported to another camp. They were received by a German camp commander. He stood on top of a barrel and called them German pigs. A murmur went through the POWs, but the Belgian bayonets kept away anyone who came too close to this German accomplice. The prisoners were treated well and received good food. Good food was very much needed to replenish their hungry bodies and to be able to do the hard work ahead.

They didn't stay long in this camp before they were transferred to a work camp close to the city of Marchienne-au-Pont. At the railroad station the Belgian soldiers formed lines on both sides of their path. The prisoners had to run through this path to a gathering place. The path made a 90 degree turn after about 100 yards and then they had to run another 10 yards to reach the gathering place. The soldiers stood fairly close together apparently afraid someone might escape. It was at night but there were plenty of electric lights all over the station.

Walter's rail car was to the middle of the train so many POWs had already made the run. Walter's turn came to run through the espalier. When he came to the corner, the soldier standing there lifted his rifle and hit him in the side above his hip with the butt of his gun. It hurt Walter and without thinking, he instinctively jumped at the Belgian soldier. The soldier fell backwards and when Walter saw someone coming he turned and ran as fast as he could to the gathering place. The POWs built a wall around him, but a Belgian officer came right in front of him. He waved his pistol under Walter's nose and said something in French, which Walter didn't understand. Walter shrugged his shoulders and shook his head as though he didn't know what was going on. Walter was thick-skinned and apathetic and looked the officer straight into his eyes. The officer left him alone.

They arrived at a well organized mining camp. All POWs living here worked in the mine except for: the German camp leadership, the doctor, the clergy and the men working in the kitchen. There were already many POWs working in the camp when Walter arrived. A high fence enclosed the camp. By the entrance was a little monument that listed the names of the men who had already died in the mines. The men who just arrived were given a couple of days to get to know the camp. They slept in barracks. The men were divided into shifts and Walter had to work the night shift. The food was good and plentiful. They had a canteen where they could buy items with the little money they earned for their work. After they started working, they got soap to clean their black bodies. They were given plenty of soap and they exchanged some of the soap with the civilian workers for bread.

They had a Lutheran minister in camp. He held religious meetings every Sunday. He also held interesting meetings on weekdays, but not about religion. He presented interesting topics and Walter attended some of the meetings. Walter also attended the church services on Sundays in addition to Walter's own scripture study and his continued work on the concordance of the book "Doctrine and Covenants." Here Walter was able to get the right kind of paper to make large size maps for his Bible study. After the Red Cross delegation visited the camp, they got books for a library. While most men were interested in novels, Walter continued his interest in classical literature. He was part of a group of men studying Goethe's "Faust." It was just a small group, but they had great conversations.

The highlight was, of course, receiving mail from home for the first time. The good news for Walter was his mother and his sister were still alive. But that was the only good news. His mother had to give up her apartment to a group of Russian soldiers for a time. When she vacated her home her main concern had been the family genealogical records Walter's father had gathered over the years. (The records needed to be made temple ready. It was the first task Walter did when he came home, and he sent the records to the mission home when they were completed.)

As time went by Walter's mother got her apartment back. She was alone, but soon took in a refugee couple and gave them a room. This couple came from Czechoslovakia and had tried to find a place to live. They couple lived with her until the end of her life and Mrs. Helene Werner was a great blessing to Walter's mother and his father after his return. Russians had taken Walter's father to a concentration camp and Walter's mother hadn't heard from him. She wrote that the mission president had contacted her and wanted to know when Walter would be coming home. He wanted Walter to serve a mission. Yes, Walter would like to go, but for the time being it was just a dream.

In their barracks they had two bunk beds standing together. Walter had an upper bunk. After the lights were turned off it was really dark in the barracks. Walter would kneel in his bed and thank the Lord for all He had done for him. One night his neighbor in the other bunk bed talked to him after his prayer. Apparently he had watched Walter very closely. He told Walter he used to pray too. Walter asked him why he didn't do it now. He told Walter, "I'm not at the front anymore and in no danger. There is no need for prayer. Here I am safe."Walter asked him if he was not a little ashamed of himself for calling on the Lord for help in times of need, but in good or safe times he forgot to thank him in prayer. Walter had many gospel discussions but no one was interested in learning more.

The POWs working in the night shift gathered every evening except Sundays at the gate to be picked up for work. They were counted and then under guarded protection they went to the mine. Walter thought that the guards were not afraid any of them would run away, they were there for the prisoners' protection. People surely didn't like them and let them know whenever there was an opportunity. At one time a man with a motorbike drove directly into the group of POWs but no one was injured.

The reception at the mine was not friendly either. Walter stood next to the elevator and took a look at the steel cords which pulled the elevator. Walter was concerned because the cords looked terrible. Steel laces were hanging by, and not just a few. Walter wondered if the mine ever had a safety inspection. With much concern, he rode with others in the elevator to the 1800 foot level. All the men carried a battery powered light around with them. Without the light, if you held your hand before your eyes you wouldn't be able to see your hand. As a newcomer it was a funny feeling walking along the tunnel to his place of work. The tunnel was chiseled out of the mountain and support was built in only a few places. The first few days Walter had no helmet and because of the meager light he could not see what was hanging down from the ceiling. He hit and hurt his head many times. In the middle of the tunnel was a conveyor belt. From the belt he could see some pieces the size of a shoe sole were cut out. At the end of the tunnel men were drilling holes for explosives.

Walter learned that only the morning shift produced the coal. The other two shifts did the clean up and the preparation. He was told his task would be taking down the supports which held up the ceiling. The ceiling was held up in three different ways.

1. Iron stems which were very heavy but easy to take down. Walter just had to hit the iron stem at a fixed place and it fell down. It sounds easy but was hard work because there was no place in Walter's working area where he could stand upright.

2. The other stems were small tree trunks. Walter liked to remove them best because these trunks were only used on solid tops. He seldom had rocks coming down on him at those places.

3. The third method was used only on the brittle ceiling places. Two four-foot long trunks were placed three feet apart on the bottom and then two other trunks were placed across them in the other direction. That process was done all the way up to the ceiling. It was very dangerous to remove them. With the pick Walter would move one trunk to the outer edge and with the next strike at that trunk the fixture would break apart and some parts of the ceiling would follow.

All the work was done on a sloped bottom. To move out of the way of the falling rocks, Walter had to move uphill which made it harder. There was not much room to maneuver because the bottom and the top were only about four to six feet apart. Every workday the dayshift broke the coal out by using hand-held air hammers and moved the mine face about three feet. The afternoon shift cleaned up what was left to do from the morning and set up pillars to hold the top in place. Walter, in the nightshift, had to remove the pillars which were placed the day before and not needed any more. The ceiling could collapse and Walter would be buried under the rocks.

Like the pencils in the picture the trunks were laid in brittle spots of the working area of the coal mine

Many times Walter barely escaped being buried. One night he couldn't move away far and fast enough. An exceptionally large amount of rocks came down and buried him. Walter was not able to move because the load was too heavy. Every worker nearby left their place as fast as possible, being afraid of being buried also. When these men passed by Walter's comrade and fellow POW Franz Rambow, they told him what had taken place. Franz jumped into the chute and slid down to the place where Walter was buried and started digging. Walter's body was lying flat on the floor and his head next to a stem. Maybe he could see part of Walter's head, because Franz started digging right where Walter's head was. He freed Walter's head from the rubble and with the help of others they freed him. The fall of the rocks hurt Walter, but he was not injured. Walter prayed every day for protection and peace of mind. The Lord showed him He heard his prayer.

At the next day after Walter had his meal and his rest before he went back to work, the friends with whom he went to the Lutheran church took Walter aside and counseled him. They wanted him to see a doctor and stay in camp. To do that, he would have to lie. Walter felt fine. "Maybe," they said, "the Lord wanted to tell you not to work anymore. Are you not afraid to go back into the mine?"

No, Walter was not afraid to go back to work and yes, he believed the Lord wanted to tell him something. The Lord wanted him to know He was with him and would protect him. Walter went back to work the next day.

The civilian men in the mine who worked with Walter came from different nations. Walter didn't think anyone who worked with him was from Belgium except the foreman. It was a rough group with low morals. Walter didn't know what they did when they were standing together, but when Walter came near them they would go away. Often Walter had discussed his belief with them. Later they would come and ask him for counsel in their married life and with their children. What did Walter know about married life? He told the men the way he thought it should be and what the scriptures said. Walter was surprised that they would ask him for help. After all, he was just a POW, a German, single, and twenty-three.

About two months later, while Walter was taking out the stems, he heard a big noise. The ground shook and he was enclosed in a big cloud of dust. After it had cleared a little Walter went up the chute to see what had happened. He found the entrance where the chute started was covered with an immense pile of rocks. Walter turned and went down the chute to see if he could get out the other way. He met five men on his way who told him the other end, our exit, was also closed. They couldn't escape. They were trapped and needed help to get out. They hit the steel air pipe with a hammer. The noise made others who worked on a different place aware they were still alive. The other group returned the same signal to let the men know they had heard their signal.

Walter asked himself what would be the best thing to do in their situation since he didn't know how long they would be trapped. His first thought was of his lamp. He turned it off. It was very important to save his light; without the light he would be lost. Next he wondered how they would get out of that place. There was no way to leave the mine without help from the outside. Then Walter felt he might need all his strength for when they would be rescued. Walter looked for a place to sleep. He found a place and fell asleep, but his co-workers woke him up. They were going up and down the chute and couldn't settle down because of fear of what could happen. Walter told them to save their strength and rest but they were afraid and couldn't sleep. Walter told them to let him sleep. It was nice and warm in the mine. The usual air movement was not working. It made it nice to rest but was very dangerous because of gas packets which could explode or gas they could inhale which would kill them. Walter slept well until he heard voices.

After about six hours, men from the other side of the breakdown had opened up a way. To see what they did, Walter and the others crawled up a mountain of rubble and through a hole where they could see more men crawling up to them. It was a relief to see those men. Walter wondered how they would open the way to their working place and move the mountain of rocks away. After a few days, the mountain of rubble was gone and things were back to normal.

There was very little going on in the camp or in the mine. One day was the same as the day before, except for Sundays. Besides going with his friends to the Lutheran church, Walter continued his Bible study and working on his concordance of the Doctrine and Covenants. It was also the same routine at work every day. Walter was more careful but he still had close calls. On the 23rd of March 1946, he took the stems out and placed them close to the chute. He had carefully looked at the ceiling and didn't see any cracks before he took out the iron stems. However the stem fell and as some rocks came down with it, Walter fell too. His head was squeezed between two big rocks and he couldn't move. Every worker fled to a safe place except his German co-worker, Franz Rambow, who came again to his aid. He was able to lift one of the rocks a little, just enough to get Walter's head out. It was just in time because another rock fell and hit Franz's hand but not Walter's head. More men came and got Walter free. Walter is sorry to say while he had only some skin damage Franz had to go to the hospital and some fingers from his hand were injured.

Not long after this Walter had another accident. While moving the stems a rock fell on his left hand and injured it. On the way to the hospital Walter made the decision not to work in the mine any more. Walter felt it was not safe enough and he was not interested in having his name on the board by the entrance. He, with many others, decided to go on strike until safety improvements were made. They stood as they normally did by the entrance and when the order came to move on they didn't proceed. This action caught everyone by surprise. They explained why they wouldn't go to work and they were dismissed to return to their barracks.

The next day all strikers were called into the middle of the camp. The Belgian camp director, an officer of the Belgian army, gave the strikers a lecture and promised improvements. He also told the men if they didn't return to work they would be placed in a penal camp. After his lecture a few of the men returned to work but most of them, about 300 men including Walter, didn't move. They were dismissed and returned to their barracks.

The following day they gathered at the same place. This time the guards used force. After some of the men were knocked down, some men gave in. The rest of them had to stand in the sun all day long. They were told they wouldn't get anything to eat until they returned to work. After being dismissed that evening the strikers met and discussed what they should do next. The men in the camp were divided; some of the men didn't participate in the strike. Some were for the strike but many were against it. Many of the strikers decided it wasn't worth it and went back to work. There were about 100 men who stood there in the morning and didn't move. The POWs stood there with their empty stomachs in the sun and they were guarded by the soldiers. At noon no move was made to feed them. The Belgian soldiers kept their promise: no food. Shortly after noon Walter saw some movement from the kitchen personnel. Big containers were brought out and a cook called loudly, "Come and eat." Without delay all the men went over and had a good meal. The guards watched what was going on and then moved back into their quarters. The strikers were left alone for the night.

In the night Walter experienced heavy pain in his abdomen. It felt like his intestines were twisted and locked. When he bent down it felt like something had to unlock in his belly before he could straighten out his body. It was extremely painful especially when he came up fast after he had bent down. It appeared to be in the place where he was wounded in the war. Walter went to the camp doctor and he admitted him to a hospital. Walter was not told what the examination showed, but was kept in the hospital for about ten days. After he recovered he volunteered to work in the hospital kitchen.

16

ENJOYING FARMING

When Walter returned from the hospital he didn't find any of his friends (the strikers) in camp. They had apparently returned to work or were transferred to another camp. He also learned that some of the men in camp were sent to work on a farm. Walter talked to a few POWs who returned from farm work. He was surprised to hear that they hadn't returned because of the work, but because of the women. Walter dismissed the women talk, and he liked what they said about work. Walter was told to return to the coal mine, but he told the camp director he wouldn't go. When asked about farm work he agreed to go there.

A few days later a farmer picked Walter up. He had a large farm and had many farm workers plus two POWs working for him. He raised wheat, sugar beets, and other crops. He also had a large pasture and many cows. His two POWs took care of over 300 pigs. They were glad that they could turn that work over to Walter. They showed Walter how to feed the pigs, clean their pigsty and where Walter had to prepare the food. This work kept him busy all day long. In the morning, before breakfast Walter had to feed the pigs. With big containers he went from one pigsty to another. The number of pigs in a pigsty determined how much food they got. It took him much longer than the former men who did the feeding. They placed one container in the pigsty whether there were 20 or 40 pigs in it. The farmer was surprised when Walter came in for breakfast after the other workers had left. Walter told the farmer that as long as he did the feeding, the pigs would get what they needed, regardless of how much time it took. Walter still found time to learn to milk cows and to work with horses. Walter loved to work with horses. At times the farmer took Walter along to the pastures to pick up cows which would soon give birth to a calf. Some nights Walter stayed up to help with the birth of a calf. He worked from early in the morning until late at night, and he loved it.

The farmer liked Walter's work, but he was disappointed that Walter didn't work on Sunday. Walter fed the pigs on Sunday, but he declined to do any other work. Walter held his own church service and intensively studied the scriptures. One Sunday, at harvest time the farmer came back from his Catholic services. He told Walter the priest had told them it was alright to work on Sunday. Walter told the farmer there were no blessings for work on Sunday and a priest couldn't change the commandment of the Lord to keep the Sabbath day holy. The farmer gathered all his men and went to the fields. Clouds came in the sky and there was a cloud burst. He and his men came back wet to the skin. Walter stood at the door and reminded the farmer, "Remember the Sabbath day and keep it holy." The farmer felt miserable because of the storm and Walter's comments didn't make him feel any better.

The farmer had outside help with most of the harvest but some of his helpers had to do some work too. Bending over and harvesting sugar beets was hard on Walter's back. He was very glad when all the beets were harvested. The men loaded the beets in reserved railroad cars and filled them; however, one car was only about half full. There were still some second grade sugar beets lying in the field. These beets were a little larger, but had only half the content of sugars as the good ones. The farmer and all the men stood and they had a discussion about the sugar beets. The men told the farmer to fill the car with the second grade sugar beets. Walter didn't go along with the others. He reminded the farmer of his good reputation. He told the farmer honesty would pay off. The farmer did as Walter counseled him.

In the winter months the farmer was delighted that Walter repaired his equipment and prepared everything for work in the spring. During this time Walter learned to speak Flemish and to communicate with the farmer. It was interesting when they discussed gospel doctrine. The farmer's Bible was written in French. At that time Walter could not read or speak French, but he had his own German Bible. To make a point Walter opened his Bible, found a scripture for the subject they discussed and looked for the same scripture in the farmer's Bible. Walter pointed with a finger for the farmer to read what Walter tried to explain. It worked out well.

Above the place where Walter cooked and prepared the food for the pigs was a small room where the POWs slept. It was a very uncomfortable and cold room and the POWs didn't like to stay there. All private rooms were off limits for them. They could use the room where the working hands were fed only for Sundays and after work. One day, unexpectedly, military police checked on the POWs. They frisked them, apparently for money, but didn't find any. Someone must have complained about Walter's two comrades' bad behavior in the tavern. Shortly after the visit of the military police the two POWs were transferred back to the POW camp.

For his Sunday study Walter moved from the room above the pigs' food kitchen to the workers' eating room in the house. After a while Walter spent more and more time in the eating room. This room was not ideal, but better than the other. One Sunday the farmer's wife came and told Walter to use their living room for his study. She was always nice to him so when she needed something done he would do it for her. She gave draperies and other things to make his room more comfortable and friendly. Without having any premonitions of trouble Walter accepted her invitation, a move he would soon regret.

Walter was bent over his books when he felt arms around his neck and the farmer's wife's cheek against his. Walter was so involved in his study he didn't even hear her coming into the room. She was a young and attractive woman, only twenty nine years old and perhaps she felt neglected by her hard working husband. Walter had heard about love-hungry women in camp. Walter never thought anything like that could happen to him. He didn't want to hurt her, but on the other hand he didn't want to do what she wanted him to do.

Slowly Walter got up and tried to kindly push her away. She

went all over him and trapped him in a corner of the room. He had no choice but to grab her hard by her arms and place her on a chair. Quickly he took his books and paper and left the room, realizing he wouldn't hear a friendly word from her again. That's the way it was. From that time on she hated Walter and whenever possible made his life miserable. She let Walter know he was just a little POW and she called him "dirty German." Walter didn't say a word to the farmer, but he gave him some hints to give more attention to his wife. Walter doesn't even know if he understood his hints. The farmer adored his beautiful wife and many times told Walter how most men and women in the community had other lovers, and proudly told Walter that neither he nor his wife had lovers.

As the time went by Walter made many friends in the community. Many had worked during the war in Germany and had enjoyed their stay. Walter was a frequent guest at some of their homes. Living conditions in Belgium were good. America had sent a lot of food and material to this nation. Of course not everyone had plenty and some offered Walter money if he would sell pigs to them. Most everyone knew he was the only one who knew how many pigs the farmer had. It was never a temptation. Walter couldn't sell what didn't belong to him.

One evening the farmer stormed into Walter's room. He grabbed him, turned him around and shook him. He was really upset. "What did you do with the sack of flour you stole from me?" he asked. Walter didn't even know where the farmer kept the flour. He told Walter the sack had a hole and a small trail went right to Walter's Belgian friends' apartment. He went over to Walter's friends' apartment, but didn't find the sack. Knowing they were friends of Walter he thought Walter might have the sack of flour and that he was involved with the theft. The farmer and Walter went over to Walters' friends place. The friends' told the farmer they didn't know anything about the flour. They permitted him to check, but he didn't find anything.

Now Walter was upset with the farmer and he let him know. It hurt him that he would think Walter would be involved in something like that. The next morning as Walter passed by his office the farmer called Walter in. He was friendly and nice and excused himself for his behavior of last night. He told Walter he believed that he had nothing to do with the theft. He had thought things over during the night. "Do you remember the sugar beets?" he asked. Walter didn't, but his mentioning of the incident reminded him. He continued, "You were honest then and you are honest now."

The farmer and Walter worked well together, but every time they talked he would say, "You will try to run away to get home." Walter had no intention to leave. It was just too difficult for him to reach his home. Besides Walter had heard harrowing stories about the Russians, and his mother hadn't heard from his father who was in a Russian concentration camp. That showed Walter how the Russians treated their own people and the Germans. The farmer had even contacted the camp, asking them what he could do to prevent Walter from leaving. They told him neither he nor they could do anything about him leaving. He mentioned Walter's leaving so often that Walter finally made plans to leave, even though his heart was not in it.

Walter collected a little money, clothing and a map from people in the village, and one night when everyone was asleep he started walking toward the German border. He walked all night and in the morning he hid in the underbrush of a field. Even though Walter was in good physical condition, his problem with dragging his left foot began again after the long walk during the night. Before, he had really not felt problems with his foot. The war injuries had healed. After the next night's march, Walter was limping so badly he had to change his plans. He walked to the Meuse River with the intention to cross the river and was surprised how wide the river was. He decided to go by rail and went to the railroad station in the city of Namur to buy a ticket. As he saw the many people who bought tickets and boarded the train he realized he would be caught right away. He told himself there must be a bridge over the river.

Walter found the bridge. Instead of waiting until there was a lot of traffic on the bridge, he walked right over it. A man crossed his way and said something to him in the French language. Walter should have ignored his words. He didn't understand a word but he answered and said “Oui (yes).” The man turned toward Walter and shouted “dirty German.” Walter ran to reach the other side of the bridge but in no time he was surrounded by a large crowd. The crowd was shouting and hollering but Walter didn’t understand a word. No one laid hands on him. He was surprised and wondered where all the people came from. The man who started all this tried to tell him he had caught many Germans before. A policeman made his way through the crowd and took Walter to the police station. They took the map from Walter, but didn’t find the money. They asked all kinds of questions, but treated him very well and they gave him a good meal. After Walter was placed in a single cell he hid the money in the sack of straw that he later slept on. He had a good night’s rest. In a way he was glad his walk to reach his home was over. He had a lot of pain in his foot and would have had a hard time reaching his home.

In the morning Walter was taken to a POW camp. The people in this camp were mainly men who had escaped from POW camps in France and tried to reach home, but got caught in Belgium. The men Walter talked to in camp couldn’t understand why he would leave a camp here in Belgium where the POWs were treated fairly and fed well. They had left the camps in France because the treatment there was inferior. All POWs worked in a quarry in Belgium and this work was not to Walter’s liking. After a few days in the camp Walter was brought before the Belgian military court. The camp commander who held the court questioned him. Walter took the opportunity to request his transfer to his former POW camp. The commander told him he would be treated here just as well as in his former camp. Walter insisted on being transferred and on the next day he was transferred by train to his former camp. Needless to say Walter was the attraction in the rail car. His clothing was marked with large letters PG (prisonnier de guerre meaning prisoner of war), on the chest, his knees and on his back. The guard accompanying him had to answer many questions and a few people told him to send Walter home.

In the evening they arrived at Walter’s former camp in Machienne au Pont. Walter was placed in a single cell where he was the only one incarcerated. Guards opened the door often and asked why he was in there. Walter told them he wanted to go home. They agreed with him and brought him food and chocolate. They told him, "you are going home," but they didn't know when. After all, POW's provided cheap labor. Walter had to appear again before a military court. He was sitting with the interpreter when the commander entered the room. He said something in French to Walter which Walter didn't understand. The interpreter told him the commander had said Walter shouldn't make such a sad face. "Nothing is eaten as hot as it is cooked," he said. The commander asked Walter a few questions, but Walter had the impression the commander was not really interested in what he said. He told Walter he was to stay in the cell for a while. The next day he changed the order saying Walter could be in the camp all day, but had to sleep in the cell. Walter slept in the cell a few nights and was then asked to go to a farm again.

Walter was sent with five other POWs to a large sugar beet farm. The POWs had their sleeping quarters in an old laundry. They had no beds to sleep on, straw bales served as their beds. The food was mainly bread and sugar from sugar beets, of which they could eat as much as they wanted. Of course they wanted better food. Four brothers owned and operated the farm. The farmers had a garden spot with all kinds of fruits and vegetables. They had two girls who took care of cleaning the house and preparing the food. Besides sugar beets they had plenty of rats. Walter had never seen so many rats in one place. The basement and the stables were full of them. Walter couldn't understand how the farmer could live under those conditions. Once in a while Walter saw one of the brothers sitting in front of the house with a gun shooting the rats he saw.

Their main work was keeping the fields free of weeds. One day the youngest of the four brothers came to Walter and asked if Walter would help out in the house. The two girls had left and they needed help. He asked Walter if he would do the cleaning. Walter agreed and for the next few weeks, before the sugar beet harvest, he became a house maid. He cleaned the rooms, made the beds and cleaned the windows. He did whatever needed to be done, but he didn't cook. Walter thought the brothers liked his work because they didn't find a replacement until the harvest time. Walter's fellow

POWs had their fun teasing him to no end. Walter didn't like the teasing, but the youngest of the brothers who was about Walter's age, took him along when he went to town. It was nice to get away for a short time.

One night in their quarters their "old man" woke every one up. The old man was in his late thirties and the other men were in their early twenties. He couldn't sleep well. They had left the outside door open for fresh air and the old man had seen a rat coming into our room. Walter had cornered rats before in the stables and had the rat jumped right at him. Three of the POWs jumped right on top of the table and told the others where they had seen the rat. The other three tried to kill the rat. They had to move the bales of straw apart and finally under their wardrobe they killed the rat. The excitement was over and every one fell asleep.

The harvest started and Walter's work inside the house came to an end. His fellow POWs had to work pulling and cutting the top of the sugar beets. Walter drove the horses and wagon for a crew who loaded the beets. They were all seasoned workers and got paid by how many wagons they filled. Walter didn't have to work with them, but he helped as much as he could. His team liked that and they worked hard. While Walter didn't get paid, the team enjoyed the pay they received after the work was finished. They outdid all other teams. Walter's helping out and working hard had a nice side effect. After the harvest was over his fellow POWs returned to doing field work and Walter became the right-hand man for the younger brother in his business. He took Walter along wherever he went. It was fun for Walter. He learned a little French and could communicate fairly well with his boss.

Before the winter arrived the POWs were back in camp. Many things had changed in camp. The first group of men got ready to go home and Walter hoped he would soon be released too. Walter didn't want to go back to work on a farm, even though he had enjoyed his time doing farm work. He was very disappointed when a few days later he got orders to get ready to go out on a farm again. Walter was not the only one who had to leave, but he was the one who dragged his feet the most. Walter wanted to show the commander he was very disappointed that he was being sent to a farm. When Walter had seen the commander in the past he was always very nice to Walter. Surely he didn't approve of this assignment. Walter had always placed his problems before the Lord but he couldn't understand this. Of course, Walter couldn't see at that time what a blessing this would be for him and his family.

The commander introduced Walter to a nice, friendly gentleman who had been the first to arrive to pick up a POW and was the last to leave. He told Walter later he had tried to take the first POW who came in but the commander, who was a school friend of his, told him to wait. He did the same to everyone who came until Walter came in. The commander told the gentleman to take him. He told the farmer that he would like Walter and his work. Walter couldn't communicate much with him. He had learned to speak Flemish but not much French and the farmer spoke only French. Walter tried to make it clear to him that he would work only from 6am to 6pm but not more. Walter didn't know if the farmer understood him.

At noon they arrived at the farmer's place. The farmer and Walter walked through the employees' dining room and the farmer introduced Walter to the other employees. Walter wanted to sit down with the men but the farmer told Walter to come with him. They entered his dining room and the table was prepared for five. The farmer introduced Walter to his wife, son, and the son's wife. His son was about Walter's age and size. He invited Walter to sit down at the table. As Walter sat down at the table a thought went through his mind, "Here goes my twelve hour work day. With this treatment I will not be able to decline to work more hours."

After the meal the farmer showed Walter to his room, the best he ever had as a POW. He also told Water to look around and tomorrow they would leave for work on a "Moulin" at another place. Walter didn't understand what the farmer said, but Walter understood he should look around. So he did. Walter was impressed with the interior of his house. It was well furnished and well kept. Close to the house he had a mill and storage places for animal food. Apparently he was selling food for all kinds of animals. He had a stable with two horses and about seven milk cows. Walter saw some equipment for farming and he learned from the farmhands that he farmed the land also. Walter liked what he saw, but he was still disappointed that he didn't get to go home.

The next day they went by car to the "Moulin" the farmer had talked about. On the way he talked to Walter and he mentioned the word "Moulin" many times but Walter didn't understand what he was talking about. When they arrived Walter saw it was a large mill, much larger than the one he had at his home. They went to the upper floor of the mill. They farmer grabbed one of the wrenches he had lying around and started to take the machine apart. Walter watched him a little while, but Walter saw that the farmer had little experience repairing equipment. Walter couldn't speak French and the farmer couldn't speak German or Flemish. Walter touched his shoulder and made a gesture to let him do the repairing. He watched Walter doing the work and then he went over to the stairs and called his old father to come upstairs. Now Granddad and dad watched Walter work. By their faces Walter could see they surely liked what they saw and Walter had a job.

Walter started early in the morning and quit late in the evening. In return he was treated very well. At no time did they let him feel he was just a POW. Walter liked the family and the work. The women were excellent cooks. When Walter mentioned a meal he would like, he got it. The young owner and Walter got along very well too. When the young owner and his wife went to movies they gave Walter nice clothes to wear and took him along. One of the owner's friends was a grocer who objected to Walter, a German, tagging along for dancing. They young boss told him if Walter couldn't go along he wouldn't go either. They took Walter dancing, found him a good looking date and they went. Walter felt bad for the girl. He was not a good dancer, but the girl didn't mind. Walter thought his farmer would love to see him fall in love with a girl and stay in Belgium, but Walter didn't give that idea any thought.

Walter's physical self was well cared for, but his spiritual side was longing for food. Not one of these families was interested in Walter's church or, as a matter of fact, in any church. Besides feeding the animals, Walter didn't do any work on Sunday. He held his own little meeting and studied the scriptures. On one Sunday his farmer and his family needed to be away and Walter realized it was very important that they went so he told them he would take care of milking the cows. It was done by hand and Walter had learned to do that with his first farmer. That was a great mistake! The women claimed Walter got more milk out of the cows than their men did. Walter now had to milk the cows every Sunday.

After they had finished overhauling the mill, and had checked everything over and were very satisfied with the result, the farmer gave a big party for the dignitaries and business people in town. At the party Walter stood back, out of the way. The farmer started looking for him. He wanted Walter to take part in the celebration. Walter told him some of his guests might object to sitting with a German POW at the table. "Nonsense," he said. Walter went to get dressed up. He liked the suit and how he looked. The farmer took Walter and introduced him to every guest: "This is Walter, who overhauled the mill and made it work." Everyone was friendly and shook hands with Walter. Sitting with the family, he was served the finest food Walter had ever eaten. The great variety of food and the many servings were new to him. Walter had never seen anything like this before and he loved it.

Now his daily work changed. In the morning before any one got up Walter cleaned the horses, the way he had learned to do at in his horse riding lesson and after breakfast he would go out and work in the field. He would plow, sow or do whatever was needed. After he sowed, he was eager to see when the plants came up how straight the rows of his sowing were. At noon he would go back to the mill and after a good meal he would help in the mill or prepare dry food for delivery. Walter would help with the delivery of animal food, or he would go with the son and pick up large loads of merchandise from other cities with the truck. The young owner had done that alone, but Walter asked him to take him along. His wife got too close to him and Walter tried to get out of her way. In the beginning, she taught Walter how to speak and write French, but what she wanted to teach Walter now he couldn't allow

In the middle of November, 1947 (two and a half years after the war in Germany ended) the farmer took Walter aside and asked him if he would like to stay in Belgium. He painted the future in rosy pictures. He had already talked to the government in Brussels and they told him Walter could stay and live and work in Belgium. He offered Walter good money and a nice place to stay. Walter had heard about POWs who decided to stay, but Walter had made up his mind to go home.

Walter told the farmer he appreciated what he had done for him and the good relationship they had, but he couldn't stay. He felt he needed to go home. His mother was alone and his father was in a concentration camp or dead, he didn't know. His mother felt he was still alive, but had not heard from him or the government. The communist government hadn't notified any family of the whereabouts of their imprisoned husband/father. His mother had written that the church needed Walter and Walter missed his association with the church. The farmer accepted his decision and asked Walter if he would stay to the last day before Walter was to be transferred to Germany. Walter agreed and the farmer talked to the camp commander, who had no objection.

The evening before Walter's transport to Germany, he said good-bye to the farmer and his family. The farmer drove him to the POW camp. The next day Walter was hurried through all the formalities and the next morning the last men of this POW camp were on the way home. Walter was very much aware of the political and physical conditions in Germany because the farmer's family and people in the community had informed him. He had prepared as much as he possible could for what was ahead of him. From the money the farmer gave him (which the farmer was not permitted to do), Walter bought items he might need at home. All that was given to him including his cigarette rations he kept for trading purposes. He had so much to carry around and it was so heavy that in West Germany Walter bought a little hand wagon to put his belongings in. He was then transported by train to Friedland an der Leine, close to the East and West German border. In that camp Walter was dismissed from the army on the 21st of November 1947. In this West German camp they were asked if they would like to stay and they were told that provision for their stay would be made. Many men accepted, but Walter had made up his mind that he would go to his home in East Germany. His mother and the church needed help and that was all that counted.

He did have second thoughts when he was sitting at the border with all his belongings waiting to walk across the border. The POWs from Russia were permitted to cross the border first. Walter, of course, was curious to see what these men looked like. On Walter's side everyone had something he was taking home. Of course, no one had what Walter had. They saw a small group of men coming from the east in fairly good condition marching across the border. On their belt hung an empty tin can and that was all. After these came sick men dragging their feet and the last of these men surely should have been helped to cross the border. It took a long time to get these men over the border.

The former POWs on the West German side of the border looked healthy and in good condition. Walter saw many of the men on his side turning around and he guessed applying for permission to stay in West Germany. Walter didn't change his mind. His mother and his church needed him and he walked over the border into East Germany.

III

PARTICULARS OF DISCHARGE

Entlassungsvermerk

THE PERSON TO WHOM THE ABOVE PARTICULARS REFER
Die Person auf die sich obige Angaben beziehen

WAS DISCHARGED ON (Date) .... FROM THE* HEER ....
wurde am (Datum der Entlassung) 21 NOV. 1947 vom/von der* entlassen

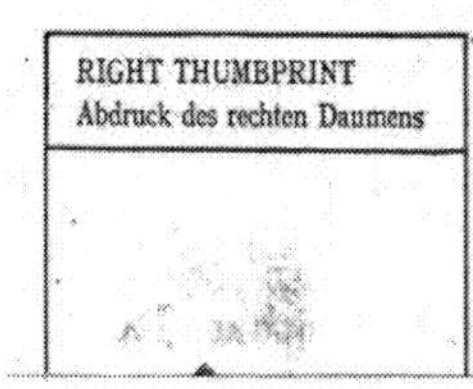

RIGHT THUMBPRINT
Abdruck des rechten Daumens

CERTIFIED BY ....
Beglaubigt durch

NAME, RANK AND
APPOINTMENT OF ....
ALLIED DISCHARGING
OFFICER IN
BLOCK CAPITALS ....

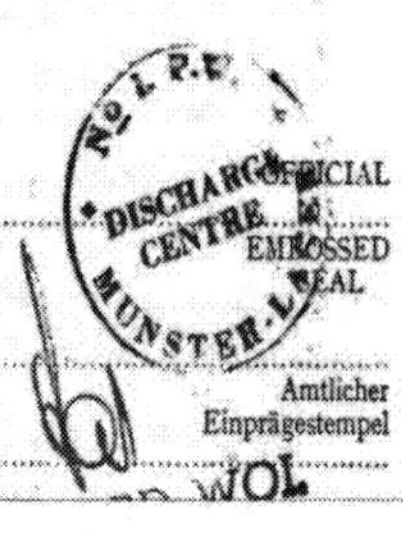

OFFICIAL
EMBOSSED
SEAL
Amtlicher
Einprägestempel

ARMÉE BELGE

CAMP DE PRISONNIERS DE GUERRE
CH II – MARCHIENNE-AU-PONT

Marchiennes, le 19 novembre 1947.

CERTIFICAT DE TRAVAIL

— ARBEITSBESCHEINIGUNG —

Je soussigné, Commandant le camp de Marchiennes, certifie que le Prisonnier de Guerre
Ich Unterzeichneter, Kommandant des Lagers Marchiennes, bescheinige, dass der Kriegsgefangene

(Nom, Prénom)
(Name, Vorname) : R o h l o f f, Walter

N. CH II
Nr 2160 né le / geb. 4-6-22 à / in Neubrandenburg

et domicilié à
und wohnhaft in Neubrandenburg (Mecklenburg)

a été employé, pendant son séjour au camp en qualité de :
während seiner Zugehörigkeit zum Lager eingesetzt war als :

Grubenarbeiter unter Tage	du / vom	9-12-45	au / bis	29-6-46
Landarbeiter	du / vom	30-6-46	au / bis	18-11-47
	du / vom		au / bis	

Cachet du Camp,
Lagerstempel.

Le Commandant du Camp,
Der Lagerkommandant,

17

HOME AND SPREADING THE GOSPEL

When he arrived on the East side of the border, Walter almost regretted his decision. He felt as if he had gone from heaven into hell. Everything was dirty and ugly. Unfriendly men treated the returning POWs like criminals. Comparing it to later experiences, Walter thought maybe the border guards thought they were all American spies. Maybe they didn't trust anyone. Walter later read in the office of a police officer, "Trust is good, control is better." Everyone's eyes were on Walter's loaded wagon. Walter didn't let the wagon out of his sight because he feared he wouldn't get his wagon home. The POWs from the North were transported to the town of Teterow in Mecklenburg, not far from his home town. Walter felt he had to do something. He saw too many eyes longing for his wagon. In the darkness of the night he made a hole in the fence and took all his belongings to the railroad station. He arrived late in the night with the train in Neubrandenburg. To Walter's delight there were only a few people on the street. He couldn't take his wagon, so he took only half the load at a time from one corner to the other, always keeping an eye on his load. What would have normally taken him 30 minutes now took him over an hour, but he got everything home safely.

On his way he had contemplated how it would be on arriving home. The house at Pasewalkerstr.11 looked just the same as it had when Walter left. There was no light and Walter assumed everyone was asleep. The house door was locked. Walter knocked at the door, but he had little hope somebody would hear him. He had left Belgium in a hurry and his concern for his belongings had not given him time to write.

Walter waited a few minutes then the door opened and Irene, his mother looked out. She must have been sleeping softly because she had heard Walter's knock. Her face showed surprise as she saw Walter. Recognizing him, her eyes lit up and tears ran down her face as she fell into Walter's arms. He was a little clumsy. He was not used to taking his mother into his arms. Walter hugged her, told her he loved her and that he was glad to be home after those difficult years.

Irene Boers Rohloff, Walter's mother

Her face looked tired and a little worn out. The worry about her husband and children was written there. Before Walter could inquire about his father and his sister he had to report to her what happened to him. Then she reported to Walter. She and Bruno (his father) had been on the way home from their garden plot about half an hour away from home when people on the street told them to go into hiding because the Russian GPU were at their door waiting for Bruno to come home. - Hiding where? They had nowhere to go.

He was not the first one to be picked up by the Russian Secret police. Upon arriving home Walter's father was taken by the Russians. His mother broke down in tears when her husband left. She hadn't heard from him for two and a half years since he was taken away. Neither the government nor any other organization would tell her if he was dead or alive. In the beginning of his incarceration she had picked up his underwear from him in prison for cleaning and had been surprised about seeing blood in his underwear. She had thought his hemorrhoids were giving him problems again. Later she had heard that during interrogations the men were struck until they were bloody.

Walter learned that she had rented out the room he had formerly used while he was living at home to a refugee couple, the Werner's. The couple was driven out of their home in the Sudetenland, which before the war was part of the Czech Republic. All Germans in other nations were driven out and had to find a place in the overcrowded, remainder of Germany. The Werner's had tried to find a place to live in different cities and with different people but no one wanted them. Mrs. Helene Werner pleaded with Walter's mother and she took her in.

Mr. Werner stayed mainly in his room, but Helene was God send for Walter's mother. Even though she had been through many hardships, she was always positive. When Walter's mother grieved, she would cheer her up. Walter learned that his mother had a lot of help from her youngest, single sister Elisabeth Boers, who was living nearby. She visited often and went shopping for her when needed. Sister Gertrud Dauss, a long time friend of Walter's family and a member of the LDS branch, also cared for her. Georg Dauss, her husband had been killed in war action in France. The branch of the church was small and brother Otto Krakow was the only man. Walter's mom proudly reported that the LDS branch meetings were held in her living room. The branch also had missionaries. An Elder

Gerhard Kupitz was their branch president and Walter could feel from her voice that she liked him very much.

While they talked Walter had his mother unpacked the many things he had brought home. There were things to eat, to exchange for food, and some sweets she hadn't had for many years. Walter had brought home yarn, wool and many other things, even spices that he was sure she couldn't get in the stores because people were still living on ration cards and everything was very limited. Walter was delighted when she tried on the nylons and the shoes he had bought in Belgium and they fitted her perfectly. Her smile and happiness was the best repayment for the long time he had carefully gathered the things together.

During the next few days Walter learned more about what had occurred while he was gone. In the last month of the war his father was drafted into the "Volkssturm," an old man's unit. He was fifty four years old and his duty was to defend Walter's hometown. They had regular trainings hours. Shortly before the Russian army arrived at Walter's hometown, his father had come to his officer and told him he would not be available because he had to take care of his family. He had taken a horse and a wagon from his workplace to carry his wife, his neighbor and their belongings. Walter's father was the only male in the group. During the night of the 29thof April 1945 they began their trip west. The roads were full of people who were trying to escape to the west before the Russian army arrived. The people had been accurately warned what would happen when the Russian armies arrived. Walter's folks didn't make it far. Soon they were passed by the Russian army. Seeing no point in going on they had turned around and gone back home. Arriving home they heard the terrible news that over two thousand people had taken their own lives. The town was not defended and a fire had started in the old town, burning down most of the town inside the wall. Who started the fire? Some said the Russians and others said the Germans. Who knows?

His father's greatest concern had been for the women. For some time the women would all sleep in one room in Bruno's apartment. He slept at the door. All went well until one day the twenty-year-old daughter of their landlord, against the counsel of her elders, paraded around on the street and was watched by Russian soldiers. That night the soldiers had come into the house and wanted to sleep with her. The soldiers saw the other women in the house and they told Walter's father, who had been standing in the door, that he could have one woman, but they would take the others. First the soldiers argued with his father but when his father didn't give in, they knocked him down. Father got up as fast as possible, but was knocked down again. He didn't physically resist; he was afraid they would shoot him. With his passive resistance he was able to protect the women and the Russians left.

One day Walter's father had met a colleague from work on the street. The Russian army had taken his home and he was looking for a place to stay. He was a handicapped man and Walter's father invited him into his home. Because of his handicap, Walter's parents had given their bed to this colleague and his wife. For many days things went well, but then Walter's parents were horror-stricken when they saw Russian secret police going in and out of this colleague's room. The Russians had found out this man was head of security and guarding the Russian POWs at the factory. They had questioned him for the names of Nazis and to buy his freedom, he had complied. Walter's father suspected this, but didn't think anything would happen to him because he had never been a member of the Nazi party. One day his father said to his mother, "I don't know, there must be something wrong. My colleague doesn't look me in the eyes anymore." Soon the Russians picked Walter's father up (July 19.1945) and threw him in the concentration camp Fuenfeichen.

At noon Walter was introduced to the missionary who was serving in his hometown. Elder Gerhard Kupitz presided over the branch in Neubrandenburg, and his companion served in Demmin, a city about 20 miles north of Walter's hometown. Elder Kupitz was a good looking young man and came from Berlin. He was about Walter's age and Walter liked his lively, positive way. While they were talking Elder Kupitz mentioned he wanted to visit the Kurt Meyer family in Cammin, a small community near Neubrandenburg. Walter offered to go along and in the morning both walked along the railroad tracks the 18 km to the little town of Cammin. The young lady Walter had visited in Tilsit, Helga, was now Frau Meyer. She and her parents had fled before the Russian army and after Helga had served a mission in the Mission office in Berlin for the LDS church she had settled with her family in Cammin. Kurt's parents had been long time members of the branch. In the confusion before the Russian army arrived and the terrible stories they heard from the people fleeing before the Russians, the Meyers had taken their lives, as many others had. Kurt was there too, but he had hidden in the old church in between the coffins which were hundreds of years old. No one went down in the basement where he was and he had lived there until the Russians stopped looking for German soldiers.

Helga was charming as ever. They talked about the past and how they would work together in the church. Her husband had some land he worked on and he had leased some small lakes where he fished and sold the catch. Walter didn't have much time because he had to return to his quarantine camp. After Gerhard and Walter arrived at Walter's mother's home Walter took the next train to the camp. No one had missed him. After he had his political and military interrogation he had a physical check up and was sent home. Sitting in the train on the way home his thoughts went back over the years he had spent being a prisoner of war. As he evaluated the time, he realized it had been a good experience for him. Walter didn't feel he had wasted his time. He felt many people obtained a positive attitude about Germans from Walter's behavior. Walter felt it helped him to understand people better when they had difficult experiences to overcome. After hardships in the beginning of his POW time, Walter was treated well. He had been able to prepare himself for his callings in the church, where he wanted to be of service as he had promised his Heavenly Father. While he had studied the scriptures intensively, he would still need to learn to explain them.

At home Walter had to report to a government agency who again wanted to know his political and military background. It seemed to him they were still hunting Nazis. Walter answered all the questions truthfully. He didn't like the people there and the dirty rooms. He got his passport and could now look for work. Walter asked the Lord for guidance. He had not forgotten what he had promised the Lord. The first company he visited was a private company with good tools. While Walter was impressed with the work and equipment there he had no desire to apply for work. At that time there were still small, private companies in communist East Germany. The large companies were called "volkseigen" which meant companies owned by the people. That was a false statement. The companies were not owned by the people, but controlled by communist party members.

Walter looked at another company and while their tools were not as good as the previous company, he felt it was the right place to work. He applied and got a job as a tool maker. Walter was one of four toolmakers. They built molds and fixtures for about seventy-five workers. They made the tools needed for the production workers. Mr. Nagel was the owner. Walter's supervisor was also the leader of the communist party in the company. He had been a communist before Hitler's rule, during the war, and now. He didn't believe in God. The company also had a union, which was more or less an institution of the communist party. Walter didn't join the union even though everyone else in the company was a member.

Everything they needed to live was obtained through ration cards. It was not enough, but the things they could buy on the black market without the card were very expensive. Walter made only 1.02 Marks an hour and he was one of the better paid men in the company. Most of the employees made less than I Mark. It was good that he didn't have bad habits like smoking and drinking. There were rations for a small amount of these on the cards, but people with these habits were always looking for more. That didn't bother him. But a pound of butter on the black market was 50.00 Marks and that hurt, especially when they were not sure if the butter they bought was really butter or if there was something else hiding in the butter.

The first project Walter began at home was looking through his father's family history work. Nothing had been mailed to a temple. His father had spent many hours and much money to gather this information. He had started with this work when he became a member of the church in 1929. In the years he was out of a job he went from one parish to the other to collect the names of his and his wife's forefathers. In the Hitler days it was relatively easy to get the information. Everyone who was looking for a good job had to prove he was not a descendant of a Jew. Records were easily assessable. Walter started to do family history when he was twelve years old and was very much interested in getting the work done. His mother had guarded the records very carefully. When the Russian army kicked her out of her apartment, she left the furniture behind but took the family history records and notes Walter's father had made.

Walter was very much impressed with the church meetings. The Sacrament meeting was held in his mother's living room, and the adult class of the Sunday School was held right after. Sunday School for children was held in Brother and Sister Krakow's home. Walter was surprised, when he visited, how many children were in attendance. Brother Krakow conducted the meeting and his wife and daughter led the singing of the hymns and gave the lessons. In Sacrament meeting they had fewer people in attendance. There were three men—Elder Gerhard Kupitz, Otto Krakow and Walter and about nine sisters—Gertrud Dauss, Ida Schulz, Irene Rohloff, Else Guetschow, Agnes and her daughter, Ruth Krakow, Erna Jeschonek and her mother. Frau Waldheim and sometimes our neighbor Frau Werner attended the meetings too. Kurt and Helga Meyer held meetings in their home in Cammin.

The missionary, Elder Gerhard Kupitz, invited Walter to help him in his effort to spread the gospel. It was just what Walter was waiting for. Gerhard had a golden family, the Caesars. In the evening after Walter's work they met the family: father, mother and the 18 year old daughter, Jutta. When Gerhard introduced Walter, Mr. Caesar, who was about five foot six inches and the tallest in the family said, "Oh, another tall fellow." "Yes," said Gerhard "and another who keeps the Word of Wisdom." They had a great spiritual meeting. The Caesars had many questions and Gerhard answered the questions thoroughly. It was a great learning experience for Walter. Gerhard did something else to help him. He asked Walter to teach the adult class in Sunday school. While Walter had studied the scriptures intensively over the years, teaching was very hard for him. He prepared well but was nervous. He even moved a table in front of him so nobody could see his shaking knees. What helped him the most was the love and appreciation these members gave him. They had known Walter when he was a child. Some of them had taught Walter the gospel and loved how he had developed.

In their meetings they discussed how nice it would be to have their own rooms to hold the church meetings. Many people were looking for rooms, but downtown Neubrandenburg had burned been down in the last days of the war. Getting their own rooms seemed to be wishful thinking. But one day Sister Guetschow told Gerhard about a hall in the old theater in the Pfaffenstrase could be available. Gerhard and Walter went over and visited the rooms. They liked what they saw. The hall was much too large for their small congregation, but the owner, Frau Fischer, gave them permission to change the room for their purpose. The district president, Brother Walter Krause, visited them and liked what he saw. The church leased the rooms. Brother Krause and Brother Otto Krakow (from the branch) were the main workers in the remodeling. Brother Krause knew where and how to get the material. Walter didn't know how he got what they needed, but it didn't take long before they had some rooms ready for use.

Walter liked his work at the factory. He worked well together with the three other toolmakers. Walter made the molds for aluminum castings and fixtures for assembling the parts. Often he had to help when problems arose somewhere in the production. He had a good relationship with all the workers. This gave him a good opportunity to discuss with the workers the teachings of the church. A few of them had had contact with the church before the war, but no one was interested to come and visit again. The company had no dining area or room so at noon or at their breaks they would sit and eat at their work place. One day during the noon hour one of the mechanics, Karl Neumann went over to Walter's place of work and visited with him. In their conversation he told Walter that he knew Walter was very religious. Then he said, "Walter, how about you coming over on Wednesday evening to my place at Ravensburgstr. 8, and listening to a discussion we have. The Jehovah's Witnesses present a lesson and you are very welcome to join and participate." Walter accepted the invitation and asked his coworker if he could bring a friend. He was delighted that Walter would do that.

Needless to say Gerhard was all for it. The Caesar family was still their only golden contact and they wanted more. They looked forward to Wednesday evening. When the day came they arrived early. They introduced themselves to the Neumann family and to everyone in attendance. They took a seat in the rear of the family room. There were more in attendance than at the LDS meetings. A young man presented a lesson out of the Watchtower, a magazine of the Jehovah's Witnesses. The lesson was about Adam's transgression. Gerhard and Walter's understanding about the lesson material was completely different than theirs. The witness's belief was that all miseries, contention, and difficulties in this life came through Adams transgression and Adam had destroyed God's intention for a better life. The LDS believe is just the opposite: Men will be punished for their own sins and not for Adams transgression. Adam is one of the great spirits who was called to open the way for men's progression toward eternal life. Through obedience to the Lords commandments men will be able to return into the presence of God. The two didn't participate in the lesson, but before closing the young man conducting asked them if they had any questions or comments.

Gerhard stood up and with the agreement of the young man conducting, explained the teachings of the LDS church. The Holy Ghost guided him well. Gerhard read and explained one scripture after another. Walter knew what Gerhard was talking about and, using both of their Bibles, Walter prepared and gave Gerhard the scripture he needed. The Holy Ghost has guided Walter on many occasions, but it has never again been as powerful as it was at that meeting. Walter guessed the Neumanns felt the spirit and invited them to stay after the meeting. They gladly accepted the invitation and taught them the gospel. Unknown to Walter and Gerhard, the Neumanns had discussed the teachings of the Jehovah's Witnesses and their daughter Gertrud, had joined the Witnesses group. But they were not satisfied with the doctrines and were looking for answers to their many questions.

In one of the next Witness meetings the young man who

conducted the meeting announced he needed an operation in a hospital in Berlin and his assistant would conduct the meeting. The assistant conducted the next meeting but he was not as effective as the first young man.

Gerhard and Irene Kupitz-Edith and Walter Rohloff

That meeting brought a complete change. Early in the meeting an exchange of thought began between Gerhard and some of the men. When the time came to dismiss, the material had still not all been presented in full. The young man conducting wanted to close the meeting and told them they would continue the lesson next time. Walter raised his hand and the young man gave Walter permission to speak. He invited the congregation to visit the LDS meeting the next Sunday. He told them that he and Gerhard had been with them many times, why not come and worship with them for a change. While Walter had not taken active part in the discussion, he had watched everyone's reaction to what Gerhard had to say. As Walter made his proposal he turned to the part of the congregation who frequently nodded their approval when Gerhard spoke. He asked, "Would you like to come?" They looked at Walter and said, "Yes, we will." Next Walter turned to the ones who sometimes approved and sometimes seemed to be against what Gerhard had to say. Walter asked them, "Would you come?" They hesitated a little and Walter could feel the tension in the room, but they said, "Yes, we will be there." Finally Walter turned to the leadership and asked them if they would come. Of course they really didn't have much of a choice, their congregation had already spoken. They told Walter they would come. Walter explained the time and place and that Gerhard and Walter would be delighted to see them all there.

Walter couldn't describe the feeling which came over Gerhard and Walter after they left the Neumann's home. Gerhard and Walter felt the Lord's guidance and the influence of the Holy Ghost very much. They were grateful they could be a tool in the Lord's hand to bring the good news of the restored gospel to these people. With great anticipation they looked forward to the meeting on Sunday.

While at work one noon hour, Walter looked over to Father Neumann's working place. He saw Father Neumann had bowed his head in prayer and blessed his food. Walter had never seen him doing this before. Walter knew the spirit of the Lord was with them and that the family was earnestly investigating the Word of God. Walter had very little time to talk with him at work, but Father Neumann told Walter once that he had never been as interested in the scriptures as he was now.

The branch had Sacrament meeting as usual. After the meeting, they had the adult Sunday School class. The children had Sunday School in the morning, but there was not yet enough room to have the children and adult class at the same time. They were still remodeling. Walter was nervous and excited. Nervous, because he had to present the lesson, and excited to see if they would really come. Gerhard and Walter walked up and down the hallway in between the house entrance door and the door where they held their meetings. They looked out of the door to see if their expected visitors would come, but they didn't see anyone. It was about time to start the Sunday School class when they saw a group of people coming toward the building. They recognized their expected visitors. Gerhard and Walter were excited and thanked the Lord. They welcomed the guests, greeted them cordially and introduced them to their members. The congregation sang the hymn, "O my Father." After the prayer Walter presented the lesson, resuming where the Witnesses had ended last Wednesday. While the LDS members took an active part in the meeting, not one of the guests participated. In closing Walter invited them to come again.

After they and our members had left, the Neumann family and a few others remained. They discussed the meeting and especially the hymn, "O My Father." The daughter, Gertrud Neumann, was deeply touched by the message of the hymn and wanted to know more. She felt there was something here that her church didn't have. The spirit was strong and they departed late. These are the words to that hymn:

O my father, thou that dwellest
In the high and glorious place,
When shall I regain thy presence
and again behold thy face?
In thy holy habitation, did my spirit once reside?
In my first primeval childhood, was I nurtured near thy side?

For a wise and glorious purpose
Thou hast placed me here on earth
And withheld the recollection
of my former friends and birth:
Yet oft-times a secret some-thing,
whispered "You're a stranger here,"
And I felt that I had wandered from a more exalted sphere.

I had learned to call thee Father,
thru thy spirit from on high,
but until the key of knowledge
was restored I knew not why.
In the heavens are parents single?

No, the thought makes reason stare!
Truth is reason; truth eternal
tells me I've mother there.

When I leave this frail existence,
when I lay this mortal by,
Father, Mother may I meet you
in your royal courts on high?
Then at length, when I have completed,
all you send me forth to do,
with your mutual approbation
let me come and live with you.

Text: Eliza R. Snow, Music: James McGranahan

Arriving at the same time they had previous met on Wednesday in the Neumann's home, they found no one from the Jehovah's Witness leadership there. Apparently the Neumann family had broken with them. Gerhard conducted and presented the lesson from that time until his transfer. Elder Walter Luskin replaced him and Walter accompanied Elder Walter Luskin. They added Frau Waldheim to their investigators. Walter's family had known her for some time. Elder Luskin served there for just a short time before a couple replaced him. They didn't stay long either and they were not replaced. After Elder Luskin received his transfer, Walter continued the cottage meetings in the Neumann home until five former members of the Witnesses became members of the LDS church through baptism.

Walter was on his way home from work. He was approaching the Ravensburg street where the Neumann family lived, the thought hit him very clearly: "Go visit the Neumanns," but Walter passed by the street and continued on. The thought came again. Walter stoped and debated in his mind what to do. He had seen the Neumanns on Sunday and in the cottage meeting which he still held with the former Witnesses, but he followed the inspiration and turned and went to the Neumann's home. When Walter knocked on the door

Mother Neumann opened, and in a suprised voice said, “Brother Rohloff the Lord has sent you. We have the Leader of the Jehovahs Witnesses from Berlin here. He is trying to get us back into his congregation.” Walter entered the living room, and Father Neumann introduced him to the visitor. They had a discussion and the spirit of the Lord helped Walter to explain the restored gospel. He found out that the Eberfelder Bible the Witnesses used, was different from Neumann‘s Lutheren Bible translation. Walter expressed how grateful he was for having the Book of Mormon to clarify the differences between the Eberfelder and the Martin Luther translation.

(Continued on page 206)

Gertrud Neumann Pielmann:“My Testimony” (given 1994)

Even as a little girl interesred me the questions: where was I before my birth, why I am here, where I am going when I die? Of course I went with my questions to my mother. Only for the question: “Where I am going after I die?”she could give me an answer: “To heaven, to our dear God.“

All members of our family belonged to the Lutheran Church. My mother knew there was a God and she taught us children to pray. At least before we went to bed we would say our well learned formal prayers. There came days where these questions stood in the background, but always when someone talked about God or Church, I was interested.

Then it happened after World War II at the end of 1946 or beginning 1947 a young man knocked on our door and told us, he had a joyous message. He was a Jehovah Witness. He was overjoyed to find someone who listened to his message. He explained to me the teaching of his church so graphic and so convincing that I agreed to be baptized. I was at that time eighteen years old and not so entlightened as the youth is now.

I had so many questions no one could answer to my satisfaction, but one thing I remember as if it was today, right after my baptism I knew it was not right what I had done. I was not happy, not satisfied, but sad and unhappy. Before I was baptized, I thought I would understand everything better and maybe get an answer to my questions, but it was not so. Every evening I prayed: "God when you are there, did I do the right thing? Why I am not joyous, happy and content? Please show me the way, what I can do, to feel that I did right. Often I sat in bed and cried.

God heard my prayers, and in a wonderful way He gave me an answer. Some weeks past, when a young man returned from a prisoner of war camp and looked for work, he found two places, but which one of the two should he take? He believed in a living God and asked him and took the same company my father worked for. He took every opportunity to give his testimony of the gospel to every employee.

My father talked about him at home and I wanted to know, to what church this man belonged. My father asked, but after work he forgot the name and told me he belonged to the demons. It couldn't be and my father asked the next day again. He wasn't a demon, he was a Mormon. I didn't know the Mormons, never heard about them.

It was of interest to me and I asked my father to invite this young man to our home. At that time we had the meetings of the Jehovah's Witnesses in our home. The young man accepted the invitation right away and asked if he could bring somebody else. So it came, that my father's colleague, it was Brother Walter Rohloff, and his friend Gerhard Kupitz, a missionary who worked here, attended the meetings of the Jehovah's Witnesses in the home of my parents.

After the meeting I asked the two brethren my questions. They told me about the world of spirits from our pre-mortal life. They talked about our life purpose, that it was a time of probation and one day we will return to our heavenly home. In short, they explained the plan of salvation, the plan to be happy. When I heard this it was as if I had always known this, maybe subconscious. It had to be explained to me again. I was so grateful and felt so content. I received an answer to my questions.

On the 11th of March 1848, I visited a meeting of our church for the 1st time and on the 8th of August, 1948, I was baptized. My mother was baptized with me and Sister Auguste Knorp, who was at that time a friend of our family and in an advanced age. Three other friends of the church were baptized.

I was at that time so enthused and I thought all my friends and my coworkers would feel that same way. I took every upportunity to tell them from my conversion. How disappointed was I when they only smiled and started to tease me. It hurt and gave me pain. I considered changing the company I worked for. Again and again I prayed to my Father in Heaven to help me to find another place of work, but the Heavenly Father gave me the strength to remain. With time my coworkers quit teasing, the conditions improved and my work was more appreciated. Today I know I shouldn't change my place of work.

At that time a new colleague was hired. He was just released from a prisoner of war camp and was hired to drive the manager. Our manager told him: "That girl in front belonged to an impossible sect." That interested him and so it came to gospel discourses. He accepted the gospel and was baptized and became my husband.

It sounds all so easy, but without the help from our Heavenly Father and His blessings I wouldn't stand here and have the strength to be faithful and firm. I would like to tell you I found the church and how beautiful the ways of the Lord are, which he has prepared for us.

The testimony we have from the gospel is made of many building blocks. When someone would ask me which building block is for me the most precious, I have to say again and again, it is the way of my conversion. From this I learned that the Lord hears and answers prayers, that the Lord needs man to help mankind. We need our voices to give our testimony and our hands and legs to help.

I ask the Lord to give all of us the necessary strength to be true and faithful and to be willing to be a tool in his hands.

(Continuation from page 204)

The visitor stated he had read the "Book of the Mormons." Walter clarified the title of the Book of Mormon, but he repeated the title in the same way as he did before. Walter told him if he had read the Book of Mormon in the same way, as he read the title he couldn't learn anything. During the ongoing discussion the man couldn't control his temper and Father Neumann had to ask him to leave his apartment. After visiting and praying with the Neumanns, Walter went home.

The district president, Walter Krause, frequently visited the branch and was always a welcome guest. Gerhard and Walter enjoyed introducing him to the investigators. Brother Krause had a great testimony of the gospel and knew the scriptures better than anyone else Walter knew. Quoting the scriptures freely in his talks and discussions, it was a joy to listen to him. He not only knew the scriptures, but he was also well versed in German literature. It seemed to Walter he knew Goethe's Faust from the beginning to the end. One Sunday, after the branch had lost their missionaries, Brother Walter Krause took Walter aside and asked him to become the branch president. Walter told him he would accept but he felt very awkward in that position. Walter told him he knew the scriptures, but had yet not learned how to teach them to others. He told Walter he would learn and that the Lord would help him. There was still some time before the sacrament meeting started. Walter went into a small, windowless room, knelt down and presented his problems to the Lord. He told the Lord he had accepted the call but needed His help to present inspired thoughts from Him. Walter was really concerned and asked the Lord for help. Walter had asked the district president for Brother Otto Krakow as his first counselor and for some time to name his second counselor. Walter and Brother Krakow were presented to the membership and the members accepted them as their new leaders. Brother Krakow was asked to speak and Walter followed him.

Walter started with his talk as the same old, shaky Walter. Suddenly he felt the spirit coming over him and he was able to express himself clearly, without any inhibitions. The Lord had answered his prayer. From that day on he was able to express himself well. After the meeting Otto and Walter were set apart by Brother Walter Krause. Walter congratulated Otto on his new calling and Otto looked into Walter's eyes and said, "I appreciate the trust you have in me. From this day on I will keep the Word of Wisdom." He did. He was not only Walter's faithful counselor, but they became best friends. He was an untiring worker who gave all he had to the Lord's work. Walter learned much from him. Without him Walter couldn't have done the work he later did. He even lent Walter his bike, in those days a valuable possession, when Walter went preaching the gospel to nearby cities and villages. None of them had much, but they helped one another.

Agnes and Otto Krakow
Otto was branch president in Neubrandenburg for 25 years

At work Walter had made good progress. The few years he had worked before helped. He was asked to make fixtures, molds and patterns. They had repaired or remodeled the machines they used in their production because the Russians had shipped the good machines to Russia. Walter was not a member of the union, but had to attend their meetings. In the meetings the employees were indoctrinated with communist doctrine. Everyone was trained to think along the party line. Everyone had to be careful what he/she said. Walter's supervisor told him in one conversation that he would not hesitate to put Walter in prison if he did or said something against the party. Walter had some discussions about the gospel with him and the owner of the company, but God didn't exist for them. Everyone knew of people who had objected to the party and were picked up at night and never heard of again.

Everybody looked for food. The trains to the villages were overloaded with people who visited the farmers searching for food. While there were some improvements from the past years, hunger was still around. Money was not worth much; trading worked best. Walter gave these problems very little attention because his mother took care of him. Many times Walter took carrots or beets to work for lunch. Two of his colleagues started evening school to become an engineer. They invited him to join and participate in the classes. Walter thought it over, but declined. To be accepted in college he would have to deny his church affiliation. To be a member of the party would have helped. Walter would not be able to work, study for a degree and do his church calling. His goal was to strengthen the church in this area and bring the good news of the restored gospel to the people. Walter had not forgotten the promise he had made to God.

Once at home Walter was so involved working to make a living and in church bringing the gospel to interested people that he didn't do much letter writing, but after a while he wrote to his favorite family from Schneidemuehl who were now living in Cottbus. They returned his greetings by inviting Walter to visit them. Walter was excited to see the Birth family again and took a week vacation during the last days of March 1948. He used the crowded railroad to visit with the Birth family. There was great joy as they met. Walter had always enjoyed his visits. They had a nice apartment now and Father Birth worked hard even though he had lost his right arm. He already had a large business in town. Of course, they had much to talk about. They shared their story with Walter of all that had happened since he had last seen them.

18

THE BIRTH FAMIY ESCAPING THE RUSSIAN ARMY

Walter had visited with the Birth family for Christmas 1944 and left shortly after to return to his unit on the German western front. Father Birth (51 years old) had already been drafted at that time. The family was a little helpless without their father. Many people left the town to avoid being present when the Russian army arrived. All the refugees who came through the town reported the terrible things they had gone through. Ruth, Edith, Irmgard and Christel had asked their mother to leave, too, but she was afraid she wouldn't see her girls alive again. In their uncertainty and fear they asked the Lord in prayer for help. Miraculously, the next day their neighbor visited and told them he would be taking a train to Berlin and could take Mother Birth and the small children along. It was the answer to their prayer. The older girls convinced their mother to leave. They would stay and keep their business going, and assured their mother the Lord would protect them. Mother Birth took the train with her daughters: Margaret, Eva and Brigitte and her sons: Werner and Peter. From Berlin they traveled to Dresden. Some time back a friend of the family had offered his house in Dresden-Doelschen to them for refuge. The plan was for the entire family to eventually meet there.

By law they had to keep the grocery store open. Edith and Christel took care of that. Irmgard worked in their father's glass business and Ruth returned to work in a government office. The girls saw many of their neighbors packing and fleeing westward. They would have liked to do the same but they were afraid of the punishment they would receive for closing the store and they didn't want to be cowards. They felt they would be safe for a while.

How wrong they were they found out when the Russian's bombarded the city two days after their mother had left. The girls started to prepare to leave following that bombardment. They packed a children's sled with food and warm clothing. It was January, 1945, and sleds were the best transportation. Edith's cousin, Wilford Kindt, came on his bike and asked if he could go with them. The military police had let his stepmother with the small children and his sister, Sigrid, leave. Wilford was fifteen years old and the police wouldn't let him leave. He was told he should become a soldier and defend the city.

The sisters also took their maid, a girl from Ukraine, along. She was more fearful than the sisters because she knew about Stalin and was full of forebodings. Edith took the scriptures belonging to her and her father along. At the last minute she thought to take her wedding dress and the ration cards (theirs and the ones they had collected from their customers). They took a last look, not realizing they would never see their cozy home again. There was no time for sentimental thought however, only time to hurry out. Their decision to leave was inspired by our Heavenly Father.

The sisters loved this town, the surrounding land, and the forest with the beautiful lakes. Only a short bike ride away they could go swimming. They had grown up here and it was a terrible feeling for them to leave everything behind. Everything in their home had a meaning for them. Here they had sung, played games, and made music. Here they had had a harmonious family life. Walter remembered well that as he had left the family to go back to the front, their father was playing the piano and all were standing around the piano singing, "God be with you till we meet again."

Big grenade craters covered the streets, but as the sisters traveled through the city the shelling had stopped. The streets were full of people trying to escape before the Russian army could catch up with them. While they were still in Schneidemuehl, Edith met one of their customers. She told Edith, "I am in the Nazi party and not permitted to leave town. Why don't you go to my brother in Lebehnke? He has a large farm and will gladly take you in."A neighbor, Frau Rieger, was with them. On her sled she had a large down comforter. It started to slip off the sled and Christel gave her a hand to fasten it. At that moment someone called, "Tanks ahead." Everyone went for cover. In this confusion the girls lost Christel and Christel lost Frau Rieger. Christel saw the girls in the distance, but because of the large crowd of fleeing people she was not able to reach her sisters. Now she was all by herself. She had nothing with her, not even money. Money wouldn't have made a difference anyway. It was almost worthless. The only thing she had in her winter coat pocket was a sandwich.

Edith, Ruth and Irmgard felt terrible and looked everywhere but couldn't find Christel. They worried about her and hoped to see her at the farmer's place in Lebehnke, but in Lebehnke there was no Christel. Their only consolation was that she had the name and address of Mrs. Guenzel in Dresden, where they were planning to meet.

The sisters walked through the deep snow on the highway near the Kueddow River. It was about 20 degree minus centigrade. They were warmly dressed, but their shoes were not made for walking in the snow. Pulling the sled was hard on them, but they didn't feel it much. All they could think about was getting away from the Russian army. They stopped in Lebehnke and found out the farmer was packing too. Unknown to them, the Russian army had already conquered the small town of Schoenfeld, only eight miles east on the other side of the Kueddow River. Every able-bodied person was fleeing before the Russian army.

Men from the German army had set up quarters in the farmer's house. The farmer made room for the sisters and Wilford so they could stay in the living room for the night. Early in the morning the farmer left with only what he could place on his wagon. There were still horses in the stable, cows needed to be milked, and chickens running around. The farmer left everything behind as he tried to escape the Russian army. After the farmer had left, the German soldiers made themselves comfortable and started killing the chickens. The soldiers would have loved to see the sisters stay with them, but the sisters were not interested in becoming their maids.

They could hear the thundering guns coming close. What should they do? If they continued on their way and walked, they surely would soon be overtaken by the Russian army. Then they remembered there was a railroad station about one and a half miles away. Maybe there was a train that they could take. Edith asked Wilford, who had a bike, to go and see.

There was a train at the station and Wilford was told to enter because the train would be leaving any minute. He explained to the men that he would go and tell his cousins and they would all come back. The men told Wilford he was a fool. "What is more important to you, saving your life or losing your life with your cousins?" But bless Wilford, he took the risk and hurried back as fast as he could to tell the sisters there was a train. After the train had unloaded the soldiers, the train would be filled with refugees and a few officers. He said that by now the train may have gone. Edith said, "The train is an answer to our prayer. If God will, we will reach the train."

They hurried as fast as they could. The soldiers at the farm had given the sisters boots to wear. The boots were warmer but it was harder to walk. From a distance they could hear the whistle of the train giving the signal to leave. They were just a short distant from their goal. Would they make it? They could hardly travel any faster. Then soldiers from a nearby anti-aircraft unit saw their effort and came to help. With their help the group made it to the train. They were barely inside when the train started to move. Out of breath and exhausted but emotionally moved, their thanks went up to our Heavenly Father.

Unknown to the sisters, Christel was in the same train. In the confusion in Schneidemuehl when she couldn't find her sisters she went on her way to Lebehnke. She knew her sisters would be going that way, but she didn't remember the name of the farmer. She had gone straight to the railroad station. She sat there all night waiting for a train to come. In the morning a freight train arrived, loaded with soldiers to reinforce the defense. The soldiers were unloaded and wounded soldiers and officers were taken on the train. Then the fleeing people who crowded the railroad station were permitted to enter the train. The sisters never saw Christel until they all met in Dresden-Doelschen.

Under normal conditions it took the train from Schneidemuehl to Berlin two to three hours. It took this train eight long days. The conditions in the freight cars were very poor. There was no food, no heat, no water and no toilets. The sisters had brought food with them from home and they shared it with other people. The three sisters were young and strong and they helped wherever help was needed. When the train stopped at railroad stations, they took half-frozen babies out to get them warm again. Babies, small children, and the elderly had the hardest time and many died. They were asked many times if they were from the Red Cross. Of course they were not, but they felt good that they could give help and comfort to people in need. It was February and very cold. Everybody was tired, hungry and cold. The train was so slow that people were afraid the Russians would catch up with them. Some people thought they would be faster if they left the train and started walking. Edith never considered walking. She thought the train was still the safest place. Some of the soldiers and Ruth went to look for straw and food at various stops. When they came back sometimes the train was gone. They went along the tracks and caught up with the train.

The train made many detours and in Neustettin many high ranking officers came into the train. They were really a blessing to all refugees. They had to be in Berlin as fast as possible and that gave their train priority over others. Because of that they passed by trains which had been standing at railroad stations for many days.

Edith wrote in her diary: "It was one o'clock in the morning. Everybody around me was asleep. I was sitting on my hard sled and my back was hurting. The train had been standing here at this station already for more than 20 hours and they didn't know why. We had no radio and we didn't know how far away the Russian army was from us. What was our fate? The fear of falling into the hands of the Russian army never left us, but when I prayed, a calm feeling came over me. While sitting with my thoughts, I heard refugees singing in another train. Death had taken their little baby and they found solace in this hymn:

Lord take my hand and lead me upon life's way
Direct, protect, and feed me from day to day
Without your grace and favor I go astray;
So take my hand, O Savior and lead the way.

Lord, when the tempest rages, I need not fear,
For you, the Rock of Ages, are always near.
Close by your side abiding, I fear no foe,
For when your hand is guiding, in peace I go.

Lord, when the shadows lengthen and night has come,
I know that you will strengthen my steps toward home.
And nothing can impede me, O blessed friend!
So take my hands and lead me unto the end.

(Text; Julie K. von Hausmann in German, Music: Friedrich Silcher)

A melancholy feeling came over me. Tears were rolling down my cheeks. I remembered this beautiful hymn from the days when we were singing it at home or in church, but now we were sitting here in the dark and the future was bleak. But somehow this hymn lifted me up and made me feel good. The horrible pictures of other refugees who had contact with the Russians faded and a positive outlook returned, knowing the Lord was with us. Standing here at the railroad station and knowing the Russian army came nearer with every hour had aggravated my fear, but now I felt good in the knowledge that with the Lord's help we would reach our destination. When the train started rolling again, my fear was minimized."

After eight days they entered Berlin and came right into an air raid. Their train stopped outside the station and entered after the air raid was over. They changed trains in Berlin and traveled to Dresden as if it was in peace time. They couldn't believe it. It was warmer here and no snow. They didn't know what to do with their sleds. They took the sleds with them to the last station of the streetcar.

Here another problem arose: How could they get up the mountain to Mrs. Guenzel's home? A passing man saw their dilemma and asked them where they wanted to go. They told him, "To Doelschen."

"To Doelschen, that's on top of the mountain." he said. "Stay here and I'll get my car and take you up." The sisters were more than grateful for the offer. Having been nine full days on the road without a clean bath and then walking in this warm weather in their winter clothing didn't make it comfortable for them. The friendly man returned and drove the sisters up to Doelschen. Mother Birth was very thankful to our Heavenly Father to see her three girls. She felt it was a miracle the three made it to Dresden unmolested. Christel had wired a telegram from Berlin. She would be arriving that same night. It seemed for now that all of the family except for their father would be safely together in Dresden.

Doelschen was a small village in the mountain overlooking Dresden and was about 15 minutes away from Dresden. Dresden was a beautiful town, maybe the most beautiful of all towns in Germany. The famous "Zwinger" and other irreplaceable architectural buildings, historical and fine arts museum were well known in the world. The surrounding mountains, river and forest were beautiful and the Birth family loved it. They wanted to stay there until the war was over and they could go home again. It turned out much differently than they had planned. As they say in Germany, "With fate you can't make an eternal contract, misfortune comes fast."

On the night of the 13thof February 1945, the air raid sirens woke everyone up. Edith slept in a neighbor's house but it was close enough to reach her family. The rest of the family had never experienced an air attack. Edith remembered the air attacks in Berlin when she was a missionary and living there. She went over to her family to calm everyone down, but she wàs frightened too. This attack was far worse than the attacks she had experienced in Berlin. Some windows in their house were broken and the roof was damaged. They were lucky. Doelschen was not the target, but downtown Dresden and the railroad station with the thousands of refugees were.

After the attack they went out of the house and looked over to Dresden. The city was burning like a torch. The Allies had dropped explosive and incendiary bombs. These bombs set the buildings and even the streets on fire. Fleeing people were sucked into the fire. These people became living torches. After the attack some of the men in the village went to the city to help to extinguish the fire and to help the people who were buried in the rubble.

Shortly after the first, a second air raid started. It was like the first but much worse. Not one of the men who went to help returned home. Because of the large amount of refugees in town, no one really knows how many people lost their lives. The estimates go as high as 35,000 people.

After the two terrible air raids, Mother Birth, the children, and Mrs. Guenzel were so scared they didn't want to stay another night, but where could they go and find a peaceful place? They didn't know anyone here in the village and they hadn't visited the LDS branch in town yet, but mother was determined that she wouldn't stay here another day. Then Edith thought of a missionary companion she had in Berlin, Gretel Dzirson who lived in Geyersdorf in the Ore Mountains. They packed their few belongings and walked the 15km to the nearest working railroad station. No bus or streetcars were going so they had to walk. It was a walk through the ruined and damaged streets, a horrible picture. It was very hard for the 50-year-old Mother Birth. She was not in good physical condition but she wanted to go and the kids helped her on the way. Shortly before Pirma they boarded a train. They changed trains a couple of times. After two days, they arrived in Buchholz-Annaberg.

One train stop was especially well engraved in Edith's memory. The people in the town of Grossenhain wanted to help the refugees aboard the train. Edith asked the women if they were working for the Red Cross. They told her, "No we are not." They said they noticed the train coming through their town and they recognized that the people on the train were refugees who had to leave their homes and land. They felt sorry for them and they wanted to help. They asked the people in town to make sandwiches in the evening and in the morning girls would pick up the sandwiches and bring them to the train to feed the refugees. All in the train were impressed with the goodness of these people.

In Annaberg Edith called Sister Gretel Dzirson in Geyersdorf, a village nearby, and explained to her the misery her family was in. Gretel didn't know a thing about the Birth family's arrival prior to that call. She organized her home so that every one of the eleven tired family members had a place to sleep. The next day, Edith, with Brother Gerhard Kupitz, who was recovering from a war injury and was in town, walked over to the mayor of the village and explained their situation. With the help of this friendly man everyone in the family found a place to stay. It was heartwarming to see how these people were willing to help. Of course because of the size of this family, they had to split the family up. They got rooms with different families, but everyone in the family had a roof over his head, furniture to use and a bed to sleep in.

They had no more air raids like in Dresden but they had low flying airplanes which would shoot at everything that moved. Many times they were attacked by these planes on their way from Geyersdorf to Annaberg to attend their church meetings. Seeking shelter meant falling to the ground in their Sunday dresses. Because of the danger involved, some Sundays they would stay in Geyersdorf and attend their meetings in the Schaarschmidt family home. From the first day the family liked the Ore Mountain region. They loved to walk through the mountains, the fields of flowers, and the green meadows. Living there for six months was a special experience for them. They loved the people and they felt so good to be with members of the church. Yes, mother Birth missed everything she had lost, her home, her business, and especially her husband, but she had her family. For the first time, she began to study the Book of Mormon. She read it from the beginning to the end. She gained a great testimony of the truthfulness of the church.

Edith immediately looked for work. The butcher's wife would soon deliver her baby and needed help to replace her in the business. Edith got the job and served the butcher's customers. Everyone had ration cards except the Russian soldiers who occupied the land now. They took what they needed and sometimes with force. One day Edith had five visitors from the Russian and the Czech army. They wanted all the sausage she had. She gave all that she had, but the soldiers were not satisfied; they wanted more. Edith told them she didn't have more. The soldiers told her they would check and if they found more they would kill her. Edith's heart was pounding but she stayed with her story. After the soldiers left the owner came and told her he had watched what was going on. Unknown to Edith he had worked all night and had made sausages. He had plenty. Had the soldiers looked through the house they would have found the sausage and Edith would have been in big trouble. Edith thanked the Lord for watching over her.

The next day Edith had another problem. While she was at work Russian soldiers went into her bedroom and stole her dresses and her winter coat. Here in the Ore Mountain region people were poor, but trusted each other and left their doors unlocked. Church members came and helped Edith. They had material and they sewed two dresses for her. Civilization had caught up with the local citizen and they had to start locking their doors.

No one had heard from Father Birth. Everyone knew Schneidemuehl was a fortress and plenty of fighting had been going on. Now it was occupied by the Russians, but that was all that they knew. Of course they prayed every day for the well being of their father and hoped he was still alive, even though he was probably a prisoner of war. A shock came when their cousin Wilford Kindt got a letter from a friend. He reported he had heard that Father Birth had been killed in action and was buried in Koenigsblick, a forest near Schneidemuehl. The girls wanted to protect their mother and tried to find a way to gently tell her the sad news. Mother Birth had already lost two sons, Gerhard and Nephi, in war action and now her husband. They all tried not to show their sadness and sorrow to their mother. When the children were alone, sadness overcame them and tears rolled down their cheeks. It was hard to take. They all loved their father dearly.

Somehow Mother Birth felt her daughters were keeping something from her and wouldn't tell. Mother knew Edith kept a diary and she went to the house where Edith was living to look for the diary in Edith's room. She took along Edith's brother Peter, then six years old. She found the diary and found what she was looking for.

She went with Peter to her room and cried and cried and prayed for a long time. After a time, a certain feeling came over her that her husband and the children's father wasn't dead but needed the prayers of the family. She called all family members together and they decided they would fast and pray for their father every Friday. From that day on the family fasted and prayed every Friday for thirteen weeks.

Mother Birth was often inspired by feelings and by the still small voice. In 1942 her mother was working in the field when a light rain fell and she got wet. She didn't feel well and was lying in her room in bed. The family was sitting together in the living room when all of a sudden Mother Birth jumped up with the words "Mother is dying." She went into her mother's room and found her mother had died.

In 1944 the family hadn't heard from Nephi who was on the battle front in Russia. They started to worry about him. Then one night mother woke up hearing a voice which said, "A royal heart ceased to beat." She knew right away that Nephi was killed. It was true. Nephi never returned home from the war.

Many in the LDS branch didn't understand why they were fasting for their father. They said, "You know he is dead, why are you fasting?" Mother was not moved by their remarks. She knew father needed help and she would keep fasting until she felt it wasn't needed any more. No one could take away this power of faith. She didn't make her children fast. She gave them an option to fast or not. All her children supported her and their father and kept fasting every Friday.

The war was finally over after almost six years. Germany surrendered on the 8th of May 1945. The Russian and American troops met on the Elbe River. All of Germany was occupied by the Allied or Russian troops. Germany was divided between the victorious nations: Russia, USA, Great Britain and France. All the land east of the Oder River was given to Poland, except a part from East Prussia that went to Russia. All Germans who were still living in this land had to leave. Germany was over-populated before the war and now it became a real problem. The Birth property was now in Poland and there was no way they could return. They now belonged to the large group of homeless people. They were still living in Geyersdorf but the arrangements were not ideal. The large family was separated in many households.

In July, 1945, they had visitors from the LDS branch in Cottbus. Brothers Fritz Lehnig and Brother Walter Krause invited all refugees to move to Cottbus. Brother Paul Langheinrich from the mission presidency was with them. In Cottbus the brethren had converted a part of their meeting house into a refugee camp. Many LDS members coming from the eastern provinces, which were now part of Russia or Poland, found a place to stay there. All LDS refugees living in the Ore Mountains followed the counsel of the brethren, but it was hard on them to leave Geyersdorf. They had lived there for six months and loved it. However, they realized their current living conditions- being guest, no food, clothing or stamps - couldn't continue. They felt this move was an answer to their prayers.

Edith wrote in her diary about the trip. Here is what she wrote: "There were 31 women and children (including two babies) and one young man who had lost one leg in the war. We left on the 17th of July 1945. Two young sister missionaries Lucy Meyer and Ingrid Bendler were in charge of leading us to Cottbus. My sister Ruth and I helped. It was a large undertaking because no regular trains were running. In Annaberg we boarded a train which would take us to Riesa. It was raining hard and the glass in most of the train windows was broken. Some windows were covered with cardboard. The roof was leaking and passengers who had umbrellas opened them. As they traveled through the cities we saw the damage the air raids had done. Whole blocks of homes were damaged or destroyed.

19

THE MORMON REFUGEE SHELTER

It was terrible what the war had done to our beautiful homeland. It took us all day to reach Riesa, only about 80 miles from where we boarded the train. Here in Riesa we stayed all night at the railroad station. It was the safest place to be. Thousands of people were still on the road looking for a place to settle. The next morning we were hungry but Sister Wetzker helped us. She still had some cream of wheat she shared with us. We found some empty cans, made a fire and we had a good tasting soup. Then we waited for a train. At 12 o'clock a passenger train arrived, overcrowded like every train. We managed to get everybody into the cars. We had to help our mother get in through the window. The train carried us only to Pristewitz. Again we had to get out. We obtained some potatoes and beans and again cooked soup on an open fire. Then we waited. I will never forget that day. Tired, hungry and dirty, we were waiting for a train that would carry us nearer to Cottbus. It was getting dark and finally we got a message. The next train would go to Cottbus. What a happy thought! At 10 pm a train arrived, but it was not a passenger train; it was a freight train. It was a train with Russian soldiers. Fear gripped us. There were many young girls in our group and the Russian soldiers didn't have a good reputation. Rape was common." (End from Edith's diary)

Why did they take the train? Another night on the street was just too scary. Edith doesn't know about the others but she never prayed so long or so constantly in her life. What a scene it was with the refugees sleeping in the same car as the Russian soldiers. They all lay down on the straw, the soldiers on one side of the car and they on the other. Her mother couldn't sleep and was watching everything. What she saw amazed her. Every one lay down except the Russian officer. He was up keeping watch and if a soldier so much as raised his head, he would order him to lie down. He was their guardian angel. Nothing happened that night.

The train still didn't arrive in Cottbus, but stopped in Ruhnau. At 6 am in the morning another freight train arrived loaded with coal. They climbed into the open cars. It was not very comfortable to sit on the hard coal and in the open air, but they were on their way to Cottbus. They were very grateful for the Lord's help and guidance.

The camp in Cottbus used the Church meeting rooms and was prepared by the city to give refugees a place to stay. After Walter was wounded in Russia and recuperating in a hospital in Kirchain (near Cottbus) he had visited the branch in Cottbus in August, 1944, and Brother Fritz Lehnig showed him what the city had done. He told Walter then that this would be a good place for the saints who had to leave their homes in Germany's eastern provinces to find a place to stay. The city had placed bunk beds in the large meeting room and had built in sanitary installations. Little did Walter know that one day his friends, the Birth family, would be homeless and find shelter here. Brother Fritz Lehnig cared like a father for all these refugee families. Most of the members in the camp had no ration cards, but he provided food for all. He had connections with the Russians and also with the farmers. Tirelessly he worked and risked his life for the stranded members.

After Edith and Ruth took their mother and their younger brothers and sister to the LDS camp in Cottbus they returned to Annaberg. At that time not all of the Birth family gathered in Cottbus. Irmgard and Christel each had a job (with the help of Brother Waechtler) on a farm in Rittnitz. Edith, Ruth and Eva were called on a mission to do genealogical research in the Ore Mountains. With help from Sister Erika Fassmann they went from one parish to another and collected genealogical information. The girls didn't broadcast they were Mormons, because some ministers didn't give

Mormons permission to do research in their church records. In one parish the minister found out about their LDS faith and he wanted to talk to them. They didn't know for what they should prepare. What would he ask? They fasted and prayed until they met him. It was a very interesting meeting. Edith recorded:"We discussed the teachings of the LDS church. He was very surprised when we discussed the Christ-Jehovah concept, whom we believe, as he did, to be the same person. After our discussion he praised us for the knowledge we had of the Bible. He let us continue our research." (End of Edith's report). After six months of genealogical research they returned to Cottbus.

During a visit to Zwickau, Edith met Brother Schulz from Berlin. He told her that he met her father in the mission home. He was released from the Russian prisoner of war camp and looked very different than before. He had lost weight and had lost his right arm. He looked old. That was the first time the family heard anything positive about their father. He wasn't dead. He wasn't buried in Koenigsblick. He was alive. He was on his way home. He went to the mission home in Berlin and there, of course, he found where his family was living.

On the 8th of August 1945, Father Birth arrived in Cottbus. It is hard to describe how the family felt when they saw their father. How Mother Birth must have felt when she saw her husband and the father of her children come home. Her feelings were right. She had continued to believe that her husband was alive and would return. Now he was back. She learned that during the time when the family was fasting for him, their father had been deathly ill with an infection in his arm. The Russian doctors tried to save him with medication, but his condition got worse. For thirteen weeks he lay in bed with a high fever and lost eighty pounds. The lady doctor thought he would die any day. She felt the last thing they could do to help was to amputate his right arm. After the amputation his condition improved from day to day. The Lord had heard and answered the family's fasting and prayers. Father Birth's life was spared. His return brought joy to everyone in the camp.

On his second day at home Father Birth went to get permission to start his own business. This would be his third start. His first was right after the First World War. Then the little family was living and doing business in Podgorz by Torun, Posnan. This area later became part of Poland. When all Germans who didn't become Polish citizens had to leave the land, they fled to Schneidemuehl. Here, Father Birth, after some years, started his own business with the help of his son, Gerhard. Later Nephi and Irmgard helped too. He lost everything during the war, even his right arm. All that didn't slow down Father Birth. He started a third time. When Walter visited the Birth family in 1948, Father Birth already had the largest glass business in town. His son Werner was his right arm. Only thirteen years old, Werner had become an excellent craftsman.

Not only Werner, but also Irmgard had learned the trade. She helped in the business as she had done in Schneidemuehl. On the same day he started his business he looked for and found an apartment. He found one in fair condition close to the church. It needed repair work but they could move in right away. After Father and Mother Birth had moved in, they went to visit their daughters Ruth, Edith and Eva who were still living in Annaberg and Irmgard and Christel who were living in Rittmitz. Their reunion was great. Tears of joy rolled down their cheeks. Prayers of thanks were offered from grateful children to their Father in Heaven. The Lord's protection made this reunion possible.

The intention for the Birth family was to have every family member home for Christmas 1945. The three sisters, Ruth, Edith and Eva, wanted to do something special. From their meager ration cards they saved a portion of flour, sugar and margarine. They wanted to surprise the family and bake some Christmas cookies. They ate their potatoes without salt and the cabbage without fat. Then came the day they all returned home to the nice, large apartment rented and renovated in which to celebrate Christmas. Oh, were they hungry for something sweet. They had missed sweets for so long, it was a wonderful treat. The highlight of their Christmas celebration was they were all together again. They all were alive and healthy. They even had a Christmas tree. They didn't have much, but here they were, celebrating the birth of our Savior and looking forward to a better tomorrow.

On the 1st of March, Ruth Birth was called on a full time mission. She worked mainly in the mission home in Berlin. Berlin was surrounded by Russian occupied territory. Because it was Germany's capital city, the Allies had divided Berlin into four parts: the American, the English, the French and the Russian sections. The mission home was in the English section of the city, meaning in West Berlin. The Russian's didn't cooperate with the other Allied nations. There was now a West Berlin and an East Berlin. East Berlin and East Germany were now Russian sections. The mission staff, including the mission president, President Walter Stover, needed a special permit to enter East Berlin or East Germany. Ruth, after fulfilling a successful mission, she was released as the young women mission leader, didn't return home to Cottbus where her family was living. She was afraid if she left West Berlin she wouldn't be able to return. She worked for six months in the West German mission home and then went to work in England. She worked there for a time and then immigrated to the USA. She began what all in the family wanted to do and she helped some of her family to get sponsors to enter the USA.

Father Birth's business made good progress. When he started his business in the 1930s, he had Gerhard to help him and later Nephi. Now Irmgard (22) and Werner (13) worked with him. Work was plentiful but not material. Glass was hard to come by and most of the available glass was hand blown and of poor quality. As a substitute he used plastic which let some light, but didn't allow someone to look through.

Because of his past business experience, there were many business people who knew of his abilities and they did what they could to help him. An example is when Father Birth needed glass. He went to the factory but they couldn't give him glass because the machines didn't work and needed new bearings. He went to the bearing factory and they had bearings, but needed fabrics. Father Birth went and got fabrics and took them back to the bearing factory. They gave him the bearings and he gave those to the glass making company. They repaired their machines and he got the glass and did the work for his customers.

The glass association was contacted by the railroad. They

had a messy job to do and wanted it done for little pay. The association president asked the businesses in town if they wanted to do the job. No one wanted that messy and poorly paid job. Father Birth was a newcomer in town and they asked him if he would do it. He accepted the job. He knew he wouldn't make money on the job, but he also knew the railroad always had something that needed to be done. He did the job well and he got a great customer in return.

Edith's recollections of her personal experiences during those years are as follows. "In these days where hunger and illness were wide spread, you could hardly get a seat in a railroad car. People found a place anywhere in the car, standing room only inside and where anyone could stand the place was occupied. People even sat on the top of the train cars. Most people traveled to buy food. The saying was, "Soon the farmers will put carpets in their stables from all the items people exchanged to get food." Every train had a couple of cars which were reserved for the Russian army and no one else could use these cars.

We had an LDS district conference in Leipzig and my two sisters and I wanted to go. We couldn't find a seat anywhere on the train, so we sat down in the car reserved for the Russian army. To the conductor who checked the passengers I was bold and told him, "I am an "Americanski". I couldn't speak a word of English, but they left us alone. A Russian army officer came in and talked with me. I told him I was a Mormon and was on my way to a district conference. He told me there were Mormons in the Soviet Union, but very few. Later I learned he was right; there were LDS members in Armenia. We safely reached Leipzig and attended the conference. It was a great conference and I met many of my good friends. We also saw my cousin Walter Kindt who was in Leipzig on a full time mission.

My father came home from work one Saturday afternoon and my mother told him we had nothing to eat. We were out of bread, potatoes, flour-everything. Father didn't say a word. He went down on the street, paused a moment, and said, "Heavenly Father, thy servant David said, he was young and became old, but he never saw a righteous man's son crying for bread. Father, my children are hungry. My wife and I can fast, but the children need something to eat. Please help." He walked down the street passing the business they normally patronized and saw a single carrot laying in the window. He walked in and asked,

"Do you have carrots?"

"Yes," the business owner said:"how many do you need?" Normally you needed food stamps to buy these carrots. Father thought, "Don't hold back. Take as much as you can." And he said "100 pounds."

"Yes you can have it. Come by on Monday."

"No," my father said, "I need the carrots today."

"Well you better hurry, we close at 5 o'clock. I only have one request, don't tell anybody where you got the carrots."

Herzele's father went home and got Werner and a sack. They picked up the carrots. On the way back home Herzele's father sent a heartfelt

"Thank you" to our Heavenly Father for the carrots.

At home father said to my mother. "We have carrots! Please take 10 pounds out and send them over to Brother Schroeder. They have a large family, too, and surely need something to eat." Not only the Schroeder family got carrots but also other families had carrot soup that week. My parents would help wherever they could. Our house was open to others in Schneidemuehl and now here in Cottbus it was the same. No one would leave our house without being fed. We were always taught that what you give away will come back to you many times over.

In May, 1946, my nineteen years-old Sister Eva got sick with typhoid fever. She passed away in only eight days. She didn't want to die; she wanted to live, but our Heavenly Father called her home. Every day we visited with her in the hospital through a window. No one was permitted to get close. Every time we visited she would beg us, "Please don't let me die." It was very hard for us to see her fading away and not be able to do anything. All we could do was cry with her and pray.

My parents got a white casket for her and all the young girls from Mutual were dressed in white blouses. It was a beautiful funeral, but we missed her so very much. She was so young and so beautiful.

I remember very well my birthday in 1946. We had one pound of flour and we used it mostly for soup at lunch. We needed it for the soup but everyone in our family had a craving for cake, so we made a cake. We had two eggs. We had no sugar but we had a sweetener. We had no fat but we had a candle. We used the candle to grease the baking pan. We made the cake and it tasted delicious. We all enjoyed it even more because it was homemade. It's amazing what hunger does.

At another time I was sick with a high fever and diarrhea, but that didn't keep me from walking 14 km with Sister Wetzker to see a farmer. We knew we would get a free meal. It was only a watery soup with some flour or a warm potato with salt but it reduced the hunger and hunger won out over reason. All people lost weight and many people died of hunger typhus. My mother lost 50 pounds. I had a nutritional deficiency and every day I got a milk injection and vitamin tablets. I read in my diary, "New Years Eve 1946 and not even a dry slice of bread in the house."

I don't know if you can imagine what it meant to us when the first product from the LDS church welfare came to us. Things we hadn't seen for years were now on our table. There was wheat, canned milk, beans, sugar, corn and many other things. We didn't know what to do with the canned corn. We had never used corn to feed people; we used it only to feed animals. We learned fast to enjoy corn. On our ration card we got milk only when we were sick. We felt so rich and blessed with these products. We said a special prayer for the good people who had worked so hard and made it possible for us to enjoy the products. We said if we always had wheat to eat, we would be very grateful."

(End of Edith's report)

Walter enjoyed his stay with the Birth family. He was impressed with the progress they had made and how comfortable their place was. On Sunday he went to church with the family. Cottbus had a large branch of the LDS church. The room was filled and they had a beautiful choir. Besides this choir they had a youth and a children's choir. They started the day by attending the teacher training class. Father Birth, being an outstanding teacher, presented the lesson. When Father Birth wanted to write some thoughts on the black board Walter jumped up to help him, expecting him to have problems writing with his left hand. Father Birth pushed Walter out of the way with the words, "How can I learn to write using my left hand when you do it for me?" Walter didn't like being pushed but he was pleased that Father Birth still wanted to learn.

During Walter's visit he met the two newlywed couples. Christel Birth had wed Werner Koenig on the 6thof May, 1947, and Irmgard had married Werner's older brother, Heinz, on the 28thof November, 1947. Both lived in an apartment close by their parents. Christel didn't work and stayed home and Werner had his own upholstery business. Irmgard worked for her father and Heinz worked on developing a delivery business. As in the past, Walter spent his time mainly with Edith. She had kept in touch with him over the years and, as in the past, they studied together and did other activities. Walter enjoyed renewing his friendship with the Birth family and invited Edith and Brigitte to visit him at his home.

In August 1948, Brigitte and Edith visited Walter in Neubrandenburg. They also visited their former sister-in-law, Helga Meyer in Cammin near Neubrandenburg. While Brigitte stayed with Helga, Edith and Walter visited investigators and branch members. They also attended the baptism of some of their investigators. The 8thof August 1948, was a great day in the LDS branch. The Caesar family and the Neumann family and two other former members of the Jehovah's Witnesses group asked to be baptized. All of them had attended church meetings for some time. Walter had continued to take an evening each week to teach at the Neumanns' home and was waiting for them to make the decision to join the church through baptism. Now the time had come.

Walter looked for a nice place on the shores of the Tollensesee for this sacred occasion. He invited his district president, Walter Krause, and also asked Elder Gerhard Kupitz to return to his former field of labor. It was a beautiful day when they stood at the edge of the forest at the lake shore to perform the ordinance. The place was near where sixteen years earlier Walter and his mother were baptized and confirmed members of The Church of Jesus Christ of Latter-day Saints. They did the same to these investigators. Most of the branch members were present and warmly welcomed the new followers of Christ.

Brigitte and Edith had enjoyed their stay and before Walter told them goodbye at the railroad station he invited Edith to come and visit him again.

Walter visited with the friends of his youth who were married now and had a family. They listened to Walter's message but showed no interest in becoming followers of Christ. One evening Walter came home from visiting members and investigators, his mother told him she thought their landlord's oldest daughter, a few years younger than Walter, might be interested in the gospel. Walter wasted no time and contacted her. Her name was Erika Standke. She was a nurse and worked at the local hospital. Yes, she wanted to know more about Christ and what her purpose was on earth. Walter spent some time with her teaching the gospel. Erika's mother and sister were not interested but that didn't keep her from investigating the teachings of the church. She attended the church meetings regularly. After a Sacrament meeting she asked Walter for baptism.

The branch had some other investigators in Cammin near Neubrandenburg and Erika was baptized with the other investigators in the Camminer Lake. Walter felt inspired while still on the lake shore to ask Erika if she would be willing to lead the genealogical work in the branch. She accepted and she did the redeeming work for her forefathers and helped others to do the same until the end of her days on earth. While Erika and Walter were talking she thanked Walter for saving her spiritual life. Then she asked Walter if he remembered saving her earthly life when they were children? Walter did not remember, but when she told the story it came back to him.

Walter's family had leased a garden spot at the Datze River. Walter's sister and Walter and the children in their neighborhood used to play and bathe in the river. Not one of them could swim. Erika went thoughtlessly into the deep part of the river and almost drowned. Without hesitation Walter jumped into the river and pulled her out. They both nearly drowned, but made it to a safe place.

20

COMMUNIST UNION LEADER AND A MORMON?

Walter was the only non-union member in the company. Later in the year his supervisor called him into his office. To Walter's surprise he told him that the union was not working and needed new leadership. Walter told him he was not a member of the union and was really not interested enough that he had even noticed what was wrong with the union. He told Walter he wanted him to be the new leader. Nothing was further from Walter's mind and he declined. Walter told him he couldn't serve God on Sunday and then work against God on weekdays. They had a long discussion in which he explained to Walter why he wanted him. The employees had not received any extra help. They had not seen shoes, clothing and extra food yet, but he felt the large companies had them and they should have them also. He told Walter it was not the union who was against God, it was the party. The employees, mainly women who had lost their husbands in the war or whose husbands were still prisoners of war and had not returned yet, needed help. He felt Walter could give them the help they needed. He also told Walter he would not have to do any political work. He would take care of that. Walter told him that he would give him an answer tomorrow.

Walter made the tools for these people and knew all of them. Yes, these poor women needed help. They worked hard for a small amount of money. Any help they could get would be a blessing for them. Walter didn't mind doing the work for them, but what he didn't like was the communist doctrine. Walter believed it was the work of Satan. He wrestled with this overnight and prayed hard. In the morning Walter had the feeling he could do plenty of good. He believed the promise his supervisor made about politics and gave him his consent.

A few days later Walter saw a notice on their blackboard. Elections would be held for leadership in the union and Walter's name was on the ballot. He still hadn't joined the union, but was on the ballot. A secret vote was taken and when it was over the supervisor told Walter he had all the votes but one. The way this was done showed Walter the union was just a ball in the hands of the party. It was thrown in the direction the communist party wanted, but Walter had promised to work for the people and he would.

First, Walter discussed with the people their needs. Food was on top of their list. Walter checked everyone's ration card and he found many were eligible for a better one. He went to the proper places (which took him a while to find.) After long arguments he got what he wanted. It was difficult to explain to the workers why not all of them got the same card. Walter, as a toolmaker, didn't get a better card, but a mechanic did. Their older toolmaker complained. He thought he was worth much more than a mechanic and that he should get a better card, but there were rules and Walter had to abide by them. Walter thought the man held resentment against him from then until Walter left the company.

An interesting thing happened at this time. The owner of the company took Walter into the warehouse and showed him a large quantity of copper hidden there. He invited Walter to take as much as he wanted and sell it on the black market in Berlin. Walter knew it was possible to do. The brother of his counselor in church did it and made good money with it. It was against the law and the punishment was heavy. Copper was a metal both East- and West Germany needed badly. He told Walter no one knew about this and he wouldn't tell. Walter didn't even consider the offer. He declined and told him it would be dishonest to do those things. Walter didn't want to burden himself with doing something illegal. He also wasn't sure if the boss wanted to use this situation to control him. Walter didn't even consider the offer.

Shoes and clothing were next on the list. Up to that day no one had received a permit for these products and it had been three years since the war had ended. Walter went all over town. Slowly he acquired one permit after another until everyone received what they needed. People in West Germany got help from the USA, but Russia couldn't help. They had their own problems in rebuilding their war-torn land and took from Germany as much as they could. Next Walter found out that companies having a canteen got extra meat and groceries. This was not an easy battle to get food and groceries. The people who handled the permits for these items definitely didn't like him. Since they had no canteen the agency said, they didn't need the permits. Walter told them everyone had the same rights. They would divide those items between the workers. It would be an extra allotment in addition to their ration cards. Walter got what he wanted, but it was not easy to distribute these items to his co-workers. Almost everyone thought someone else got something more than they did.

After completing those tasks, the most common complaint Walter heard was that the workers felt they were underpaid. Walter agreed with them. He made 1.02 DM an hour at that time. A pound of butter with the ration card cost 2.50 DM. That meant Walter had to work more than 2 hours for a pound of butter. Butter on the black market was at least 50.00 DM. Walter went to the owner of the company about the wages and he agreed to sit down with Walter, the supervisor, and the accountant. They discussed every worker's salary. Walter asked for permission to have every lead person present when they discussed their salary. All agreed. From one group of workers Walter asked for two representatives. This group was the one which did most of the complaining. As they came in, the owner asked why they wanted more money. Both women replied that they didn't want more money, that it hadn't been them who asked. Yes, they were the ones who complained the most. The owner didn't say a word and Walter asked the women to just come in, sit down, and then tell the owner and the supervisor what they told him. Walter helped them along. After they were through he was able to get an increase in salary for everyone but one man. In looking at the records, Walter agreed that he was overpaid.

Walter's work was noticed by others. Maybe his supervisor being the head of the Communist party talked about it. Maybe he thought Walter would change his mind and become a member of the party. One day Walter was called into the office and two high ranking party leaders were there. They tried to convince Walter of the advantage he would have if he joined the party. After a long debate, Walter told them he couldn't in good conscience sing on Sunday "Nearer my God to thee," and during the week sing the "Communist International" which denied the existence of a God. They left him alone.

When Walter quit the company and moved to Cottbus, the Communist party leader (his supervisor) asked him to come into his office. He thanked Walter for the work he had done for the people. He told Walter in his whole life he had never seen a union leader do so much for the people. Walter thought it was a nice compliment coming from a Communist to a Mormon. At that time the owner gave Walter a certificate in which he praised Walter's work for the company with a special mention of his personal conduct saying that Walter was a pleasant and amiable colleague.

21

EDITH, WALTER'S HERZELE AND ETERNAL WIFE

Edith accepted Walter's invitation to visit and came in November, 1948. Walter enjoyed her visit. Over the years she had become a good friend. After she returned from her full time LDS mission in November 1943, she was engaged to a young LDS man from Chemnitz. Edith and her fiancé wanted to get married during his next furlough. Helmut Kinder was stationed in France, but was later transferred to Russia and there he was killed in war action. During the time Edith was engaged Walter respected that commitment, but she was still a good friend. They studied the scriptures in the morning and they went visiting and did other things together. Walter talked with her about everything, including girls.

Besides visiting other members of the church, they visited Sister Erna Jeschonek (51). She was someone special. She had an open mind and was very well informed. They could talk to her about anything. Walter loved to talk to her after a hard day of work. After visiting with her he was always uplifted. She made everyone feel good even though she was handicapped. She was a blind woman and one side of her body was paralyzed. She lived on the third floor of her building. Walter could easily carry her down the stairs and place her in a wheelchair. She had a noble mother who took great care of her. Most members of the church who lived in town or were visiting loved to visit with her. She was a central point of the branch life. When district conferences were held in their branch rooms, the two women would insist they could take visitors in and care for them. Edith and Walter visited with her and while Walter was at work Edith spent quite a bit of time with her. As always, Edith and Walter enjoyed their time together.

A short time after Edith had left, Walter visited Sister Jeschonek again. She politely asked him how his bride was doing. Walter told her he had no bride. Edith was a good friend of his, but not his bride. Walter had not yet even considered marriage. She was disappointed in him. She felt he and Edith were made for each other. She couldn't understand why Walter didn't court Edith. She told him how much she had enjoyed visiting with Edith and what a gem Edith was. She advised him to think it over.

Because Walter admired Sister Jeschonek, her words made a big impression on him. He chose to walk home through the lonely garden plots. It was about a half hour walk and gave him plenty of time to think about that conversation. The thought that he could ask Edith to become his wife had never occurred to him. Yes, he loved to be with Edith. Somehow they harmonized well together. Walter admired her integrity, her love for the gospel of Jesus Christ, and her willingness to serve others. Thinking it over Walter thought, "I have to see her and look at her to see if we could spend an eternity together." As Walter reached home he knew what he would do. Walter told his mother he would take a week off from work. He dropped in at work in the morning and told his supervisor that he needed to take a week off.

No one was surprised that Walter came to visit again so soon. Everyone greeted him as usual, more or less as part of the family. Walter thought Mother Birth had a suspicion of why he was there, but she didn't say anything. Edith had to work during the day and Walter visited with her sister, Irmgard, who did picture framing in her father's business. Walter also visited with Irmgard's husband, Heinz Koenig, who was repairing his large truck. Werner Koenig had received his masters degree in upholstering and he and Heinz owned their own business.

The evenings Walter spent with Edith. They had a great time

together. As they spent more and more time together, Walter had the feeling she was the one the Lord wanted him to take as his wife. No, it was not a love like in the movies. It was the feeling that he could share with her pleasure and pain, happiness and hardship. He felt he could trust her and could make her happy. But how could he tell her that? Two days in the evening before the end of Walter's vacation he took the step. He took her in his arms and asked her to become his wife. After her consent Walter gave her their first kiss. He confessed his love to her and she told him she had known he would marry her. Six months before this, she had a dream. Walter came into her room while she was lying in bed. He bent over her, gave her a kiss and told her she would become his wife. She didn't think it would become true. That was the first day of their life together and after more than 63 beautiful years Walter still kisses her daily and confesses his love to her, as she does to him. At a later time she showed Walter the entry in her diary, which they still have to this day.

Later that evening Walter walked into the living room where Father Birth was working on his postage stamps. Walter walked over to him and told him what had happened. Walter asked if he would give Edith to him to be his wife. He looked straight into Walter's eyes, took his hand and with tears in his eyes he said, "Walter, I have always loved you as if you were my own son." He and Mother Birth had shown Walter their love for a long time. Walter had called them "Mom" and "Dad" when they were still living in Schneidemuehl. As mother came in, father told her what had happened. She had a happy smile on her face. Edith came in and they all started to make plans for the wedding. Walter wanted the wedding to be within a month. He couldn't see why they should wait now they had made up their mind. Mother wanted it in May. Walter didn't want to wait that long. They all agreed on the 10thof February, 1949, as the wedding day, eight days before Edith's birthday.

On his train ride home Walter had time to think about the upcoming event. He thought about how much love Edith had shown him when he departed. He thought about what the future would bring. He wondered how she and his mother would get along. He didn't want her to be a servant in his house. He wanted her to be his wife and be respected as such by everyone.

Walter didn't know how he would pay for anything. He had saved in the years he was working and in the army and he still had his savings book, but the government had frozen the account. He couldn't and never got a penny from it. He couldn't save money now. All the money he made he gave to his mother to pay for food and the obligations they had. Then he worried how his mother would take this news. They hadn't heard from Walter's father and didn't even know if he was still alive. It was now three and a half years since he has been picked up by the Russians and not one word had been received about what had happened to him. Walter had prayed before his decision whom to marry and he prayed now. He had the same feeling as he had over the years, "Don't worry. Keep the Lord's commandments and listen to the inspiration of the Holy Ghost. The Lord is with you."

Walter didn't think his mother was really surprised when he came home and she saw the ring on his finger. Father Birth, realizing that Walter had no money. He was generous and bought the rings. Walter told his mother what had happened in Cottbus. She must have thought, "Why didn't he take one of the girls in our LDS branch?" There were some very nice girls in their branch, but the thought had never occurred to Walter to ask one of them to become his wife. Walter asked his mother not to worry. He said they would make their home with her if she agreed since it was her apartment. Walter knew Edith would get along with his mother and both would enjoy their time together. On Sunday in church everyone knew he was engaged. He was not used to wearing a ring and played with the ring on his finger all the time.

Edith visited with Walter and his Mother for Christmas in Neubrandenburg and those 14 days were really the only preparation days they had before their marriage. Of course they had dreams but the reality was clear, they wouldn't be able to get an apartment of their own. Like so many other newlyweds, they would have to move into his mother's apartment. A good thing was they wouldn't need their own furniture, they would use his mother's. For the years Walter was a prisoner of war he didn't get paid or receive any reimbursement. In the year since he was home he hadn't been able to save. Father and Mother Birth realized this and before Edith left home her mother gave her 200.00 DM, which was a fortune for the couple when Walter made only 1.10 DM an hour. This money was to help her in case of need.

They made plans with his mother about how they would handle the new living arrangement. During the day Walter went to work and in the evenings he spent time with Edith. During the day Edith and Walter's mother got along well. Walter was busy with his church calling, working, and taking care of the welfare of the workers. Edith and Walter knew each other from their many years as friends. Now they started to build and prepare their lives living and loving together. They started to forge of two people, one. They knew that loving was not enough; it would need work to make it a happy union. They both had the desire to make their partner happy and to serve the other. With good intentions they looked forward to their wedding day.

After 14 beautiful days, Walter took Edith to the railroad station and on the 10thof January, she went home. She was busy at home. She went to work with her mother to do all the preparations for the wedding. Walter's mother and Walter were too far away to give a hand and financially they were not able to help. Truly, the couple started out with nothing but love. They worked hard and asked Heavenly Father for His blessing. With His help they were sure they would make it.

Before Edith married Walter, she was the sales lady in her father's art store. Besides that, she studied music and took voice lessons. Because of her beautiful voice her teacher advised her not to marry, but to become an opera singer. For Edith, it was much more important to be a wife and become a mother, than to stand on a stage and entertain. Before she came to visit Walter in Neubrandenburg she sang at a Christmas party. She also sang the solo parts in the different choirs of which she was a member.

On the 8thof February, Walter took the train to Cottbus with his mother, Gertrud Dauss (a dear friend of their family) and her daughter Gisela. Walter went to marry his "Herzele," (little heart) now his special name for Edith. Edith, her mother and friends had done all the work for the wedding. Her father had exchanged glass for food to make their wedding something special. Father Birth took a big risk doing this and had some difficulties later, but was able to settle everything peacefully. Many friends of the Birth family came and Walter had invited Gerhard Kupitz to be his witness. Because there were so many missionaries, the branch president organized a special church meeting on the evening before their wedding. Herzele and Walter took part in the program, she singing a solo "Jerusalem" and Walter giving a gospel message. The meeting was very spiritual and very much to the couple's liking.

In Germany, the night before the wedding, people would wish the couple luck by throwing glasses (all kinds of glasses) in the entrance to the building. The tradition was that the groom carried the bride-to-be over the broken glass to protect her. Walter didn't like the poltergeist (goblin) tradition but there were some who attended the evening meeting and liked the poltergeist (meaning those who threw the glass).

Church weddings were not binding in communist East Germany. They had to go that morning to the civil registry office to be wed. They chose as their witnesses Herzele's father and Walter's friend Gerhard Kupitz. Walter would have loved to have his father as a witness, but they still didn't know if he was alive. Walter thought a lot about his father during those days and would have loved to introduce his Herzele to him. His father had met her on his visit to Schneidemuehl and at a district president's conference in Berlin while Herzele was an LDS full time missionary. In the civil registry office they were sitting around a table when the official got up and quoted, "Noble be the men, helpful and good." He gave *a short* and meaningful sermon which gave the couple good counsel for their married life. Then he performed the ceremony and made them legally husband and wife. They kissed each other and Walter told his sweetheart he loved her and he was grateful that she would be his eternal companion. Those present congratulated the couple and they left looking forward to their church wedding. They would have loved a temple wedding, but there was no temple in Germany at that time.

People say it brings good luck when it rains on your wedding day. They had plenty of it, but Walter would have gladly given it away if it would have been in his power. A carriage took them to the church. They had to walk a short distance to the church entrance in the rain. On the stairs Herzele stepped on her dress and almost fell. Walter held her tightly and prevented that disaster. Herzele looked beautiful in her wedding dress. Brother Norbert Lehnig went the extra mile and travelled to West Berlin to buy a beautiful flower bouquet for her because Walter was not able to get one in town. It made her even more beautiful. She had shared her dress with her sisters Christel and Irmgard who married before her and she would share it with other friends who married after her. Walter had bought a suit for this occasion, but the women didn't like the suit. He doesn't know what kind of material, for sure not wool, it was made of, but the women said it wasn't good looking and joked that it would sprout out leaves if it should rain. The women decided he should borrow a suit from Brother Hagen; a suit of much better quality (made before the war). It did fit Walter and he felt handsome in it.

As they entered the church meeting room, Walter saw it was filled to the very last chair. They were late and the poor people had to wait, but in their eyes Walter saw only love and admiration for his sweetheart. His Herzele was very much loved by young and old alike. He didn't know the program but Walter was sure the leaders of the branch would make it special. The organ played and all arose when they entered the room. The ones who offered the prayers asked the Lord to bless and lead the couple through their life.

Herzele's cousin, friend and district president from Leipzig, Walter Kindt, was the main speaker. He talked about and thanked Edith for how she had taken care of him, his brothers, sister and father, while his mother was sick in the hospital. In the morning she would ask the kids to get up and without objection they would go to school, even though she was just a little older than they were. She had the meals prepared for them and their father. He said she followed their mother's wishes while taking care of her. He thanked her for the friendship they had even up to that day. For Walter he had instruction how to handle this pearl of great price.

After the speech a beautiful choir sang and then Brother Fritz Lehnig, Herzele's district president spoke, telling Walter more of Herzele's strengths and examples of service. In reality they didn't have to tell Walter that. He knew Edith better than they were aware off and he was already a great admirer of hers. He strongly believed the Lord guided him in his choice and they would make a good team. Brother Fritz Lehnig then repeated the wedding ceremony that the government official had performed earlier.

Walter and his Herzele

A carriage took the couple to the photographer and then they had a delicious meal at the Birth family home. In the evening they had a wedding celebration prepared by the activity committee of the LDS branch. A professional band invited everyone to dance. In between the dances they inserted some dialogues and told some jokes. It was very entertaining for the members of the church and the friends of the family. Herzele didn't miss a dance all evening. Herzele loved to dance and Walter preferred everything else before dancing, but he did dance with her four times. Missionaries were not permitted to dance, so with those present he took time and discussed LDS doctrine. No one wanted to quit, but at 1:00 o'clock in the morning the wedding party walked over to the Births' home, which was nearby. Here the good women had bakery products prepared and every one enjoyed the tasty cakes. Finally at 4:00 o'clock the party was over.

It had been a beautiful and lovely wedding day and Herzele and Walter enjoyed every minute of it. Walter didn't know how Father Birth was able to get all of the food. They knew the family got a few extra ration cards, but what was served definitely didn't come from ration cards. Mother Birth, Herzele and others must have worked long hours to prepare the meals. All Walter could do was say, "Thank you." They still love to remember all the ones who worked so hard to make it a memorial day for the couple. Their thanks went to our Heavenly Father for His blessings and to their families and the brothers and sisters in the Lord's church.

At noon when Walter got up, he didn't feel well. Maybe the cold bath he took before he went to the Standesamt (city hall) caught up with him. Walter thought he was just too lazy that morning to go down to the cellar, pick up the fire wood and bring it up to the third floor to heat the water heater. But he was sick and stayed in bed for a couple of days. He was able to attend sacrament meeting on Sunday. In the meeting Herzele was released from five callings and she told everyone goodbye. Wherever they moved in the future and had to say goodbye it was hard. It was really a blessing to live and serve together with Latter-day Saints in a ward or branch.

They took the train to Neubrandenburg the next day, arriving in the evening. They went in Walter's mother's apartment and as they turned the light on, they saw the table was decorated with wedding presents. They were touched as they saw with how much love the table was arranged. The greetings and good wishes for their marriage and especially for Herzele, made them feel very happy. It was a good beginning for Walter's Herzele.

For Herzele a new world opened up. It was hard for her to leave her family and friends and move into a different environment. While she had met her new neighbors, living with them was a different story. She was with Walter's mother more or less all day. The three room apartment would now be divided between the refugee couple, Mr. & Mrs. Werner, Walters mother, and Edith and Walter. The two larger rooms were occupied by the Werner's and the young couple. Walter's mother took the smaller room. The use of the only kitchen the women shared. There never was a problem in the kitchen.

However, Walter's mother's small room had a problem. The only entrance to her room was from the young couple's room. When she wanted to do anything outside her room, even just go to the bathroom, she had to walk through their room. The three families shared one bathroom. How uncomfortable Walter's mother must have felt when she had to cross their room, especially at an inopportune time. Hopefully she remembered how it was when she married and there were no apartments for young couples just as it was now for Edith and Walter.

Walter had heard how many of the young wives were treated by their mother-in-law. Walter wanted everyone in the family to have the same rights and for Herzele to be an even partner. Walter told his mother that Herzele would now handle the money he brought home. His mother was shocked. Herzele heard about it and told Walter she was okay with his mother taking care of the money and she told Walter's mother and mother smiled again. That is not all. Walter had helped Herzele with the dishes, which his mother said his father never did, but they wanted to be together and why shouldn't Walter help? On the way for a walk Walter told Herzele that his mother's face told him she wasn't happy that they were going out. Herzele stopped and said, "Let's go back." Of course Walter objected because he wanted to go. Herzele said, "Do you know how it feels when the one you love is not with you and you don't even know anything about him for that long a time?" Mother and Herzele worked well together, studied the scriptures together, and both loved Walter.

22

LOVE THY WIFE AS THYSELF

(Eph 5:33)

Father Birth had given the young couple a small radio for a wedding gift. Few in East Germany in those days had a radio. It needed not only an antenna, but also had to be grounded. Walter needed to attach a ground wire from the water pipe to their radio which they had on their night stand next to their bed. He pushed the wire under the bed to Herzele and asked her to plug it into the radio. She didn't understand what he said and didn't move. He repeated his request but she still didn't move. Than in a loud, army voice Walter ordered, "Plug the wire in." Without saying a word, she did. Walter's mother and their landlord, Mrs. Marie Standke, were standing and watching them, expecting this to lead to their first fight.

They were wrong. Herzele didn't say a word. Edith and Walter had made it a habit to lie together at night and talk. They did the same thing that night. After a while Herzele said,"Walter, today.." She didn't get any further. The sound of her voice made Walter aware that there was something coming which he had already forgotten. Walter stopped her from going on. He knew he had handled things wrongly and now he felt bad about the mishandled situation. He took a deep breath and apologized and promised it would never happen again.

In the first days of April 1949, Herzele felt sick, but after some days she recuperated and Walter arranged for her to visit her family. While she was gone Walter and his friend Otto repainted their room. "We" implies that Walter helped with this, but in reality Otto did the work. Walter also bought a lamp which Herzele had shown him she wanted and he hung it up. The day Herzele came home, Walter placed a flower bouquet on the table. Herzele was delighted and praised their work. She felt they needed something more to decorate the room. They had seen in one store a beautiful little doll, but far too much money for their budget. Walter still made just 1.10 DM an hour, but they bought it anyway. Walter had to work more than 2 days to pay for the doll. They didn't mind, they loved the little doll and placed it on their bed.

The government had now arranged a new kind of store called H.O. (Handels Organisation) stores. The nation had now three kinds of stores: Private stores, which were dying out; "Konsum" stores owned by the government where you could buy everything for which you had ration cards; and H.O. stores also owned by the government. Here you could buy items from other nations, mainly from West Germany, products other stores didn't carry. You needed no ration card to buy here; all you needed was a large amount of money. They splurged and paid 10 DM (10 hours work for Walter.) for a little 100g chocolate, Swiss Tobler "Trumpf Ecken." Together they went on a walk, enjoying Mother Nature and the rich tasting chocolate. They had very few material goods, but they made the best of it. They loved each other and that was most important for them.

Walter was still teaching the adult class in Sunday School, but he was not satisfied with his performance. He couldn't get the participation he wanted to have. He didn't see any spiritual growth in the class. At Walter's request he was released and his Herzele was asked to teach the class. Surely enough, it didn't take long for her to reach all the goals Walter had set for himself. She had a great way of working with the members of the class and she made friends wherever she went. Soon one of the sisters asked her if she prepared the talks Walter gave in church. No, she didn't, but Walter liked that, it made him feel good that people thought so highly of his wife. Of course, it was not a great compliment for him.

Walter never cared much about the clothing he wore. It had

to be clean, but what he wore didn't bother him much. Not so with Herzele. Before he got married he wouldn't wear a necktie, he would just turn his sweater around. Now upon her insistence he wore a tie. Walter had a new jacket which had been given to him while he was a POW but it had two large letters in the back: P G, for Prisonnier de Guerre (French for POW). Walter liked the style of the jacket and one Sunday he wore it. They were both on their way to teach the gospel in different villages, but were riding the same train to their different stations. Walter had to conduct the meetings and teach in Neustrelitz and she would be teaching in Cammin. On the way she recognized the jacket Walter was wearing. She was upset and after a short argument she wouldn't talk to him anymore. While waiting for the train on the railroad station Walter took her in his arms and asked for her forgiveness. He told her their lives were too short to waste a minute not being in harmony with each other. From that time on Walter didn't wear that jacket on Sunday.

Walter's greatest desire was to bring the restored Gospel of Jesus Christ to the people. At home he would take his lovely wife along and visit members and investigators. One day they visited with Brother Adolf Kuhfeld, who was inactive. He had a nice family, but had married outside the church. He was the one who gave the talk on the Word of Wisdom that made Walter's father change from a chain smoker to one who never smoked again. He clearly remembered that event well, but he was now a smoker. Walter and Herzele discussed the gospel with him and they were able, with the Lord's help, to change his attitude towards the gospel. In one of their visits the spirit was so strong he jumped up, got his pipe, broke it apart and promised he wouldn't smoke any more. He soon became an active member of the church again and his family was baptized.

So far the branch had Sacrament meeting, Sunday School and Relief Society, but no Priesthood meeting. Walter's counselors were a little skeptical when he told them they would have Priesthood meeting on a weekday evening with the Relief Society. His counselors said that the three wouldn't be enough to have a meeting. Walter said, "We will have nine brethren attending the meeting." He visited every Brother of the branch and when they started the meeting they had eight brethren in attendance. While Walter was teaching, Brother Gaertner walked in. It was an uplifting meeting and they continued the meetings in the future.

Up to that time, Walter didn't have the Melchizedek Priesthood but was a priest in the Aaronic Priesthood. Because of that he didn't have the authority to set people apart or give priesthood blessings. He had to ask visiting brethren to do so. It was becoming more and more difficult to conduct the affairs of the branch without being an Elder. In June, 1949, Elder Walter Krause, the district president, visited the branch and while there he asked Walter and Brother Otto Krakow if they would like to become elders in the church. After they agreed, their names were presented to the congregation for approval. Then they received the Melchizedek Priesthood and were ordained as elders. Now they could fully function as a branch presidency. Herzele, Walter's mother and Walter celebrated the ordination by Herzele baking a cheese cake. Walter didn't know where she got the ingredients from, but they enjoyed the rare occasion.

Herzele became ill. The doctor told her she had pneumonia. To get well she had to be wrapped many times a day in wet sheets and be watched over. Walter had to work. His mother was not strong enough to wrap her, but then Frau Werner offered her services. She was an angel. Frau Werner gave a hand wherever help was needed. She took care of Herzele for three long weeks until Herzele had recuperated.

While Herzele was sick, Walter went to work during the daylight hours and in the evening he did his church work. One evening he had invited their branch secretary, Sister Gertrud Neumann, to come over and to do the reports. After they had completed their work Walter told Herzele that he would walk Sister Neumann home. Herzele didn't object, but Walter could see in her eyes she was disappointed. She wanted to spend some time with him. While Walter walked with Sister Neumann through the hallway and to the door, many things went through his mind. He hadn't realized what he had been doing. Every day when he had come home he had spent very little time with his wife. All day long Herzele was lying there, and waiting for him to come, hoping to spend time together. Walter realized at that moment how unfair he had been to his wife. He decided he would change that. At the door Walter wished Sister Neumann a good night and a safe way home, then he went back to his sick wife. Without telling his sweetheart, he repented and from that day on he spent more time with her.

While Herzele was recovering from her illness Reverend Reinhold, a Lutheran minister, visited with her. She arranged time for a visit with him and Walter. At the appointed time he came and he wanted to know more about the "Mormons." His church had a discussion on the seven sects of corruption and the Mormons were one of them. He told Walter that in the outline he had to present to his congregation there was plenty of negative information about the Mormon Church, but at the end the outline talked of the outstanding accomplishments of the Mormon Church. He thought the outline was wrong. Either what they said in the beginning was wrong or the end was incorrect. He didn't believe that a bad tree could bring forth good deeds. He told Walter he came to him because he wanted to know more about the Mormon Church.

They sat down and discussed Mormon doctrine. Walter was surprised on how many things the Reverend agreed with him, which were really in contrast to the Lutheran faith. They both had their Bibles in front of them and used the Holy Scriptures frequently. At first he tried to lecture Walter a little, but after Walter saw him looking over at his worn out, well-marked Bible, his attitude changed and they became equal partners in the discussion. He came back a couple of nights and after the last visit, Walter saw he was very much impressed with the teachings of The Church of Jesus Christ of Latter-day Saints. He told Walter he knew the Lutheran Church was built like a house of cards and could break apart anytime. Walter invited him to join the LDS faith. He answered,

"What should I do for a living? This is all that I know to do. I can't change."

Walter responded that the Lord would be with him and help him.

He didn't invite Walter to his lecture, but Sister Edith Schade attended. She was very much impressed with the Reverend's presentation and told Walter about one man saying that in the temple in Salt Lake City women were mistreated and raped. The Reverend Reinhold told the audience he didn't believe that. If anyone wanted to know more or had further questions he asked them to contact Walter and he gave the audience Walter's address. Sadly, no one contacted him.

In those days they had an adult class in their Mutual program on weekdays. Because of Walter's pleasant experience with the Reverend Reinhold, Walter decided to invite him to give a presentation to the adult Mutual class. He gave a good presentation on the teachings and history of the Lutheran Church. In the end he asked for questions. As the class asked their question Walter was impressed with the scripture knowledge of his fellow branch members. When Reverend Reinhold left, Walter walked him to the door. He told Walter how much larger his congregation was then his. But then he added, "I only wish I had two in my large congregation who had the scripture knowledge your members have."

Very satisfied with the first meeting of this kind, Walter decided to invite the minister of the apostolic faith to give a presentation. Because of the shortage of rooms, representatives of this church had approached Walter to rent their rooms for a time on Sundays for their services. Walter had agreed to rent them the rooms.

Herzele and Walter went over to the minister's home and presented the invitation. His first question was,

"Does your superior know about this invitation?"

Walter told him, "No, they don't."

He warned Walter that when he gave his presentation Walter's members might join his congregation. Walter told him he was not worried about that and Walter asked him to take this opportunity. He thought for minute and then he said,

"I better not. Our members might come over and join your church."

Walter very seldom dreamed, but one night he did and in the morning he told Herzele about the dream. He dreamed that on his birthday he held their baby in his arms and gave it a blessing. That was a great message for both of them because they wanted a baby. They checked the calendar and they found out his birthday was on a Sunday. Next they checked with a doctor and it was true, Herzele was pregnant. They gathered items together for the baby. During the waiting time they visited with Walter's uncle, Arnold Rohloff, and he gave them a basket in which they could place the baby.

During the first days of April, 1950, Herzele told Walter she no longer felt life. They were concerned, but hoped everything would be all right. Walter was working in their garden spot about 20 minutes from home when Tante Werner came running and told Walter his Herzele was in labor. As fast as his feet could carry him he hurried home. The women of the house were standing around Herzele. Walter's Herzele was lying in bed in pain. Helpless Walter stood there and stroke with his hands over her hair and told her how much he loved her. Walter gave her a blessing. The midwife finally arrived and the women prepared for the arrival of the baby. It was hard for Herzele to deliver the baby. The baby moved slowly and Walter had to help Herzele by lifting her body up to aid in the delivery. After the arrival of the full grown baby, Herzele asked: "Is it a boy or girl?" Walter couldn't answer right away as he tried to control his emotion. Then he told her, "The baby is dead."

She cried and Walter cried. This was the baby they had been waiting for. Tearfully she asked Walter, "Why me? All my life I served the Lord, from my youth to now. I have kept the Lord's commandments. Why can't I have a healthy baby?"

Walter comforted her as best as he could and tried to find an answer for her and for him. Then an answer came into his mind and Walter explained to his despairing wife, "Why shouldn't we go through trials and tribulations? It is part of our life on earth. The Lord must think very highly of us, and knows that we can bear this tragedy without losing our faith in him." Walter loved his Herzele dearly. This hour brought them nearer to each other than anything before.

The midwife was a God-fearing woman and did not understand why they couldn't have a healthy baby. Another woman she had just delivered in the past few days had given birth to a healthy baby and her husband had cursed her for not aborting the baby.

For some days they grieved over their loss. A few days later Herzele had complications from the childbirth. She was admitted into the hospital quarantine station building. For a while she was very depressed. All feared the worst. She was sure she wouldn't make it and she recommended to Walter whom he should marry after she died. But the Lord heard their prayers and slowly she improved.

It was not easy for Walter to visit her. Visiting hours for the hospital were during the daytime and on Sundays and were strictly enforced. Visitors had to pass through a small, controlled entrance, one person at a time. Walter couldn't make the afternoon visiting hours because he had to work so that left Sundays. He tried to enter the hospital after work, but the guard wouldn't let him pass. Of course that was no hindrance for Walter. The fence around was not high enough to keep him out. While the guard was watching the door and kept everybody out of the hospital, Walter jumped the fence in the rear and visited with his Herzele every day after work. To reach Herzele's room he had to pass the nurse station. He did okay at the beginning of his daily visits, but then one day the nurse caught Walter. He told her what he did and that he would like very much to use the door to see his wife. She understood Walter's action and only objected that he was by-passing her. Well, the next time Walter saw her before he saw his sweetheart. Herzele loved Walter's visits. She recovered and was soon as positive as before, enjoying life and making friends wherever she went.

Walter thought it would be good for Herzele to come along when he went to visit the different places where he taught the gospel and held church meetings in homes. After working until noon on a Saturday, they went to the railroad station with the intention of buying a ticket to the city of Waren. A long line of people were standing in front of the ticket box. Walter and Herzele would never make their train if they joined the people in line. With a platform ticket they could get on the platform so they bought one and they passed through the gate by showing their tickets. On the platform they saw their train was just starting to move. Walter got his Herzele into the last car and with the help of the postmaster, Walter made it too. As Walter knew from prior experience, the postmaster's car was not checked by the conductor because people were not supposed to ride in that car. He made sure to buy their tickets from Neubrandenburg to Waren at the next station where they had a longer waiting time.

In Waren they had only one member family. They held a cottage meeting with the family and a few friends the family had invited. After the meeting they stayed with the family and discussed gospel principles and encouraged them to stay close to the church. Sister Beyer and her daughters were refugees from the city of Stettin which was now in Polish territory. Sister Beyer was ill and wanted to die. The two daughters were older than Walter and very talented. Their friends had immigrated to Utah, but had left the church. These former friends encouraged the Beyer's to leave the church. They mailed anti-LDS literature and tracts to the Beyer family. Walter and Edith discussed gospel principles with them and answered their question. Showing the Beyer's the untruths the tract's proclaimed helped them stay close to the Lord's church. They felt the Lord's spirit during the discussion and stayed as guests in their home for the night. Whenever possible the Beyer's visited the branch of the church in Neubrandenburg, but it was a long and difficult trip for them.

The next morning was a beautiful morning. In a motor boat they crossed Germany's second-largest lake, Lake Mueritz. They enjoyed every minute of that ride. The scenery was outstanding. In Alt Gaatz they left the boat and met with friends of the church. These friends had invited their neighbors and friends. The room was filled with refugees from the former eastern part of Germany. They were not members of the church, but were investigators interested in hearing the truth. In those meetings Walter and Herzele had to do everything-conduct, pray, teach and preach. The Lord's spirit was with Walter and Edith as they gave their gospel message and their testimony of the truthfulness of the gospel and of the restoration of the gospel through the Prophet Joseph Smith. After the talks they had a lively discussion on gospel principles. These people were looking for the truth. Walter regretted that he couldn't visit this place more often. He felt it would have been a fruitful field.

Walter and Edith held meetings and had baptisms in Neubrandenburg, Cammin, Godenswege and Neustrelitz. They also held meetings in Waren, Alt Gaatz and Laerz. The railroad connections were just too bad and the places too far for Walter to reach the last three places more often. It was a matter of time and money. Walter had only Saturday afternoons and Sundays for visiting these places and he paid his travel expenses out of his own pocket. With the small income he earned, his finances were limited. Walter's mother was a great help in caring for their wellbeing. She knew many places and people and traded whatever they didn't need for things they did.

From Alt Gaatz they walked to Laerz, a nearby town. A member couple lived there and they visited with them at their home. They had invited their neighbors and Herzele and Walter discussed with them the restoration of the gospel. Walter was not favorably impressed with these people. He felt these people came to the meeting because of the church welfare plan, not for the gospel.

In Neubrandenburg there was just a small branch of the church. About 100 members were registered in the books, but only 30 to 40 attended. Walter's counselor conducted the meetings in Neubrandenburg and Walter did missionary work and conducted meetings at other places. Usually Walter would leave on Saturday afternoon and return before sacrament meeting on Sunday. Some weekends he held a meeting on Saturday evening in Neustrelitz, then on Sunday went to Cammin and Godenswege and then to there own sacrament meeting in Neubrandenburg. Other weeks he would travel to Neustrelitz, Laerz and Alt Gaatz. He wouldn't make it back in time for sacrament meeting when he went that far away. He visited the member family in Waren whenever possible.

Finances were very limited, but brother Otto Krakow helped Walter out by lending him his bike. One Sunday Walter remembers especially well. He had held a cottage meeting in

Neustrelitz (over 30km away) and then went on the bike to Cammin (about a 10km detour) for sacrament meeting. This worked out well most of the time, but on this particular Sunday it snowed hard and the road from the highway to Cammin had not been plowed. In all the snow Walter had to carry his bike. He arrived in Cammin wet all over and late. But the good brothers and sisters and investigators had waited for him. After Walter cleaned up he conducted the meeting and gave an uplifting gospel message. They had a really inspiring time. Brother Kurt and Sister Helga Meyer in Cammin, worked hard to establish a branch of the church there. The Meyer's conducted regular Sunday School and Sacrament meetings and on a weeknight held Relief Society. Through these efforts the membership increased in Cammin and Godenswege with several baptisms.

In Neustrelitz there were no members. They, Trudi Neumann who often accompanied Walter, held the meetings in the home of the Jahnke family and Trudi and Walter stayed for the night at their home. Mrs. Jahnke had her father living with her and he joined the church, but she wanted to wait until her husband came home. He was a POW in Russia. It was the only baptism Walter had there and he didn't see much hope for any further progress.

One weekend, while visiting Neustrelitz, Walter was really discouraged. Before he went to bed he knelt in prayer and told the Lord about his dismay, concern, and problems. Walter asked the good Lord to lead him to people who were interested in His gospel. Walter prayed hard and sincerely. Usually he slept to the last minute in the morning and had to hurry to the railroad station to get to Laerz and Alt Gaatz, but this time he repeated his request in prayer from the night before and still had plenty of time to get to the train. He was early and sat down in an empty compartment. He took out his Book of Mormon and prepared his sermon for Laerz and Alt Gaatz.

Shortly before the train started moving, a lady took a seat across from him. After a while he saw the lady was uneasy and kept moving back and forth on her seat. Walter asked her if she did not feel well.

"No" she said, "I forgot."

Walter said, "What did you forget?"

"I forgot the book you are reading," she said.

"What do you think I am reading?"

"The Bible" she said.

"No, I am not reading the Bible. I am reading the Book of Mormon."

"The Book of Mormon?" she asked.

"Are you are Mormon?"

Yes," Walter said, "I am a Mormon."

"We have been looking for Mormons for a long time. May I have your Book of Mormon?" she said.

Walter loaned her his book until he had to leave the train. It was the only copy of the Book of Mormon he had and he needed it back. Walter made an appointment for the following Saturday to see her in her home.

On Saturday at the appointed hour Walter knocked on the door of this good lady. Her husband opened and after Walter introduced himself he was invited in with the words,

"Come in, you servant of the Lord."

After entering Walter asked him, "How do you know that I am a servant of the Lord?"

"May I call you brother?" he asked.

Walter agreed. "Brother Rohloff, we have been looking for the Lord's church for a long time. That very morning when you met my wife in the railroad car, we had knelt in prayer' and he pointed at a place in the room, 'and asked the Lord to lead us to his servants when they were in the neighborhood. My wife made your acquaintance on that day. I know you are the Lord's servant."

They had a great conversation and the spirit of the Lord was with them. He was handicapped and Walter learned in the discussion that he had a great desire to become whole again. Walter was invited to return and he arranged to have their next meeting in their home.

Walter invited his district president, Brother Walter Krause, to be with him. Brother Krause had a great way of explaining the gospel. It was an inspirational evening. Brother Krause gave him a blessing and invited him to join the church, but things turned out differently than they thought. The couple had applied to move to West Germany and when they received permission they had to move immediately. Walter never heard from them again. Maybe they joined the church in West Germany.

At home after Sunday School, Brother Wehse Jr. was waiting for Walter. His mother was sick and she wanted the elders to come and give her a blessing. Sister Martha Wehse (82) received many visits from the branch members. Often they would go over and have a cottage meeting in her home. She loved to hear and sing the hymns and she liked a good gospel doctrine discussion. Walter went to give her a blessing as she had requested. When he entered her apartment and saw her lying motionless in bed, he thought it was her last hour on earth. Walter gave her a blessing and to his own surprise in the blessing he promised her health. Walter gave the blessing as he was inspired and he was disturbed when he promised her health. How could he promise her health when she was lying there like a dead person? After a few words with her son, Walter went home. He told Herzele how he felt and they both decided to fast and pray and place their worries in the Lord's hands. After work the next day they went over to visit Sister Wehse. After Walter rang the bell, to their surprise, Sister Wehse opened the door.

"Sister Wehse," Walter said, "you are up?"

"Brother Rohloff," she said, "you gave me a blessing and promised me health."

And healthy she was. It amazed Walter. He sat at Sister Martha Wehse's feet a few years earlier when his family jointed The Church of Jesus Christ of Latter-day Saint. She taught Walter about the teachings of the Savior, Jesus Christ. Now with the Priesthood authority vested in Walter, he had been able to give her a blessing and through the Lord's prompting he promised her health.

Having more to eat was on everyone's mind. The trains were always crowded with people who were out to trade anything for food. Living in an agricultural state helped Walter's family. It was not far for them to go to trade, as long as they had something to trade. Walter's mother was an expert and Walter had no idea what she traded, but she always had food on the table.

A great help in those days was the food and clothing received from the church welfare program. Every member got canned foods, flour, sugar, and many other items. From the shipment the church sent to the members, 50% went to the East German government. Most of the time the food was brought to them by trucks the church rented for that purpose. When the church did send food items through the government they had problems. Before Walter would contact the government about the missing food, he would check to see who was in charge. If it was a lady, Walter would go and negotiate with her. If a man was in charge, Herzele often went. It worked out well. They always got what they wanted.

One time a sack with sugar was missing. Walter talked with the agency in charge. They told him the Americans had plenty and he should contact the Americans for more. Walter explained to them how the welfare plan worked. He told them that this had nothing to do with being rich or poor; this had something to do with spending your spare time helping the needy without getting a penny for it. Rich and poor did that in the church and we were benefitting from their selfless work. Their attitude changed and they responded, "That is what we want to do here."

Walter had to travel to Neustrelitz, but he got the sack of sugar. Thanks to the welfare program of the church they were never without food. There was only one time when they could offer their guests only hot potatoes (Pellkartoffel).

It was October, 1950, and they still hadn't heard from Walter's father. Apparently the government did not feel obligated to notify the family of a person they incarcerated and what they did to them. It was now five years since his father was picked up by the Russian secret police and they had not heard a word from the government or from anyone else. It was hard on Walter and Walter's mother and she worried about her husband. They all believed one day he would return.

Walter on a boat tour on Lake Tollense near Neubrandenburg with Herzele, Gertrud Dauss, Max and Gertrud Pielmann, Otto Krakow

Walter had had a dream about hia father a year before, in which he saw him walking along the street and coming into the house in which they were living.

It was a great blessing that Herzele understood the feelings and sorrows of Irene her mother-in-law. She always was concerned about mother's well being. They both loved one another and they got along very well.

23

THE STASI WANTS WALTER

The living arrangements in Walter's mother apartment had become an unbearable condition for both his mother and the young couple. His mother needed to get her room back, but where could the couple go? Then they received a letter from Herzele's mother. She told Edith there was a job opening in town for Walter and that it might improve Walter and Edith's finances. She had two separate rooms in her apartment that they didn't use and the couple could have them. While Herzele was reading the letter to Walter and his mother, Walter thought it over and felt a change would be good. This would return the living room to his mother and she wouldn't feel so much like she was in prison. She would not have to cross the young couple's room when she wanted to leave her room. She would have her own living space back.

Herzele and Walter would also benefit by having their own living and bedroom. The three decided Walter would go and see how he liked the living conditions and the work. He took a few days off from work and traveled to Cottbus by train. First, Walter applied for the job and got it. Then he looked at the rooms and was impressed with them. They would have their own apartment. While the rooms were on the same floor and belonged to Mother Birth's apartment they were completely separate. Herzele would have to use her mother's kitchen, but Walter didn't see any problems with that. They had worked well together in her mother's business in Schneidemuehl.

Back home Walter told his mother and Herzele about the

rooms and the job. Walter's mother had nothing against the young folks moving. Walter told her they would continue to help her with her finances.

They made all the preparations necessary to make the move. Walter told his supervisor at work and the owner of the company of his intention. They wished him well and gave him a letter of appreciation which praised his work as a toolmaker and included a special note at the end wherein they emphasized that he had always been a kind and pleasant staff member.

Herzele and Walter didn't have much furniture. Father Birth had asked Gerhard Gaertner, an excellent carpenter whom he knew from Schneidemuehl, to make bed frames and later he had him make a wardrobe. Father Birth was always very generous to the young couple. Besides their possessions, Walter wanted to take some of their firewood with them. How could they transport all of it?

Walter's friend, Otto Krakow, worked for the railroad and he arranged a railroad car for them to use to move all their belongings to Cottbus. He helped load the car and locked and secured it.

Before the couple moved the LDS branch presidency were meeting in the home of Walter's counselor, Karl Neumann. While they were discussing branch business someone knocked wildly at the door and yelled, "Stasi, open right away! (Stasi was a comparable organization as Hitler's animosities Gestapo.) They had heard of things like this happening in the dark many times, but never expected it could happen to them. Brother Neumann opened the door and Walter heard a voice saying

"Is a Mr. Rohloff here?"

"Yes," Walter said, "I am here."

"You have to come with us to Stasi (National Security Service) headquarter," they said.

Walter took his coat and was ready to go when his Herzele came in.

"What is going on?" she wanted to know.

Walter explained to her that the two men were picking him up and taking him to Stasi headquarters. She grabbed her coat and said,

"I am going with you!"

"Oh," Walter said, "you better not. Let me go alone. You know what can happen."

"I will go with you," she said, "and if it should be, I will go with you to Siberia."

(Siberia was the hated place where the Russian government sent their criminal and political prisoners). Walter tried hard to change her mind, but she took her coat and Walter helped her in.

They walked arm in arm flanked by two officers through the streets to the Stasi headquarters. The thought went through Walter's mind: That was the way his father had been picked up and they still didn't know if he was alive or dead and that was over five years ago. It was a strange feeling, but Walter didn't feel fear and couldn't see any fear in Herzele's face. They tried to find out what the Stasi wanted from Walter, but the officers would not talk. They entered the hated building were Walter's father had also been arrested and interrogated. They walked along a hallway until they reached a large, sparsely furnished room. While Walter and Herzele stood in the door frame they saw by the window two men sitting at a desk. One of the men who brought them in saluted and reported. Walter didn't understand what he said. The officer he had reported to looked over at Walter and then turned back and said to the reporting officer:

"I know that man. He is not an American spy, he is a religious fanatic."

Then he turned to Walter and said, "Rohloff, you can go."

They gave no explanation or excuse. Walter didn't ask for an explanation either. He and Herzele were more than glad to leave that building. Walter and Herzele had heard enough stories of innocent people who were picked up by the Stasi and held prisoner. They didn't have to look far for an example. Walter's father was one of them.

Our love never ends

A few days later they arrived in Cottbus and after they moved their furniture into the room they felt at home. Walter started to work at the Urania Fahrad Werke and Herzele worked as sales lady in her father's art store. To their great surprise, a few days after they arrived in Cottbus, Herzele was told to write a short life story for the Stasi (National Security Service). They already knew that Walter had moved.

24

CALLED TO SERVE

The company Walter worked for used to make bikes, but now they made parts for tanks and other war equipment. It surprised Walter that they were doing this since Germany was not permitted to have an army. Of course the union had an explanation for everything. The German Democratic Republic had to protect themselves from the aggressive, capitalistic Americans. All employees had to attend the union political instructions, whether they were a union member or not. Walter didn't report his union membership and was not willing to renew it. These meetings were held to inform the employees of the superior government they had in comparison with West Germany. Walter knew of no one who believed their teachings, but no one said a word and that included Walter.

At church Herzele was called to teach and Walter was asked by the district president, Brother Fritz Lehnig, to accompany him on his visits to the different branches of the church. Walter was soon called to be the district mission president and later he was also called to be the district Sunday School president. Brother Lehnig had no counselors and used to counsel with Walter when he felt he needed advice. Many times they took the district Relief Society president, Sister Kaethe Voigt, along. Brother Lehnig was a strong-willed and tireless working man. He was a convert with a strong testimony of the gospel and had fearlessly worked and protected the Saints in the early years after the war. Through his efforts many LDS refugees from the eastern provinces, now Polish territory, found a place to stay. To visit the branches they used his old car, an Opel that he kept in good condition. It had no heater or defroster. It was a unique experience in winter to go with him in his car. He had blankets in the car, but Walter would have to jump out of the car to clear the windows. He called Walter his ice breaker, because Walter was always assigned to speak before him in the meetings. Walter loved him for the enthusiasm he had for the Lord's work and he learned much from him.

The Russians had a uranium mine in Buchholz-Annaberg in the Ore Mountains and were always looking for workers. Rumors had it the food and money were good, but the health, safety and working conditions were terrible. Companies were required to transfer men to the mine. Walter's boss was told to send a man there. He came to Walter and told him to go. Walter had to take a health test and while the doctor gave the test he ask Walter if he wanted to work in the mine. Walter told him, "No, I didn't want to go there." Walter showed him a statement from a medical examination he had when he was discharged from the military. It declared that he had a 30% disability from the war. The doctor gave Walter's company a report that Walter was unfit to work in the uranium mine. What a relief for Walter and Herzele. Walter was not afraid of the work but he did fear the poor health and safety conditions there. Walter's boss was upset because he had to find someone else who would go.

Besides Walter's callings in the district, he was asked to teach the eleven-year old boys in Primary including Peter Birth, Walter's brother in law. When Walter had day or afternoon shifts he took time off from work to teach the boys. In compliance with the directions of the communist government they had to teach the boys religion, but anything else, including outdoor activities, the youth should receive by joining the Communist Young Pioneers. The branch had about ten fine boys in that age group. Walter didn't want the boys to become more indoctrinated by the communist party than they already were in school. Walter took the boys in the forest, where they went hiking and did other scout activities. The scouting program was prohibited by the government. At one time, the boys and Walter went on a bike ride to the Grossee, a lake about 30 km away from town. Walter had come from a nightshift at work and hadn't slept yet. Arriving at the lake he was so tired he needed to take a nap. When Walter woke up from his very long nap, they had to leave and go home. On the way home Walter had a flat tire on his borrowed bike and no repair kit. The boys offered Walter their bikes, but he walked the distance home. Walter was sure the boys had a lot of fun, as they told him later.

Brother Guido Schroeder had found a family who was interested in the teachings of the church. He asked Walter's father-in-law Friedrich Birth and Walter to teach this family. Going alone with Father Birth was fun and teaching that family: father, mother and a teenage son, topped it off. They became golden investigators and they had fruitful discussions. After several meetings with the family, one time when Walter and father Birth arrived, the minister of their church was present. They included the minister in their discussion. Of course Father Birth and Walter were interested why the family had invited their minister, but they didn't ask. Visiting with the family the next time the family asked for baptism into the Lord's church. They became very active in the church and the father later became a member of the branch presidency. The father and son were very musically inclined. The father conducted a musical band and played the violin. The son played the oboe. The father later organized a musical band with members of the branch and they played in Sacrament meetings and for dances. He was also called to direct the choir. The branch had at that time an adult, a youth, and a children's choir. Walter's sister-in-law, Margaret Birth, conducted the youth and children choirs.

Herzele and Walter had wanted children from the beginning of their marriage and not just one child. Their prayers went to their Heavenly Father and one day Herzele felt again she was pregnant. They had been told by the doctor with the next child all would be well, but that didn't eliminate the fear that their first experience would be repeated.

After five months Herzele felt there was something wrong. She hadn't felt life for several days. Walter and Herzele went to the doctor and she was admitted to the hospital. On the day she was operated on, Walter waited and waited and waited and didn't hear anything from the nurse or doctor. After a long wait a doctor came and told Walter that Herzele was now safe. The doctors had performed a difficult operation. The fetus had already decayed. If even a little of the decayed tissues had entered her blood stream it would have killed her. The doctor told them not to give up and they believed him.

After Herzele went home she didn't feel well and felt tired. An x-ray showed she had tuberculosis. The family fasted and prayed and Walter gave her a blessing. She continued with her daily activities. To improve her condition the doctor prescribed her milk (milk was only available for children and needy patients), which the couple hadn't seen for years. Walter thinks he benefitted from the milk more than she did. Walter loves milk and Herzele didn't care for milk. Doctor's examinations later didn't show any trace from tuberculosis. How blessed they were to live under the wings of the Almighty.

The Rohloff family
Walter, Herzele, Diana, Mario.

25

BRUNO HOME FROM CONCENTRATION CAMP

They heard good and bad news from Neubrandenburg. The good news was Walter's father was still alive and his mother got permission to visit him once a month. She was notified her husband was in a penal institution in Waldheim. The bad news was his father had been sentenced to ten years in prison. They later learned his trial was held on the 15thof May 1950, five years after he was picked up. It was done in a mass court sentencing. The lowest penalty was ten years. The family would have to wait five more years for him to come home.

To get his father released from prison Walter sent, with the help of Father Birth's clerk, Mr. Klandt, a letter to the president of the German Democratic Republic and requested the release of Walter's father. They also changed his home address to Walter's sister Elfriede's in Bad Toelz, West Germany.

They were all excited for Walter's mother to go and see her husband and Walter's father. After her first visit she reported that he was alive but in very poor condition. Walter asked his mother if she would let him go once to visit his father, realizing it was a great sacrifice for her. She agreed and Walter went when the time came.

The prison in Waldheim was a heavily guarded prison for hard criminals. There were security guards everywhere. Walter was led into a room which had a table in the middle reaching from one wall to the other without a pass-through in between. Down the middle of the table stretching from wall to wall and up to the ceiling was a chain link fence. There were three places in the fence where there was a small opening large enough to put a hand through. In front of these openings were chairs on both sides. Three visitors were invited to enter the room and take a seat at the table. Walter went to the chair the farthest away from the door. There was a guard standing next to each chair on both sides.

After a while a door on the other side of the room in the farthest corner from Walter opened and three prisoners walked in. Walter couldn't make out which of the three was his father. All three were undernourished and dragging their feet. One of them said "Buby" and Walter instantly recognized his father's voice. Walter's tears were near when he saw his father in this poor condition. All his life his father had been heavy and Walter's mother had called him, "Dicker (stout)." But now he wasn't stout, he was only skin and bones. His body was broken, but his eyes sparkled as Walter talked to him. Walter could see that he had not given up.

Walter's father was very much interested in what was going on in the world. He wanted to know how mother was and thanked the LDS branch in Neubrandenburg for their prayers. He congratulated Walter on his choice to take Edith as his wife. He had met Edith when she filled a mission for the church in Berlin and he had attended a conference for district presidents. He knew the Birth family from Walter's reports when Walter had visited the Birth family and he had met Father Birth in church meetings. He was interested in what Walter did to make a living and what Walter's callings were in church. He shared with Walter his testimony of the truthfulness of the restored gospel of Jesus Christ. He knew there was a living God and he was watching over him and making his life bearable. The good Lord had kept him alive. He knew our Heavenly Father would give him the strength to make it through these tough days and years. The half hour passed quickly and they had to part. It was Walter's only visit to his father.

Herzele and Walter received an invitation to meet with their district president in his office. When he wanted to talk to Walter, he did that when he met Walter in church or when Walter was with him visiting the various LDS branches. It was in August, 1952, when the invitation came. What surprised Herzele and Walter the most was that he wanted to see them both. Meeting him in his office, he told them the mission president had called him and told him to ask Walter if he would be willing to go on a full-time mission for the church. The mission president, a Brother from the USA, couldn't enter the German Democratic Republic because he was stationed in West Berlin and needed a special permit to enter the Republic.

Walter had discussed this many times with his Herzele and she knew it was his wish from his youth to serve a full-time mission for the Lord. Walter told him he was willing to go. Next he asked Herzele if she agreed with Walter's desire and if she was willing to support Walter. Her answer was also in the affirmative. After this he let them go home to think about it more.

There was not much to think about. Herzele had filled a mission for the church and she wanted Walter to have the same opportunity. The only problem they really had was how they could continue to financially help Walter's mother. As they had promised, they had mailed her a little money every month so she could cover her expenses. That would not be possible any more. As a missionary, Walter had no income and was living on his savings and with what other people supported him. But they trusted in the Lord and they started preparing. They notified Walter's mother and she knew of Walter's desire and was very supportive.

The mission president, Arthur Glaus, could not come to Cottbus so Walter went to Berlin. On the 21st of August, 1952, president Glaus set Walter apart as a missionary for The Church of Jesus Christ of Latter-day Saints. Walter asked him for missionary instructions, but he told Walter,

"Brother Rohloff, let your conscience be your guide."

On the 5th of September, 1952, Walter, now 30 years old, left home to travel by train to Gera, his first field of labor. Walter said goodbye to his sweetheart and Walter was glad she was close to her parents. While she would miss him, her close relationship with her parents, brothers, and sisters would help her. For Walter, plenty of work would be the best medication when he would miss his Herzele.

Missionary work, as most LDS members understand it, could not be done. Going from house to house was not permitted by the government. In every field Walter served he was either branch president or a counselor to the district president. While he loved to talk and teach investigators, his main interest was the well-being of active or inactive members. His goal was for every branch of the church to become independent. Most of the branches were small with few or no priesthood bearers. The branches which were larger became independent and grew into wards.

Walter's first field of labor was the LDS branch in Gera in the state of Thuringia. His first companion was Elder Werner Baumgard. He gave Walter a short report of what was going on in the branch. The membership was divided in two groups: members who had been living there for many generations and refugees, members from Silesia. They hadn't found a way to live peacefully together. On Saturday the district president, Elder Rudolf Hegewald, also a missionary, met with the two missionaries in Gera and asked Walter to become the branch president and he recommended Walter's companion as a counselor and a member of the branch as the other counselor. Walter was told beforehand of his calling and he had thought and prayed about the calling and asked the president for two members of the branch as his counselors instead. Elder Hegewald agreed and Walter was sustained as branch president on the next Sunday.

During the week Walter visited with Brother Darnisch, a former district president from the city of Breslau in Silesia and Brother Kretschmar a former local district president from Thuringia, and asked both to become his counselors. Both agreed without knowing who the other counselor was. The two counselor's, age, could be Walter's father, but they worked well together. This reflected well on the activities of the branch. Walter and his companion visited the branch members, and encouraged them to live a Christ-like life. But very soon on the 1st of October, Walter was released even though there were some vocal objections of some branch members. He had to travel the next day to Gotha to preside over the Gotha and Erfurt branches.

While the Gotha branch had few Priesthood bearers and needed help, disharmony in the Erfurt branch was what made the mission presidency release the local brethren and call Walter to be the branch president. It was a large branch with many priesthood brethren. The branch had a church-owned building and there were only a few of these buildings in the entire mission. It was not a church designed building and had the former branch president living upstairs, to the dislike of some members. Here, Walter, came in contact for the first time in his life, with a person who was a spiritualist. She had held meetings with others in her apartment, but she wanted to get away from this group. Her father had used her as a medium and had sexually molested her. Upon her request, Brother Herbert Gulla and Walter gave her a blessing and she felt better after. The Sister missionaries worked with her.

Walter and Herzele worried how they could help Walter's mother but the Lord did it the best way. On the 7th of October 1952, one month exactly after Walter had left for the mission field his father was sent home by the communist government. Not only was the family grateful, but many people in the East German Mission and the leadership were grateful for the return of his father from the concentration camp. The mission president notified Walter to go and see his father. It must have been a great day for Walter's mother. It had been more than seven years since she had lost her husband. For more than six years she hadn't known if he was dead or alive. Now he was home. All her worries had an end and her faithfulness begot the blessing. For Walter, the dream he had three years before was now reality. His father was alive and home. He looked much better than when Walter had seen him in Waldheim.

One of his first questions he asked his father was, "Why didn't you go and stay in West Germany, where treatment of returnees' from a concentration camp is much better than here in the East?"Bruno Walter's father answered, he rode the underground train through West Berlin and could have left the train in West Berlin without difficulties. But he felt he had an obligation first to his wife, my mother, who he said would never leave her home town and then to the branch of the church in Neubrandenburg. He told Walter the branch members had fasted and prayed for him and he felt he had a moral obligation to help and support the branch. Walter doesn't know how his father felt after being home for a while. He was sixty-one years old and he needed to work to be able to get retirement. There was no good work available for concentration camp returnees. The only work he could find was night watchman and that was not to his liking, but he took the job. He never complained. He was very careful about what he said. Walter wanted to learn more about his life the last seven years, but he wouldn't talk about it. He was afraid he would have to return to prison.

The man Walter dearly loves. His father visits him in the mission field

The Russians picked up Walter's father in July 1945, and imprisoned him in the cellar of the Russian Secret Service Interrogation Building. Prisoners who had gone through the interrogation before him told him to hold on to the chair he would be sitting on. He would be hit until he was bloody, but if he fell from the chair the guards would kick, step and trample on him. Father held on to the chair through all the hits he received. They wanted to know if he was a Nazi or if he had mistreated Russians. Every time he answered "no" they hit him and he would bleed. Over the days the hits became harder and he was told if he would sign a paper, which he couldn't read because it was in Russian, they would stop. The hits got harder every day and to end this treatment, he finally signed the paper. When finally on the 15thof May 1950, he was brought before the court, he learned the paper he signed stated that he was a Nazi and he was to be sentenced to 10 years in prison. He had never been a Nazi nor had mistreated any Russians.

The statement of his former friend, whom he had invited to stay in his apartment, was the only evidence against Walter's father.

Walter dearly loves his father and mother very much

That man was an informer for the Russian Secret Police (GPU). He had been in charge of the security in the factory and the company had employed Russian POWs. To save his skin, he gave the names of other Nazis to the Russians along with Walter's father's name. At one time during the interrogation, between questions and hits, Walter's father was asked if he knew that man. "Yes," Walter's father said, "I know him. He is a sick man and he lost his home and I invited him and his wife into my home. He lives there and sleeps in my bed."

"You mean to say, that man sleeps in your bed?" the interrogator said.

Yes," Walter's father said, "that is so."

The man questioning Walter's father shook his head and let him go for that day. It was too much, even for the interrogator, to know that someone who was being helped by another person would turn against the helper.

Walter learned that he was arrested on the 19th of July 1950 and after his bloody interrogation he was brought to the Fuenfeichen criminal camp near Neubrandenburg (8thof October 1945). From there he was moved to the Buchenwald criminal camp (October1947). Fuenfeichen and Buchenwald camps have been former prisoner of war and concentration camps. And then he came on 9th of February 1950, to the criminal prison in Waldheim. On the 15th of March 1950 a court sentenced him to 10 years in prison. About a year later his wife, Walter's mother, heard for the first time, that he was still alive and she got permission and could visit him once every month. Than on the 6th of October 1952 after being 7years and 3 month innocently in criminal camps he was released from criminal prison and came home. Through all the difficult days, when people were dying by the thousand, his testimony of the truthfulness of the gospel never left him. A few month before his death, 3rd October 1961 he wrote his testimony:

> "When I was beaten up and lying in a cellar, when I tore apart my last shirt to poorly cover the wounds on my legs, when in illness I was lying between life and death, and when thousands sank into the grave; I continued to believe that Mormonism was and is the truth. This realization never left me. All that happens to us is working for our good if we love God."

On the 11th of April, 1953, Walter was released in Erfurt and Gotha as branch president and Erfurt again became an independent branch. Walter became the companion of his former district president, Elder Rudi Hegewald. Both were transferred to Leipzig and Rudi talked Walter into riding a bike to get there. Rudi was an excellent bike rider and Walter was more than glad to have the ride behind him when they arrived in Leipzig. On Sunday, Rudi was sustained as the district president of Leipzig and Walter was sustained as his counselor. During the first month in Leipzig, Rudy and Walter visited many members of the branch. Later Walter traveled on his bike to the many small independent branches in the district.

In Dessau, the government wanted to close the branch and Walter talked with the responsible men in the government and the closing was prevented.

In Aschersleben, a brother had a large family, but his wife had died and he was heartbroken. He mentioned many times he would like to jump into the grave and to be with his wife. Walter took much time with him to comfort him in his sorrows. The brother couldn't see how he alone could care for his children, and go to work, and make enough money to raise his children. Walter explained to him: God was his father and God loved him like a father loves his son. Walter promised him that he would see how true this was after only a short time. It was hard for him to understand, but he calmed down.

Another sad story occurred in Magdeburg to the parent of a beautiful young boy. The child had been crawling around the home, but on the balcony he tried to climb up the railing. The father and mother knew of the problem and had a close eye on him. He had tried many times without success, but one day, while mama was working in the kitchen he was successful and fell from the 4 story high balcony. The parents were heartbroken and the father blamed the mother for being careless.

Walter was asked to stay with the couple and try to calm them down. They stayed up until late in the night. It was not easy to bring peace into the hearts of the parents and especially to bring the reproachful accusations of the father to an end. They prayed together and when Walter left the next morning a little more peace had returned into their home.

In some branches of the church where Walter presided, he had to go to the government office to see the person who was responsible for religious questions. He would have to give them an outline of what the branch would do and teach in the coming month. He/she would then approve or reject his program. He/she would tell Walter what was going on between the members and once in a while he/she knew more than Walter did. He knew there were members reporting to the Stasi, but in none of the seven branches in which Walter had served for a time did he ever know who the informer was. Walter was even warned to be careful with what he said.

In one of the branches the Primary wanted to do an outside festival. Walter was refused permission from the city government. He went then to the department in charge of the state and they refused permission. Walter wrote a letter to the president of the German Democratic Republic stating that they were a free people and according to the constitution they had the freedom to choose. The president of the German Democratic Republic wrote back and explained to him that the Young Pioneers were in charge of all of those activities. He stated, the church job was to teach the children religion and anything else the communist youth organization would do. By the time Walter got this letter they had already held their "Kinderfest." Walter never told anyone of the problems and that he hadn't received permission for the "Kinderfest".

One day Walter received an invitation from the mission president to transport books, mainly hymn books, printed in West Germany into the German Democratic Republic. Walter knew it was unlawful to do this, but how else could the members get these books?

He took only as many books as he could put under his seat on the police controlled underground train. It was a cold day and he wore a large coat which covered the books well. It took one full day completing this job. Walter is not sure if the mission president knew the danger that was connected with doing this work. Walter was not the only one who helped to get these books into East Germany. He does not think any member knew how the books got into the branches of the church.

Elder Henry D. Moyle from the Council of the Twelve was in Berlin and invited all missionaries serving in the East German Mission to their mission home in West Berlin. There they mingled with the American missionaries who served in the same mission, but around Hamburg in West Germany. Elder Moyle spoke about gospel doctrine and encouraged the missionaries to do their work well and they would be blessed. Before the East German missionaries returned to their fields of labor, they filled their suitcases with food which they couldn't get in East Germany and with church books and manuals that they couldn't buy or print in the East. It was against the rules of the East German government, but they didn't care.

One of the sister missionaries showed Walter what she had and Walter advised her some of the things she should not take, which were against the law in East Germany. She was a very sensitive, nervous lady and she was afraid she would attract police attention. Walter took her belongings into his suitcase.

There were only missionaries in Walter's train compartment. Sure enough, the police came checking on the men and what they carried. The officer pointed at Walter's suitcase and asked,

"Whose suitcase is this?

'It is my suitcase" Walter said.

'What is in it?" Walter didn't want to lie, so he told him he would show him what he had. Walter reached up to get his suitcase down.

"No" the officer said, "I don't want to see it. You tell me."

Walter said, "I would rather show you what I have," and he pulled the suitcase down on a seat.

"I don't want to see it, just tell me."

"No," Walter said, "I want you to see it."

Walter used both hands and opened the locks but the cover opened just a little so the officer couldn't see anything inside. The policeman put his foot down hard and said,

"I don't want to see it," and left the compartment.

It felt like a rock lifted from Walter's heart. He had food and church literature in his suitcase. Later, when he looked through one of the manuals, it contained an article from Elder John A. Widtsoe about the evils of communism. Where would he have landed if that officer had looked through his suitcase? Walter would have been punished with a heavy penalty for undermining the communist government.

The little sister missionary was not so lucky. When she was asked if she had anything from West Berlin she answered truthfully, "No." She was always afraid and nervous when she saw police officers. The officer took her to a special compartment and turned her over to a female officer. That sister missionary had to undress. The female officer checked her and looked extensively through her clothing, but when she couldn't find anything she let her go.

Walter met with his branch president, Brother Eckert, in Berlin. He asked Walter if he had any objection to the branch presidency calling Herzele to be the Relief Society President. The branch had a large Relief Society and he knew Herzele would be a good president. He knew she had the love and trust of the sisters. So he told the branch president he had no objection. He also told him and asked him not to tell anyone else, but that after his release from his mission Walter and Herzele would be leaving for America. He smiled and Walter guessed he thought many people talked about it, but few actually did go. He asked Walter to delay their departure for at least six months. Walter agreed. He had to hear what Herzele had to say anyway.

Rudy Hegewald was released as a missionary for the LDS church, but he stayed on as the district president of the Leipzig district. Walter was transferred from Leipzig to Zwickau on the 8thof August 1953. In the building where the branch held their meetings, a room was prepared for Walter to live; he had no companion. Walter knew the large branch from a speaking assignment he had in the past. At hat time after the meeting many brothers and sisters came to Walter and talked to him. He remembered especially an elderly man, Brother Heimann, who came and told Walter that he didn't understand a word, and he didn't speak loud enough. He told him, he looked around and could see everyone was very attentive and listening to Walter's sermon, but he couldn't understand a word. Walter excused himself and promised he would change. For some time he put a note, "speak loud" with his outline in front of him.

On Sunday the district president, Brother Karl Neumaerker from the Planitz branch, visited with Walter before the prayer meeting and told Walter the mission presidency wanted him to be the branch president and asked if he would accept the calling. Of course Walter accepted. He wanted to ask for an explanation, but there was no time, because both had to attend the prayer meeting held before the sacrament meeting.

In the prayer meeting the district president told the branch presidency they would be released that day. They were completely surprised. The only meeting Walter had attended thus far was the choir practice. The branch president was the conductor and Walter saw he was much respected and loved by all the members.

In the sacrament meeting the branch presidency was released and Walter was called to be the new branch president. As far as he could see, all hands went up sustaining him. No one objected, but of course, no one knew Walter. Except for the members of the choir, he hadn't talked to anyone. After the meeting one brother after another came to Walter and told him what their calling in the branch was and also told him they wouldn't do their work anymore. Except for the

Relief Society, all refused to work with him.

Most understand that in the LDS church a calling to any position is just for a relatively short time, except for the few general authorities. Walter could well understand the negative feelings of the branch members having a stranger as their branch president, but he didn't expect something like this. The branch had many good and faithful brethren and sisters. Walter did much praying. He knew with the Lord's help he would be able to overcome the problems and they would have an uplifting time. Walter went to work and visited with nearly every member in their homes. He discussed with them their needs, their testimony, and their willingness to serve in the Lords church. He had a warm reception.

Walter was sitting in his place at choir practice, but at the usual starting time no one started. He asked the conductor why he didn't begin the practice. The conductor stated that he was not conducting any more. Walter looked around, but he didn't know who could lead the practice. Walter had been singing in choirs for some years, but conducting? Every choir member was present. Sending them home without a practice was out of the question. He got up, explained the situation and conducted the choir practice with much humor and laughter. It worked out very well. Of course the practice was good; only because Brother Voigt at the piano didn't quit.

The branch held Relief Society and Priesthood meeting on a weekday night. The brother who had been called to teach the Priesthood class was present, but declined to teach. Walter took over and when he asked a question no one answered or raised a hand. After a while Walter called on a brother and he replied, "I didn't raise my hand and I am not giving an answer." Now Walter lost his temper a little, and in no uncertain words he told the brethren how he felt. He told the brethren he had not asked for this position that he would like to do missionary work and even more he would love to be home with his wife, but he was called to preside over this branch and he would do whatever was needed to move this branch of the church forward. He said much more and then asked if anyone wanted to voice his opinion. No one did.

One of the good, active brothers had gone to visit his relatives in West Germany. He had returned from his visit, but Walter didn't see him in church. Walter visited with him and he told Walter he was having doubts that Joseph Smith had seen God the Father and His Son. He gave Walter one of the tracts of the Jehovah's Witnesses in which they had many scripture references to prove it was not so. Walter looked at the article and then he asked the brother to pick up his Bible and they would look at the scriptures. The tract author had misquoted and not mentioned some important scripture references. Walter had him open to Acts 7:55, where Stephen saw the heavens open and Christ standing next to God. Then Walter told him, "Let's see how it was with Moses in Exodus 33:11. And the Lord spoke unto Moses face to face as a man speaketh unto his friend." This brother was as old as Walter's father but he took Walter in his arms and said

> "Brother Rohloff, the Lord has sent you. Thank you for helping me to understand."

On the 30th of June, 1954, Walter was transferred to Halle to lead the branch there. He was released the Sunday before he left and a local brother was called to lead the branch in Zwickau. The choir director called on Walter to lead the choir in memory of his beginning. Over ten month ago Walter had led the choir in one performance because of the problems. Now the problems were solved and harmony was restored.

Looking back on the 26 months he served as a missionary, Walter felt he had labored hard and had been able, with the Lord's help, to bring stability to the branches. They had some baptisms at that time, but Walter didn't baptize anyone; his companion or priesthood holders in the branch had performed the ordinance. The mission was a good learning experience for Walter. He had gained a solid knowledge of the gospel while he was a prisoner of war. As a missionary Walter used this knowledge to help people gain a testimony of the gospel of Jesus Christ. Walter was grateful for the spiritual guidance he had as a missionary. Herzele's prayers and the financial help from both her and church members here in Germany and abroad made it possible for him to have a successful mission. Walter had good companions on his mission, but there were many times he wished he could have had Herzele with him. Being branch president for most of the time and having your wife at your side would have been a big help.

Back home it was a new beginning for Walter and Herzele. Herzele was very involved and busy with the Relief Society. She had made plans for everything she wanted to do before she left for America. During the time period before their departure to West Germany, Walter was Mutual President for the Young Men. To make a living he worked for his father-in-law's business. At that time when they were preparing to leave it was still possible to take a vacation to West Germany. Walter was very careful not to mention to anyone their intention to leave East Germany for good. Leaving the DDR was punished with imprisonment.

On the evening of Walter's departure he told their branch president, Brother Eckert that he would be leaving the next morning. Brother Eckert was astonished when Walter told him of his intention, but Walter reminded him of their conversation in Berlin more than six months before. Walter had placed anything he thought of importance in a suitcase. There were items that he was not permitted to take. Because of the risk involved, Herzele wouldn't take anything with which she might have problems.

26

ARE YOU FROM NEUBRANDENBURG?

The next morning Walter was on his way to West Germany, Herzele would follow Walter 14 days later. She had organized and prepared the Relief Society birthday party and wanted to be with the sisters for that program.

Walter went by train and at the border between East and West Germany in Eisenach, the border patrol entered the railroad car. Their assignment was to check everybody's permit and their baggage. Walter was alone in his compartment. He was reading the sports section of a newspaper when a lady in police uniform entered his compartment. She wished him a good day.

Walter looked up from his paper and wished her good day also. She was a young, attractive lady and asked Walter politely what he was reading. Walter told her he was reading the sports section of a newspaper.

"In what kind of sport are you interested?" she asked.

"In soccer," was Walter's answer.

"Who is the soccer champion in the DDR (German Democratic Republic)?" she wanted to know.

"Erfurt," Walter said.

"I am from Erfurt," she said and sat down across from Walter.

"You come from a beautiful place," Walter replied.

As a missionary Walter served for about six months in Erfurt. He had a habit to always inform himself about the history and beauty of all the places in which he served. Erfurt was in the beautiful Thueringer Forest and there was a lot to talk about. It was fun to talk to her and in the process she forgot to check anyone's permit and luggage. While Walter and the lady were deep in conversation the train started moving. She hurried and left Walter's compartment and the passenger car. Walter opened the door to see her jump from the moving train. She waved goodbye and wished him a good vacation. While waving back to her Walter saw the platform was full of people standing there with their luggage at their side. Walter didn't think much about it until later. Lost in his thoughts, Walter went back into his compartment.

Through the window Walter watched as the train crossed the well-marked border between East and West Germany. A high barbed wire fence with a plowed field on the East side of the fence made it hard to illegally cross the border. The field was plowed and raked and would show every footprint should someone try to cross the border. In our political meetings we were told the fence was placed to protect the DDR from unauthorized people. Everyone knew all too well that no one wanted to get into the DDR, but plenty of people wanted to leave. Every year 150,000 to 300,000 people left illegally. By 1961, three million people had left. If people didn't get vacation permits to cross the border they went through Berlin until the wall was built.

The train had just crossed the border when a lady came into Walter's compartment. Respectfully, he arose. To his surprise she took Walter into her arms and kissed him on his cheeks. Another lady did just the same to him. There were quite a few ladies standing there and smiling. Walter asked

"What is going on?"

"Come and see," they told Walter.

Opening their suitcases they showed Walter what they had carried on board. All of the items were not permitted to be taken out of East Germany. There were no harmful items - just things to make someone happy. Walter could see that all of them would have been standing on the platform waiting to be penalized, just as the many travelers he had seen standing there. While the women thanked him he thanked the Lord for being so kind and watching over him.

Walter was surprised how prosperous West Germany was. In the DDR he had read in the government controlled newspaper that West Germany was broke, with many people out of work. The articles said that no one took care of the poor. Now, as Walter looked around and saw how prosperous everything appeared he realized how much the press and the party lied. They seemed to lie more than Joseph Goebbels in the Nazi time.

Herzele's sister Irmgard and her husband Heinz picked Walter up from the railroad station in Darnstadt. They had generously invited Walter and Herzele to stay with them until they could find a place to live. The next day Walter found a job with the machine company, Paschke & Co. Walter was asked to make tools for their production. Walter liked the work and worked there until Walter and Herzele left for the USA in January, 1957.

Walter wrote Herzele that he had a job and made more money than he had made in the DDR. He told her how well Irmgard and Heinz had taken care of him and he invited her to come. She took care of her Relief Society program and came.

The first LDS church meeting Walter attended in Darmstadt was a Priesthood and Relief Society meeting on a Wednesday night. The branch members made him feel as welcome as if they had known him for a long time. The meetings were in class rooms in an elementary school and the chairs were small. They discussed how to find rooms for church services or building a chapel. Heinz told Walter after the meeting that they had talked about this for years and nothing had changed. On Sundays they used a larger room for sacrament meeting with adult chairs. During the week Heinz invited Walter to go with him and do missionary work. They found Mrs. Marotzek and her daughter. They taught her the gospel and both later became members of the church. Walter and Herzele were impressed with the friendliness of the branch members. They felt right at home.

It was Walter's third Sunday in Darmstadt when the district president, brother Fock, visited the branch. Before the meeting he took Walter aside and asked him,

"Brother Rohloff, are you from Neubrandenburg?"

Walter was surprised that someone would ask him that question, because he thought everyone knew, he had come from Cottbus. Of course Neubrandenburg was his hometown.

Walter answered, "Yes, I am from there."

The Rohloff's visiting Elfriede, Walter's sister

Brother Fock told him he had a telegram from the mission president, Kenneth B. Dyer, and he gave it to Walter. It read:

> "Brother Rohloff arrived in Darmstadt. If he is from Neubrandenburg, make him branch president right away."

After Walter read the telegram the district president asked him if he accepted the calling. Walter did and in the sacrament meeting he was sustained as branch president. Afterwards Herzele and Walter went over to the home of the former branch president, Brother Ludwig Hosch, and he turned over the books and gave him some important advice. He told Walter he knew Walter would be with them for only a short time. He and all the members would be very grateful if Walter would find a good place for the church to meet. Walter agreed with him 100%. They needed a better meeting place in order for the church to grow.

The following Sunday Brother Heinrich Sommerkorn and Brother Heinz Koenig were sustained and set apart as Walter's counselors. After the meeting they met together in Brother Sommerkorn's home and held their first presidency meeting. Of course one of the priorities was a meeting place. Walter asked brother Sommerkorn to place an ad in the newspaper for rooms to rent. Then Walter recommended asking the branch members on Sunday to fast and pray for their success in finding a meeting place. Brother Sommerkorn was critical and told Heinz and Walter they had done this many times with no results. Walter believed him but still insisted that he would place the advertisement. Side note: Darmstadt was the first branch of the church organized in Germany (1843).

Walter conducts his 1st sacrament meeting in Darmstadt

They received an answer to their prayer, fasting and to their advertisement. They were offered the whole unfinished floor in a downtown building at Ludwigstr.17, just a minute away from the center of town. It was the place where all the streetcars met. Walter looked at the place and he loved it. In Walter's opinion there was no better place for them to rent anywhere in town. The owner told Walter he would build the floor to Walter's specifications if they would lease the place for ten years. Walter called a membership meeting and discussed how they would do it. Walter encouraged everyone to voice his or her opinion and of course there were pros and cons. It gave Walter an opportunity to answer every question and after all that was said, he received a positive response. He now discussed the project with the mission president who gave Walter the go ahead. While Walter was in the president's office, Walter also asked for a piano and a harmonium. The president replied, "Either one or the other, not both." When they were ready to move in, the president gave them both instruments. Walter gave the approved floor plan to the owner and he started to prepare it. This preparation and work brought harmony to the branch. They planned together, worked together, and worshiped together.

While the branch was preparing the rooms for their use, the owner came and asked Walter if he knew someone who wanted to rent one single room. It was next to his apartment on the top floor and had a balcony facing the street. Herzele and Walter looked at the room and they liked it. It was just what they needed. They thanked Irmgard and Heinz for their kindness and help and then they moved into the room.

Sacrament meeting in rented rooms

It was just a small room. Members gave them a couch, chairs, a kitchen table and a smaller table to place a hot plate. Walter built the frame for a folding bed with a storage shelf on top. Herzele and Walter had all they needed. Because the place was in downtown and it was the main market place, all members had occasional to do business there. Therefore they, especially Herzele- had many visitors. It was so easy for anyone doing his/her shopping to stop by and see how she was doing.

Walter and Herzele had just moved into their room on the top floor of the house when they received a letter from a friend of theirs in East Germany, Eberhard Sommer. He wanted to immigrate to the USA and Walter Kindt wanted to sponsor him. They contacted Walter Kind and he told them everything was prepared. Walter let Eberhard know and he came to live with them. A short time later Manfred Adler, a former missionary companion of Walter's wanted to come. Then a little later his wife, Ruth, wanted to join her husband. Walter and Herzele invited all to come and stay with them. They had a full room. Because they were all actively engaged in church work, they needed time for preparation. Arrangements were made for everyone to have time alone. The three friends slept on air mattresses in a classroom. They got along very well. When Walter and Herzele later moved to the USA, Eberhard had already gone and the Adlers' had found an apartment in Darmstadt. Herzele's sister Gretel moved into the room with her future sister-in-law, Renate Tegge.

The branch had a full house the day they had the dedication of their rooms. President Kenneth B. Dyer was quite surprised when he saw how the branch had changed. He was the main speaker. The choir (20 voices strong) was under the capable leadership of Brother Uwe Hansen. He served in the US Army. He soon became a dear friend of Herzele and Walter. Whenever they needed help he was available. Up to that time the LDS members in the US armed forces stationed in Darmstadt had been going to Frankfurt to attend their church services. The brethren organized an English speaking servicemen's branch and they shared the rooms with the German branch. After Herzele and Walter left for America and the branch wanted to have their own chapel, the armed forces brethren and sisters were a big help in obtaining it.

With the new rooms, missionary work got another dimension. The missionaries used the rooms to give lectures on the Book of Mormon and other church doctrine. The life of the branch also changed. Now they could and did have all kinds of activities for young and old.

Celebrating New Years Eve 1957

Walter organized an investigator class. The elders taught the class first and then later Walter taught the class. It was fun to teach a class where every seat was filled. They had frequent baptisms. It was fun to live in a growing branch where the members lived and spread the word of God. Walter discussed with the district president the possibility of a proselyting evening for all members. The district president was not in favor of it. Walter asked him to stay home, watch his kids and send his wife. He did. The branch members went from door to door. After the activity they had a meeting in the church and the enthusiastic members reported. It was a very spiritual meeting. On Sunday they had a full house.

A great thing happened for the German-speaking saints when a temple was built and dedicated in Switzerland (1956). Some of the members went to the dedication of the temple. Herzele and Walter went later and organized a temple tour using two Volkswagen buses. Eberhard Sommer and Norbert Lehnig did the driving. Besides branch members they took along their friends, Gerhard and Irene

Kupitz, and their two daughters. Father and Mother Birth and Herzele's brother Werner were their guests, also. They all received their endowments on the 19th of May, 1956. While there they did some sightseeing, and attended sacrament meeting in Zürich. Walter had the opportunity to speak in the meeting.

From that time on the branch organized temple tours for members of the church living in East Germany. They couldn't get permission from their government to go to Switzerland but they could get permission to go to Darmstadt. In Darmstadt they exchanged their DDR passport with a West German one and before they returned home they got their East German passport back. Eberhard Sommer did the driving. Through this temple program, Herzele and Walter met many old friends. After they left for the USA these trips were still continued and Walter's parents received their endowments that way.

The First of our Temple Tours

The time for Herzele and Walter's departure drew nearer. Father and mother Birth came and wished them a good trip. Herzele's sister Brigitte came with her girlfriend, Gisela Voigt. The Births and Brigitte later immigrated to the USA.

The last one who came to say goodbye was Walter's father. They spent several days together. They sat around a little table in the small room and discussed LDS doctrine. Bruno, the pioneer, who was the one that opened their minds and hearts to the gospel of Jesus Christ, exemplified through very difficult situations the love he had for our Savior, Jesus Christ. In the discussion and during one small disagreement on a minor interpretation of the Lords teaching, Bruno got so involved and said "Brother, I tell you" he didn't get any further because Walter broke in and said: "Dad, I am still your boy." They laughed and continued their discussion. Father Rohloff hoped he would see Herzele and Walter in the USA. Walter's mother was not doing well. His father thought he would outlive his wife, but it worked out differently. The years in the DDR were hard on him. He had enjoyed visiting Walter's sister once a year in Bad Toelz, West Germany, but he needed permission from the government for the visit. For the last few years of his life the communist government wouldn't give him permission. They denied him his permit because Walter had left the DDR without government permission. Bruno passed away 3rd October 1961, two years before his wife.

After his passing, Trudy Pielmann sent Walter his father's last testimony which he had written down about six months before his death. In it he explained how the Lord had guided him to His church and then concluded: "After the collapse of Germany in 1945, I took a colleague into my apartment by the name Karl R. The Russians had taken his apartment. To buy himself freedom from the concentration camp, he had given my name to the Russians as a Nazi spy. I never had been a member of the Nazi party."

On 19th of July, 1945, He was apprehended. Through a pardon by the president of the German Democratic Republic, he was released on October 6, 1952. His life was full of hardships. First, he was fighting in World War 1 from the first to the last day. On almost the last day of World War I he became a prisoner of war in France till 1920. There was a short, peaceful time and then came the depression and he was seven years out of work. Next Hitler came and World War II, and after that, the concentration camp, and misery after that. Nothing shook his faith in Jesus Christ and in the restored Church of

Jesus Christ of Latter-day Saints. Until the end of his life he was an active member of the Lord's church.

Walter and Herzele stood at the railing of the ship, United States. They looked over to the shore where they saw the men loading the passenger luggage. They thought back about the happy and not-so-happy days they had experienced in their country, a land they loved.

They were so grateful that the Lord had taken them under His wings and protected and guided them up to this day. They knew the Lord would be with them in building and feeling at home in a new land. With much enthusiasm, optimism and praying for guidance from the Lord they were on their way to a new adventure.

27

EPILOGUE

Leaving the stormy sea behind, Walter and his Herzele arrived safe in Milwaukee. Two cousins of Herzele's, Hans and Walter Kindt, and their family and friends greeted them. The Kindts had everything prepared for their well-being. The next day, with the help of Herbert Ludwig, they found a good job for Walter.

Later in May one of their friends, Eberhard Sommer, decided to get married in the Salt Lake Temple. Walter and Herzele accompanied them and enjoyed visiting the temple with their friends. Two of Herzele's sisters, Irmgard and Christa Koenig, lived in Salt Lake City with their families and many of Herzele's and Walter's friends. Herzele's impression was:"It is like home. Let's move." Thus after being only a year in Milwaukee they moved to Salt Lake City.

In Salt Lake City, Walter found, with the help of Jan Luczak, work at the University of Utah and later joined the staff of Dr. Willem Kolff, who worked on the development of an artificial heart and artificial kidney. The group Walter worked with was involved in creating the first artificial heart to be implanted in a human being. Dr. Kolff was later presented with a special medal for his invention by the Queen of the Netherlands, which Dr. Kolff later presented to over twenty of his co-workers including Walter.

Meanwhile Herzele, worked as a sales lady and later she worked in a cancer research lab at the U. of U. as a research assistant. Herzele enjoyed her work very much, but chose to give the work up when they adopted their children. Through the Social Services department of the LDS church they adopted two children: Mario Walter Rohloff on the 30th of September 1964, as a one year old child. Diana Irene Rohloff joined the family in January 1967, seven days old. From them they now have six grandchildren: Cassie & Shea Stegner and Brock, Riley, Taulia and Braden Rohloff. They bring much happiness to Herzele and Walter.

— 195 —

THE UNIVERSITY OF UTAH

SALT LAKE CITY 84112

INSTITUTE FOR BIOMEDICAL ENGINEERING
COLLEGE OF ENGINEERING
AND
COLLEGE OF MEDICINE

WILLEM J. KOLFF, M.D., Ph.D., *Director*
JOHN D. WARNER, *Administrator*
Medical Center, Building 518
Phone 801 — 581-6296

March 6, 1978

Walter Rohloff

I could not possibly give a medal to all my co-workers although I love all of them. Therefore, I have decided to give one of these medals to everyone who has worked in the Division of Artificial Organs for six years or longer. It is most gratifying to see that even with this limitation, I had to give more than 20 medals.

I hope that you accept this as a sign of my great appreciation for the many years we have worked together. As of January 1, 1978, these medals are no longer coined, so they have now become a collector's item.

Sincerely yours,

W.J. Kolff

W.J. Kolff, M.D., Ph.D.

WJK:vt

After a trip to Bear Lake (1961) with the LDS German Choir, Herzele, Walter and Herzele's siblings began visiting the lake every year. The family quickly fell in love with the beautiful area and decided to purchase two acres of land which they divided up among all eight Birth children. With their portion of the land, Mario and Walter built a cabin which their family enjoys to this day.

We designed and built our cabin on Bear Lake

In Salt Lake City Walter and Herzele were called to be ordinance workers in the German and English speaking sessions of the Salt Lake Temple. They worked in their ward as teachers and later Walter was called as second counselor in the bishopric. They continued their service in ward positions after they moved to Bountiful, Utah. After living there for a little over a year, Walter was called to be the bishop of the ward. (1969) In this ward most members actively participated in the Church programs. The ward had an unusually large group of active teens and most became Eagle Scouts and missionaries for the church.

While Walter was bishop of the ward, he was in charge of the building remodeling. Later the ward participated financially with the Bountiful stakes, jointly buying the Valley Music Hall for their stake conferences. They also bought the White Farm for the welfare project, and paid their part on building a Seminary building for the Woods Cross High school. The final building project while Walter was bishop was building the chapel his ward now occupies. At Walter's release, the ward was divided and Walter's ward moved into the new building along with two other wards.

From the beginning of his calling as a second counselor through his calling as a bishop and beyond, Walter always loved scouting. He worked with those great boys for over twenty years in a variety of positions including Explorer advisor, scout master, etc. For his work he was awarded the Silver Beaver Award, the highest adult scouting award.

After their retirement, Herzele and Walter were called on a full-time mission to the former East German Republic. Their field of labor was Frankfurt, Oder and Eisenhuettenstadt. Their assignment was to find rooms for missionaries and meeting rooms for a branch and establish a branch of the church. They made many friends and completed their assignment. The Lord was with them and it was gratifying to see two new branches of the church developing.

They are grateful to their neighbors Evelyn & Roy Boulton for watching and maintaining their property and their financial obligations while they were on their mission in Germany. They were sad when the Boultons left their earthly estate for a heavenly home, but were very much surprised as were Boulton relatives, when Roy's sister informed them that Walter was the responsible person of disposing of their properties and bank accounts.

Herzele and Walter have heartfelt appreciation for their citizenship in the United States of America. They are grateful for the Lord's guidance to this noble land. For them, living at a time in Nazi Germany and later in Communist Germany was an enormous experience and made them especially grateful to live in this great land. May God bless this land and bless His Church.

A special thanks goes to the Lord. Through His grace they were born "of goodly parents," who spared no pain to raise them in the ways of the Lord. Walter and Herzele thank God for that privilege and for His son, Jesus Christ, for His redeeming work, and for His gospel that gave them and gives all people the direction to master their lives. Walter and Herzele are especially grateful for the restoration of the Lord's church "The Church of Jesus Christ of Latter-day Saints."They challenge all to follow the example of the Prophet Joseph Smith to ask God and He will give you wisdom as He promised. (Jam.1:5). What a privilege!

Walter and Herzele celebrated their 60th wedding anniversary in 2009 with family members and many friends.

The day came when Edith & Walter celebrated their 60th wedding anniversary. The tables were well decorated with fresh flowers (in February) and a table full of good German food from Siegfried's Delicatessen. Their guests enjoyed this delicious German food and live music provided by a band that invited everyone to dance. However, there were so many people, there was no room and nobody wanted to go home to make room. Everyone had a nice time, and Edith and Walter saw many friends they hadn't seen for many years. Edith and Walter were very grateful to everyone who helped them celebrate.

A few months after this celebration, Edith's abilities to stand and walk declined rapidly and she soon needed Hospice care. Her nurse Debbie reported: "Edith was on Hospice care, due to general decline. Edith had what appeared to be a stroke, with a fall. Edith lost the ability to walk; was in a wheelchair; and soon became bed bound. Her appetite decreased; her oxygen saturations decreased; and she had to wear oxygen. Edith continued to decline and became non-responsive at times. When she was awake she would look up at the ceiling and watch the angels.

"The spirit was strong in her home and it was evident that angels were present to prepare for Edith's return home. When others asked what Edith was looking at, she would reply, 'There is a room full of people. They want me to come with them and die. I don't want to die.' This was very upsetting to Edith. She did not want to leave Walter. Edith continued to show signs of her body shutting down. Breathing became irregular and labored and she was sleeping most of the time and eating very little. When the weekend came, she was not expected to live past the weekend."

Walter and Edith's son, Mario, reported: "On a Sunday I received a phone call from my dad that Mom was declining in her health and the nurses said she would probably not survive the night. After hearing this I went to be with Mom and, as I saw her lying in her bed, it was clear that the end of her days here on earth were at an end. I sat down next to her bed and I took her hand in mine, just to feel her warmth one more time. All the memories of her life with me started going through my head. As I sat there reflecting on the memories, Mom started to squeeze my hand with great fervor. It was surprising to feel the strength of her grip. Surprisingly, as I sat there, I began to feel some discomfort from the amount of pressure she was using to grip my hand, but I didn't want to let go. Suddenly she opened her blue eyes and looked right at me and released her grip. I asked her if there was anything she wanted and she responded 'YES'. I asked what it was and she simply said that she wanted to get up! I then said to her 'Then let's get you up!' I helped her sit up for a few moments and then she said, 'OK' and she stood up! Straight as a board she stood and I immediately informed my Dad who was just as shocked as I was to see her standing. This was a testament to her strength in life and a lesson I will never forget."

The following morning, her nurse Debbie observed: "Monday morning came and Edith was still with us. Shelly was the aid that would take care of Edith's personal needs. Shelly had come to bathe and dress Edith, that Monday morning. To Shelly's surprise Edith was more alert, and wanted to eat breakfast and was able to visit with Shelly. This was very unusual for someone to rally back from such a critical situation. Shelly asked Edith what happened to all the angels, Edith's reply was, 'I sent them away.' This was news that was not heard of. Most people would go with the angels, but Edith sent them away. Our Father in Heaven allowed Edith to stay for almost a year longer, before her return home to Him."

After a time Edith's condition deteriorated and Mario moved the beds downstairs into the dining room area. Herzele now had a nice view out of the large sliding door into the backyard and could watch the deer grazing. Walter's bed was placed next to hers so that he had a good view of his Herzele all the time, and when she needed help he could give help quickly. Then came the time she couldn't eat and drink any more, and couldn't even swallow. With a straw, Walter put some moisture into her mouth when needed.

On the morning of Sunday, June 3, 2012 - a day before Walter's 90th birthday - their bishop Gordon Smith came by for a visit. Walter asked him if they could give Edith a blessing and ask our Heavenly Father to take her to her heavenly home. After the blessing, Walter continued to moisten her mouth and at 5:30pm he was again bending over her, but this time he did what he hadn't done before. He lovingly stroked her hair and told her how much he loved her, and then gave her a kiss on her dry lips. Walter returned into the living room when he remembered he forgot to give her medication. He returned to his Herzele with the medication and touched her hand. The hand was cold and her cheeks were lukewarm. In this short time she went home - home to where we came from. Walter was saddened, but grateful to be with her until the last minute of her earthly life. Our

Heavenly Father had heard and answered his prayer. He thanked the Lord for this privilege and he knew their love would never end.

Auf Wiedersehen mein Herzele